CHRISTIANITY
FOR SKEPTICS
[Expanded and Updated]

Dr Steve Kumar

with
Dr Jonathan Sarfati

■ ■ ■

CREATION
BOOK PUBLISHERS

Atlanta, Georgia, USA

www.creationbookpublishers.com

ISBN: 978-1-921643-49-1
Cover design: Emily Moes
Layout and design: Nikala Drager
Illustration: Caleb Salisbury

For further information on creation/evolution and the Christian worldview go to: **CREATION.com**

CHRISTIANITY
FOR SKEPTICS
[Expanded and Updated]

Dr Steve Kumar

with

Dr Jonathan Sarfati

CONTENTS

FOREWORD
[to the first edition]

We are living in an age in which ideologies rule and rule often without much evidence for their truth. The whole world is veering left towards humanism. Neo-Darwinism, developed from the theories put forward by Darwin some 140 years ago fits with this trend, for it too believes that Natural Law, the Laws of Matter and the Space-Time Continuum are the be all and end all of reality. Thus any ideologies involving metaphysics and God are retrograde— for neither God nor metaphysics really exist. That is the view.

Yet at the same time as these 'scientifically' based trends to humanism and atheism are developing, the innate religious nature of man is asserting itself with a vengeance. Thus we have the resurgence of occultism, Eastern cults and religions old and new (Islam and New Age as examples) while the ideology of materialism political as well as 'religious' grows up all around us at the same time. Thus anti-polar and antithetical ideologies grow and flourish in most modern societies. The skeptics are often to be found in the academic scientific circles while the occult and metaphysical ideologies are widespread among the lay people, philosophers and the theologians too.

As a result of these antithetical developments confusion amongst students and thinkers has grown enormously in recent years. For they in the colleges, universities and media are confronted with both trends—and few are the clear thinkers who are in a position to help them come focusing their thought. If these tendencies go on unchecked we shall find ourselves in the position which C.S. Lewis so beautifully described namely that of the pure materialist believing in ghosts and spirits!—the materialistic occult magician.

It is for this reason that I recommend Dr Steve Kumar's book. It gives a clear and balanced view on the subjects above mentioned and will help, if well digested, to clear away some of the mists of simultaneous antitheses which so easily befog the thoughtful young academics of today.

Professor A.E. Wilder-Smith (1915–1995)

B.Sc., Ph.D., Dr.es.Sc., Dr.Sc., F.R.S.C.(London), Professor of Pharmacology at the Medical Center, University of Illinois.

PREFACE
[to the Expanded and Updated Edition]

In my days as a doctoral student in New Zealand in the early 1990s, finding good defences of Christianity was not easy. The internet was still years in the future, and New Zealand was thousands of miles away from the leading apologetics schools. Fortunately, there were some excellent books available, and foremost among them was the 1987 edition of *Christianity for Skeptics* by Dr Kumar.

This book explained many of the key points in a very readable way. And, importantly for the university environment, it didn't avoid the hard questions, and was well supported by scholarship. Dr Kumar had distilled the wisdom of some of the greatest minds in history, including leading Christian apologists, into a compact volume.

Developments since the first edition have served only to reinforce the arguments. The Teleological Argument (from design) has been massively strengthened by discoveries in the micro-universe of the cell. In addition to tiny, super-efficient machines, we now know of multiple coding languages in the same length of DNA. The force of this argument helped lead philosopher Antony Flew, featured in the older editions of this book as a leading atheist, to theism.

Dr Kumar was also prescient about the coming challenge of Islam as the 20th century drew to a close. Not long into the new millennium, jumbo jets flying into the tallest buildings in America and riots in Europe proved him right. The secularized West had proven to be a limp reed that could not withstand a belief system that fanatically believed its own truth without evidence.

Since the book, there has also been the rise of the 'New Atheists', although there was nothing really new about the arguments, already refuted in the book.

I always thought it was a pity that such a book was mainly known in New Zealand, with only about 4 million people, and mostly unknown elsewhere. Certainly the internet has been a great help in gaining information, but the problem here is the opposite of before: information *overload*, with few checks and balances, thus highly variable quality.

Thus I was happy to help update this new millennium edition, especially with the new information that has become available, as above. Christianity really doesn't require believers to check their brains at the church door, and it can withstand the toughest challenges. And as arch-neo-atheist Richard Dawkins admits, it is likely the only 'bulwark' that can stand up to radical Islam.

I hope that a much wider audience can now benefit from this book: both *skeptics,* so they can see the strong case for Christianity; and *Christians,* so they can know what and *why* they believe.

Jonathan Sarfati

Ph.D. in Physical Chemistry

The greatest question of our time is not communism vs individualism, nor Europe vs America, not even the East vs the West; it is whether men can bear to live without God.
— WILL DURANT

The mathematical precision of the universe reveals the mathematical mind of God.
— ALBERT EINSTEIN

I shall always be convinced that a watch proves a watch-maker, and that a universe proves a God.
— VOLTAIRE

1

DOES GOD EXIST?

Is it reasonable to believe in God? Can God's existence be logically proven without appealing to religious experience or a leap of faith? Is God merely a psychological projection, a primitive myth? How could anyone be sure there is a God? What evidence supports God's existence?

Our secular culture may dismiss God as irrelevant to our existence and give the seductive impression that God is on a long vacation. This popular concept may provide some humans with a sense of freedom and autonomy, but it has not delivered us from boredom, anxiety, suicide, stress, drugs, crime, addiction to entertainment, and other neuroses.[1] After diagnosing the human predicament, psychiatrist Victor Frankl (1905–1997) observes, "More people today have the means to live, but no meaning to live for."[2] According to Erich Fromm, one of the leading specialists in human behaviour, the majority of those who visit psychiatrists suffer from "an inner deadness. They live in the midst of plenty and are joyless."[3]

In the light of our social and spiritual crisis, it is not beyond reason to propose that the missing ingredient in our recipe for existence is the reality of God.[4] History has repeatedly confirmed the tragic truth that when people ignore the Transcendent they descend into the abyss of nihilism. Where God is abandoned human life becomes, in the words of English political philosopher Thomas Hobbes (1588–1679), "solitary, poor, nasty, brutish and

---

1. Federal Bureau of Investigation statistics indicate that since 1960 there has been a 560% increase in violent crime in the U.S.A. The National Center for Health Statistics indicates divorce rates have tripled and the number of children living with single parents has also tripled. The teenage suicide rate has tripled.
2. Frankl, V., *The Unheard Cry for Meaning*, Simon & Schuster, New York, pp. 20–21,1978.
3. Fromm, E., *Zen Buddhism and Psychoanalysis*, Harper & Row, New York, pp. 85–86, 1960.
4. For some excellent discussions of the concept of God, see Henry, C.F.H., *God, Revelation and Authority*, Word, Waco, TX, 1976, Mascall, E.L., *Existence and Analogy*, Longmans Green, London, 1949, Morris, T.V., *Our Idea of God*, InterVarsity, Downers Grove, 1991, Nash, R., *The Concept of God*, Zondervan, Grand Rapids, 1983, Owen, H.P., *Christian Theism*, Clark, Edinburgh, 1984, Plantinga, A., *God and Other Minds*, Cornell University, Ithaca, NY, 1967, Ward, K., *Rational Theology and the Creativity of God*, Pilgrim, New York, 1982, Yandell, K.E., *Christianity and Philosophy*, Eerdmans, Grand Rapids, 1984.

short".[5] There is no song of hope but only the cry of despair.[6]

I. THE RELEVANCE OF GOD

The subject of God's existence has serious consequences for human existence. No other issue touches our lives as deeply as this. It has a profound philosophical implication in all matters of reality. "The greatest question of our time", notes American historian Will Durant (1885–1981) "is whether men can bear to live without God."[7] Chicago philosopher and director of the Institute for Philosophical Research Mortimer Adler (1902–2001) agreed, "More consequences for thought and action follow the affirmation or denial of God than from answering any other basic question."[8]

It is vital to recognise the relevance of God before we demonstrate the reality of God. The fact of God's existence is profoundly significant for all our lives. Superficially, many choose not to acknowledge this, but upon deeper reflection are forced to admit that it is so.

Some time ago a New York police officer observed a man standing on a bridge, apparently thinking of committing suicide. The policeman approached him and said, "Let me make a deal with you. Give me ten minutes to tell you why I think life is worth living, then you take ten minutes and tell me why you think life is not worth living. If I am unable to convince you, I will let you jump." According to the story, after twenty minutes they joined hands and both jumped off the bridge.

The story poses serious questions. Is life really worth living? If there is no God, then what is the reason for our being? What is the logical ground for our values, morality, rationality, dignity and personality? If there is no God we are, in the words of philosopher William James, "Like dogs in a library observing the volumes but unable to read the print." Are we just an accidental by-product of matter which evolved mindlessly on a tiny speck of dust called planet Earth, basically just rearranged pond scum? How could we find meaning in a meaningless universe? Reason in an irrational world? Value in a material universe and purpose in a random existence? If there is no God, then should we not conclude with Shakespeare's

5. Hobbes, T., *Leviathan*, ch. 13, 1651.
6. The writings of famous atheists like Nietzsche, Bertrand Russell, Sartre, Albert Camus and Hemingway confirm this truth.
7. Quoted in Baxter, B.B., *I Believe Because...*, Baker Book House, Grand Rapids, MI, p. 29, 1978.
8. Adler, M., *Great Books of the Western World*, Vol. **II**, ed. Robert M. Hutchins, p. 561.

Macbeth that "Life is a tale told by an idiot full of sound and fury signifying nothing?"[9] How could we possibly escape the nihilism of Friedrich Nietzsche, the meaninglessness of Jean-Paul Sartre, the despair of Bertrand Russell, the nothingness of Martin Heidegger or the fatalism of Albert Camus? The absence of God in reality is the absence of goodness, truth, value, meaning, reason, life and joy. Many brilliant minds have understood this truth only too well. The rejection of God logically implies the rejection of all reality that is fundamental to God.[10] (See also Chapter 3(VI): The Agony of Atheism, p. 89.)

Although the subject of God may appear to be simple on the surface it is, in fact, extremely profound. God is not a secondary issue but an ultimate factor. The very nature of God demands an approach that transcends the normal and the contingent. One should not attempt to prove God the way we try to prove apples and atoms. The reality of God is in a category that is radically trans-natural. It is beyond and above nature. God is transcendent.[11] One must not commit the categorical mistake of equating God with the phenomena which He has made.[12]

If God is the cause of the universe, then He must be beyond and greater than the physical dimension. Therefore we may discover the effects or evidence of God in the universe but not necessarily observe the essence of God within the universe, for the profound reason that He transcends space, time and matter. The skeptic who says "Show me your God!" and demands scientific proof, is being extremely simplistic.

The story of the man who went fishing illustrates an important truth. Every time he caught a big fish he kept throwing it back into the lake and each time he caught a small one, he kept it. A mystified bystander, observing his peculiar process of selection, asked him what on earth he was doing. With a smile the man replied, "I only have an eight-inch frying pan and so the larger fish won't fit." The trouble is that many skeptics reject God because they can't fit Him into their naturalistic frying pan. The truth is there are realities that go beyond our limited paradigm but to reject them because they do not fit our limited scientific categories is to become a poor metaphysical fisherman. Our philosophical frying pan is not big enough to include all of reality.[13]

---

9.   Shakespeare, W., *Macbeth*, Act 5, Scene 5.

10.   See Küng, H., *Does God Exist?* translated by Edward Quinn, Doubleday, Garden City, NY, 1980.

11.   See Frame, J.M., *The Doctrine of the Knowledge of God*, Presbyterian & Reformed, Phillipsburg, NJ, 1987.

12.   The category fallacy made prominent by British philosopher Gilbert Ryle (1900–1976) is committed when things or facts of one category are regarded as having similar properties of another (e.g. colour to sound, truth to questions, space to time). It would be a category mistake to ask: What does yellow taste like? Can you show me the sound of music? Who made God?

13.   Many important philosophers and scientists conclude that the scientific method is not capable of handling all realities. See Clark, G.H., *The Philosophy of Science and Belief in God*, Craig Press, Nutley, NJ, 1964, Hooykass, R., *Religion and the Rise of Modern Science*, Scottish Academic Press, Edinburgh, 1972, Jaki, S., *The Road of Science and the Ways to God*, University of Chicago Press, 1978, Kuhn, T.S., *The Structure of Scientific Revolutions*, University of Chicago Press, 1970, Mascall, E.L., *Christian Theology and Natural Science*, Longmans Green, London, 1956. The statement "science can handle all realities" is also self-refuting, since that statement itself is not part of science!

The question of God's existence is a perennial one, which presses upon all of us and demands a rational response. For one to go through life without examining ultimate questions is to miss the central point of human existence. The meaning of life is to find the meaning for life and the purpose of existence is to discover the purpose worth living for. A sensible existence is only possible when we try to make sense of our lives and the universe. As Socrates so wisely proposed, "The unexamined life is not worth living."[14] Reflection can lead us to resolution. American Quaker theologian Elton Trueblood (1900–1994), in addressing this issue suggests, "If we refuse to discuss the existence of God we are simply avoiding the central issue, which is the issue of delusion."[15] Even the Australian-born Oxford atheistic philosopher J.L. Mackie (1917–1981) agrees that the issue of God's existence is worth reflecting on. He insists, "The question whether there is or is not a god can and should be rewarding, in that it can yield definite results."[16] In the final analysis, as Thomistic[17] philosopher Edward Sillem affirms, "The conclusion we reach in our reflection on this question has the most momentous consequences in the orientation of our thinking and of our daily living."[18] If there is a God, knowing Him will be the ultimate key to our existence. This truth will be the greatest truth for mankind. Unlike any other question, the question of God has cosmic significance, for it touches every realm of our existence and provides the basic reason for our being.

Since the concept of God is the greatest issue confronting humanity it deserves our most thoughtful attention. Evangelical philosopher C. Stephen Evans affirms, "Belief in God is

14. Plato, *Apology*, 38.
15. Trueblood, D.E., *General Philosophy*, Baker, Grand Rapids, MI, p. 209, 1963.
16. Mackie, J.L., *The Miracle of Theism*, Clarendon Press, Oxford, p. 1, 1982.
17. Following the approach of the hugely influential medieval philosopher and priest Thomas Aquinas (1225–1274).
18. Sillem, E., *Ways of Thinking About God*, Darton, Longman & Todd, London, p. 1, 1961.

genuinely coherent with all we know about ourselves and our universe. It contradicts no known facts and it makes sense of many things that would otherwise be inexplicable."[19]

Thirty years ago, *Time* magazine, in an interesting article, "Modernizing the Case for God", reported, "In a quiet revolution in thought and argument that hardly anyone could have foreseen only two decades ago, God is making a comeback." A generation ago there were few intellectuals in academic circles providing logical arguments for the existence of God, but today the situation has altered. As *Time* suggested, "Now it is more respectable among philosophers than it has been for a generation to talk about the possibility of God's existence."[20] The case is even stronger now, especially with the new discoveries of the cellular nano-machines in living creatures.

Great thinkers who hold to the existence of God have left a legacy of arguments for us to ponder. We will examine several of them. These arguments have been reinforced by recent developments in contemporary logic, philosophical argument and an increasing amount of scientific data. They are valuable in supporting our confidence in the reality of God.[21]

II. CONCLUSIVE COSMOLOGICAL EVIDENCE

In the opinion of many Christian philosophers, one of the most forceful arguments for the existence of God is the cosmic evidence.[22] The existence of the universe is an undeniable reality. The fact of existence is indeed a mystery that staggers the mind. Sophists may deny the reality of the universe but such an attempt is futile, for the Sophist must exist in order to deny it, therefore such an argument is self-refuting. A good case in point is the example of a student at New York University who troubled his professor with a contradictory question, "Sir, how do I know that I exist?" The professor paused for a while, lowered his glasses, gazed at the student and demanded, "And whom shall I say is asking?" The notion that existence is an illusion is logically incoherent and factually meaningless.

The most profound philosophical question, which has caused many debates and much discussion among philosophers, is "Why is there something, rather than nothing?" The

19. Evans, C.S., *The Quest for Faith: Pointers to God*, Inter-Varsity Press, Leicester, p. 131, 1986.
20. *Time*, p. 65, 7 April 1980.
21. Not long ago, Alvin Plantinga (1932–), arguably one of the brightest philosophers of our time, presented a paper "Two Dozen (or So) Theistic Arguments" at a philosophical conference and complained that our philosophers have not availed themselves of the rich material that supports a theistic universe. See also the essay by Henry Schaeffer III, "Stephen Hawking, The Big Bang, and God".
22. For an in-depth discussion on this evidence see Burrill, D.R. (Ed.), *The Cosmological Arguments*, Anchor Books, Garden City, NY, 1967, Craig, W.L., *The Kalām Cosmological Argument*, Barnes & Noble, NY, 1979, Garrigou-Lagrange, R., *God: His Existence and Essence*, Herder Book Co., St. Louis, 1934, Geisler, N.L. and Corduan, W., *Philosophy of Religion*, Baker, Grand Rapids, 1989, Hackett, S., *The Resurrection of Theism*, Moody Press, Chicago, Mascall, E., *He Who Is*, Longmans Green, NY, 1943, Reichenbach, B.R., *The Cosmological Argument*, Charles Thomas Pub., Springfield, IL, 1972, Rowe, W.L., *The Cosmological Argument*, Princeton University Press, 1975, Sproul, R.C., Gerstner, J. and Lindsley, A., *Classical Apologetics*, Zondervan, Grand Rapids, 1984, Thompson, S.M., *A Modern Philosophy of Religion*, Regnery, Chicago, 1955.

reality of the universe demands a verdict. There is hardly a philosopher worth a grain of salt who has not wrestled with this question. Every thinking person at some point confronts the problem. Philosophical theologian John Hick (1922–) writes:

> *"When we try to think about this infinitely fascinating universe in which we live we find that we are faced in the end with sheer mystery—the mystery of existence, of why there is a universe at all."*[23]

Welsh philosopher and theologian H.D. Lewis (1910–1992), from London University notes, "The question 'Why is there something rather than nothing?' is regarded even by some skeptical philosophers as a significant one."[24] This question caused considerable philosophical speculation for the German philosopher and mathematician Gottfried Wilhelm Leibniz (1646–1716). He finally came to the conclusion that, "The first question which should rightly be asked is: Why is there something rather than nothing?"[25] Indeed, the fact is that we exist rather than that we do not. Existential theologian Paul Tillich (1886–1965) admitted, "the riddle of all riddles" is the mystery that there is anything at all.[26] The question of Being, as German Nazi philosopher Martin Heidegger (1889–1976) conceded, is the most significant of all questions and deserves every effort of our intellectual energy.

The writings of great minds over many centuries such as Augustine, Thomas Aquinas, Descartes, Hegel, Dostoyevsky, Heidegger, Jean-Paul Sartre, Ludwig Wittgenstein, C.S. Lewis, and others, indicate that the question of existence is worthy of serious consideration. Ludwig Wittgenstein (1889–1951), one of last century's greatest philosophers, reflected deeply on the mystery of existence. He made this significant point, "It is not *how* things are in the world that is mystical, but *that* it exists." This is an important observation in the light of his philosophical stature. His conclusion is even more startling, "The solution of the riddle of life in space and time lies *outside* space and time."[27] According to Wittgenstein, the answer to the question, "Why is there something rather than nothing?" lies not in the something, but beyond the something. In this sense Wittgenstein claims that the fact of existence demands a ground for its existence, and the contingency of existence requires a

23. Hick, J., *Christianity at the Centre*, SCM Press, London, p. 63, 1968.
24. Lewis, H.D., "Philosophy of Religion, History of," in *The Encyclopedia of Philosophy*, Vol. **VI**, ed. Paul Edwards, Macmillan, London, p. 284, 1972.
25. Leibniz, G.W., "The Principles of Nature and of Grace, Based on Reason," in *Leibniz Selections*, ed. Philip P. Weiner, The Modern Student's Library, Scribner, New York, p. 527, 1951.
26. Tillich, P., *Systematic Theology*, University of Chicago Press, 1963.
27. Wittgenstein, L., *Tractatus Logico-Philosophicus*, Routledge & Kegan Paul, London, p. 149, 1969.

non-contingent being who is the cause of all contingency.[28]

Philosopher David H. Freeman, in his important work, *A Philosophical Study of Religion*, correctly observes, "The issue is whether the world is explicable solely in terms of itself, i.e., is the world itself ultimate, or is there a being other than the world to which the world is related?"[29] John Warwick Montgomery (1931–), the brilliant American apologist and lawyer, argues along the same line, "Nothing in this world is able to explain its own existence; thus, there must be a God in order to explain the world in which we find ourselves."[30] Therefore, the most rational option for the thinking mind in reference to the universe is the reality of God.

Edward Sillem insists, "Man cannot find the ultimate explanation of his own being anywhere but in God Himself."[31] In the same vein, English philosopher Frederick Copleston (1907–1994) asserts, "What we call the world is intrinsically unintelligible, apart from the existence of God."[32] It is no wonder that Voltaire echoed the obvious maxim, "If God did not exist it would be necessary to invent him." Speaking about the universe, Colin Brown, the British theologian at Fuller Theological Seminary, writes, "Are we to regard it as the product of pure chance, and believe that everything happens at random without rhyme or reason?"[33] No! This would be mental suicide. Even a radical skeptic such as David Hume (1711–1776) admitted the force of this argument when he wrote, "I never asserted so absurd a proposition as that anything might arise without a cause."[34] Without God the universe makes no sense.

The universe had a beginning

The weight of the cosmological argument is further strengthened by the confirmation of the majority of scientists today. In the past scientists believed that the First Law of Thermodynamics—mass-energy can neither be created nor destroyed—leads to an eternally existing universe. That the universe and everything in it has existed in one form or other forever. However, research scientist Dr Robert Gange notes,

"The older idea of an eternally existing world is now known to have a problem … that it actually had a beginning."[35]

28. See also Bergman, J., "Ludwig Wittgenstein: Darwin doubter"; creation.com/wittgenstein, 31 May 2011.
29. Freeman, D.H., *A Philosophical Study of Religion*, Craig Press, Nutley, NJ, p. 78, 1964.
30. John Warwick Montgomery, J.W., *How Do We Know There Is a God?* Bethany, Minneapolis, MN, p. 9, 1973.
31. Sillem, ref. 18, p. 182.
32. Copleston, F., *The Existence of God*, ed. John Hick, Macmillan, NY, p. 174, 1968.
33. Brown, C., *Philosophy and the Christian Faith*, Tyndale, London, p. 29, 1969.
34. "David Hume to John Stewart," February 1754, in *The Letters of David Hume*, Vol. **I**, ed. J.Y.T. Greig, Clarendon Press, Oxford, p. 187, 1932.
35. Gange, R., *Origins and Destiny*, Word Books, Waco, TX, p. 8, 1986. Dr Gange was on the staff of the David Sarnoff Research Center in Princeton, New Jersey for 25 years.

This is because of the Second Law of Thermodynamics—the amount of energy available for work is running out, or entropy is increasing to a maximum. If the total amount of mass-energy is limited, and the amount of usable energy is decreasing, then the universe cannot have existed forever; otherwise, it would already have exhausted all usable energy—the 'heat death' of the universe. For example, all radioactive atoms would have decayed, every part of the universe would be the same temperature, and no further work would be possible. So the obvious corollary is that the universe began a finite time ago with a lot of usable energy, and is now running down.

So what does this mean? We can make the following logical argument:

1. Everything **which has a beginning** has a cause.[36]

2. The universe has a beginning.

3. ∴ the universe has a cause.

The words in **bold** are important—it is not everything that has a cause, but only everything which begins to exist. It undercuts a common skeptical objection, "If God created the universe, then who created God?" The universe requires a cause because it had a beginning, as shown above. God, unlike the universe, had no beginning, so doesn't need a cause. In addition, Einstein's general relativity, which has much experimental support, shows that time is linked to matter and space. So time itself would have begun along with matter and space, an insight first pointed out by Augustine in the fourth century. Since God, by definition, is the Creator of the whole universe, he is the Creator of time. Therefore, He is not limited by the time dimension He created, so has no beginning in time—God is "the high and lofty One that inhabits eternity" (Isaiah 57:15). Therefore, He doesn't have a cause.[37]

Robert Jastrow (1925–2008), director of NASA's Goddard Institute for Space Studies and author of many important studies in astronomy, came to a similar conclusion. Writing in the *New York Times* Jastrow poses the question, "Have astronomers found God?" and suggests that they have, or are very close to it. Dr Jastrow, who claims to be an agnostic, argues that the evidence from astronomy demonstrates that the universe had a beginning at a certain moment in time. He declares, "Now we see how the astronomical evidence leads to a biblical view of the origin of the world." He notes, "The details differ, but the essential elements in the astronomical and biblical accounts of Genesis are the same: the chain of events leading to man commenced suddenly and sharply at a definite moment in time, in a flash of light and

---

36. Actually, the word 'cause' has several different meanings in philosophy. But in this section, we are referring to the efficient cause, the chief agent causing something to be made.

37. This is called the *Kalām* Cosmological Argument. It goes back to the church theologian Bonaventure (1221–1274), and was also advocated by medieval Arabic philosophers. The word *kalām* is the Arabic word for 'speech', but its broader semantic range includes 'philosophical theism' or 'natural theology'. The *kalām* argument's most prominent modern defender is the philosopher and apologist Dr William Lane Craig (1949–), *The Kalām Cosmological Argument*, Barnes & Noble, New York, 1979.

energy." His witty conclusion deserves serious consideration:

> *"For the scientist who has lived by his faith in the power of reason, the story ends like a bad dream. He has scaled the mountains of ignorance; he is about to conquer the highest peak; as he pulls himself over the final rock, he is greeted by a band of theologians who have been sitting there for centuries."[38]*

The Apostle Paul, speaking to the Greek philosophers of his day, argued that the existence of the universe provided good and sufficient reason to trust in the existence of God:

> *"The God who made the world and everything in it is the Lord of heaven and earth and does not live in temples built by hands. And he is not served by human hands, as if he needed anything, because he himself gives all men life and breath and*

38. Jastrow, R., *God and the Astronomers*, W.W. Norton, New York, p. 116, 1978.

everything else. 'For in him we live and move and have our being'"
(Acts 17:24,25,28).

The universe is a remarkable evidence of an infinite Creator. Its very existence points to the reality of a powerful God. The Psalmist understood this truth when he wrote:

"The heavens declare the glory of God; the skies proclaim the work of his hands. Day after day they pour forth speech; night after night they display knowledge"
(Psalm 19:1,2).

III. COMPELLING TELEOLOGICAL (DESIGN) EVIDENCE

The wonder and the beauty of our universe are astonishing. In every realm we observe compelling evidence of design, purpose, beauty, complexity and order. This amazing evidence convinced Albert Einstein to make the eloquent remark, "I cannot believe that God plays dice with the cosmos."[39]

For many scientists, exposure to the order of the universe, as well as its beauty and complexity, is an occasion for wonder and reverence. Philosopher of science Stanley L. Jaki, referring to the splendor of our universe, observes, "It has supreme coherence from the very small to the very large. It is a consistent unity free of debilitating paradoxes. It is beautifully proportioned into layers or dimensions and yet all of them are in perfect interaction."[40] Even the skeptic David Hume, a renowned critic of the proofs for God's existence, was so impressed by the force of the evidence that he wrote, "A purpose, an intention, or design strikes everywhere the most careless, the most stupid thinker; and no man can be so hardened in absurd systems, as at all times to reject it."[41]

One of the greatest minds of science, perhaps the greatest, Sir Isaac Newton (1642/3–1727), whose achievements still boggle the modern mind,[42] was a firm believer in the argument for design. The evidence of intricate order and complexity in the universe confirmed his confidence in the existence of an intelligent Designer. He declares:

"When I look at the solar system, I see the earth at the right distance from the sun to receive the proper amounts of heat and light. This did not happen by chance."[43]

No wonder he said:

---

39. Although Einstein did not believe in the God of the Bible, he was not an atheist either. He believed in the God of Spinoza who reveals Himself in the orderly harmony of what exists. Einstein wrote, "God Himself *could not have* arranged those connections (expressed in scientific laws) in any other way than that which factually exists." (Quoted in Weinberg, S., *Dreams of a Final Theory*, Pantheon Books, Random House, NY, p. 242, 1992.) See also Grigg, R., "Einstein, the universe, and God", *Creation* **23**(1):50–53, 2000; creation.com/Einstein.
40. Jaki, S.L., *Cosmos and Creator*, Scottish Academy Press, Edinburgh, p. 42, 1980.
41. Hume, D., *Dialogues Concerning Natural Religion*, Bobbs–Merrill, Indianapolis, p. 214, 1946.
42. See for example Lamont, A., Sir Isaac Newton (1642/3–1727): A Scientific Genius, *Creation* **12**(3):48–51, 1990; creation.com/newton.
43. Quoted in *Heroes of History* **4**:34, Caleb Publishers, West Frankfort, IL, 1992.

"This most beautiful system of the sun, planets, and comets, could only proceed from the counsel and dominion of an intelligent Being. … This Being governs all things, not as the soul of the world, but as Lord over all; and on account of his dominion he is wont to be called 'Lord God' Παντοκράτωρ [Pantokratōr], or 'Universal Ruler'. … The Supreme God is a Being eternal, infinite, absolutely perfect."[44]

The evidence from design, commonly regarded as the teleological argument, is one of the most popular arguments employed by philosophers. The great philosopher Plato observed there are two things that lead people to believe in God: the evidence from the experience of the soul and "from the order of the motion of the stars, and of all things under the dominion of the mind which ordered the universe".[45] Even the great logician Aristotle, who formulated the laws of logic and proposed that philosophy begins with the sense of wonder, was impressed by the order of the cosmos. The force of this teleological argument is evident in its impact on numerous scientists today. This argument, notes philosopher William Lane Craig (1949–), is "the oldest and most popular of all the arguments for the existence of God".[46] Referring to this evidence, the German philosopher Immanuel Kant in his famous work *Critique of Pure Reason* insists that the argument "always deserves to be mentioned with respect".[47]

The argument from design has, in spite of David Hume's earlier critique, received "strong support in recent years from astronomy, physics, and biology"[48] as philosopher J.P. Moreland correctly points out. It is brilliantly defended by able minds in the rank of Richard Taylor, F.R. Tennant, Richard Swinburne and A.E. Taylor. And through the centuries great minds like Plato, Aristotle, Cicero, William Paley, Aquinas and others have used it.[49]

Universe design: anthropic principle

Recent scientific observation is providing supporting evidence in the light of what scientists presently call the 'Anthropic Principle' in Cosmology. Astrophysicists suggest that life would not be possible if the early condition of the universe had varied even slightly. The universe appears to be designed for life. In other words it is 'fine-tuned' for our existence. For example:

- The electromagnetic coupling constant binds electrons to protons in atoms. If it was smaller, fewer electrons could be held. If it was larger, electrons would be held too tightly to bond with other atoms.

44. *Principia III*; cited in Thayer, H.S. (Ed.), *Newton's Philosophy of Nature: Selections from his writings*, Hafner Library of Classics, NY, p. 42, 1953.
45. Quoted in Craig, W.L., *Reasonable Faith: Christian Truth and Apologetics*, Crossway Books, Wheaton, p. 84, 1994.
46. Craig, ref. 45, p. 83.
47. Kant, I., *Critique of Pure Reason*, translated by Smith, N.K., St. Martin's, New York, A. 623, B. 651, 1965.
48. Moreland, J.P. and Nielson, K., Does God Exist? Thomas Nelson, Nashville, p. 35, 1990.
49. See Sarfati, J., *By Design: Evidence for nature's Intelligent Designer—the God of the Bible*, Creation Book Publishers, Brisbane, Australia, pp. 7–9, 2008.

- Ratio of electron to proton mass (1:1,836). Again, if this was larger or smaller, molecules could not form.

- Carbon and oxygen nuclei have finely tuned energy levels.

- Electromagnetic and gravitational forces are finely tuned, so the right kind of star can be stable.

- Our sun is the right colour. If it was redder or bluer, photosynthetic response would be weaker.

- Our sun is also the right mass. If it was larger, its brightness would change too quickly and there would be too much high energy radiation. If it was smaller, the range of planetary distances able to support life would be too narrow; the right distance would be so close to the star that tidal forces would disrupt the planet's rotational period. There would be too little of the blue and ultraviolet light that are most important for photosynthesis.

- The earth's distance from the sun is crucial for a stable water cycle. Too far away, and most water would freeze; too close and most water would boil.

- The earth's gravity, axial tilt, rotation period, magnetic field, crust thickness, oxygen/nitrogen ratio, carbon dioxide, water vapour and ozone levels are just right.

At "Christianity Challenges the University: An International Conference of Theists and Atheists", participants trained in natural sciences were asked what particular evidence played an important part in their conversion. Their unanimous response was, "The incredible design or order in the universe was overwhelming evidence for a divine plan and the existence of a Divine Planner."[50] "The principle of teleological purpose", observes Nobel Prize winner Sir Ernst Chain, who co-discovered penicillin, "stares the biologist in the face wherever he looks".[51] Chain was scathing of Darwinian

50. See Varghese, R.A. (Ed.), *The Intellectuals Speak Out About God*, Regnery, Chicago, 1984.
51. Chain, E., *Social Responsibility and the Scientist in Modern Western Society*, Council of Christians and Jews, London, pp. 25–26, 1970.

explanations.[52] Internationally known UK-born cosmologist Paul Davies, who was at the time the Head of Theoretical Physics at the University of Adelaide, Australia, declared that, "It is hard to resist the impression that the present structure of the universe, apparently so sensitive to minor alterations in the numbers, has been rather carefully thought out … the seemingly miraculous concurrence of these numerical values must remain the most compelling evidence for cosmic design."[53]

Canadian Philosopher John A. Leslie (1940–) argues that the Anthropic Principle provides an excellent defence for the design argument. In his work *The Probability of God*, liberal bishop Hugh Montefiore (1920–2005) offers compelling evidence of a designed universe, including the Anthropic Principle. He claims that chance and natural selection do not offer an adequate explanation for the reality of life. God, notes Montefiore, "is by far the most probable explanation".

Consider the popular analogy provided by New York University philosopher Richard Taylor (1919–2003): Imagine that you are travelling to Wales by train and as you approach your destination, you observe at the border on a hillside the words "Welcome to Wales" arranged out of white stones. What is the chance of these stones popping out of the earth by themselves, developing a white exterior by chance and then rolling together to spell out the words "Welcome to Wales"? In reality the complexity that we observe in our cosmos is far greater than the simple sign "Welcome to Wales." It is more probable,

---

52. The biography of Chain (1906–1979) noted "Chain's dismissal of Darwin's theory of evolution", and his belief that "evolution was not really a part of science, since it was, for the most part, not amenable to experimentation—and he was, and is, by no means alone in this view." As an understanding of the development of life, Chain said, "a very feeble attempt it is, based on such flimsy assumptions, mainly of morphological-anatomical nature that it can hardly be called a theory." And speaking of certain evolutionary examples, he exclaimed, "I would rather believe in fairies than in such wild speculation." Clark, R.W., *The Life of Ernst Chain: Penicillin and Beyond*, Weidenfeld & Nicolson, London, pp.146–148, 1985.

53. Davies, P., *God and the New Physics*, Simon & Schuster, New York, p. 189, 1983. But see Batten, D., Physicists' God-talk, *Creation* **17**(3):15, 1995; creation.com/physicists-god-talk.

mathematically speaking, for those stones by blind chance to emerge out of the ground, develop a white exterior, roll down and form the words "Welcome to Wales" than for chance evolution to produce the complexity of the world in which we live.[54]

Even before Christ, the Roman orator and statesman Cicero (106–43 BC) vigorously used design arguments against the evolutionist Epicurus (341–270 BC).[55] Epicurus taught that everything formed by chance collisions of particles, which could form anything, including something as beautiful as the world. Cicero replied that this was on a par with believing that if the letters of the alphabet were thrown on the ground often enough they would spell out the *Annals of Ennius*. And he pointed out that if chance collisions of particles could make a world, why then cannot they build much less difficult objects, like a colonnade, a temple, a house, or a city, that nobody doubts were designed?

It is eminently more reasonable to perceive that our universe is the product of intelligent design than it is to believe that it is a product of chance. Who in his right mind would think that an explosion in a printing shop could produce the *Oxford Dictionary*? Chance has no real basis for producing anything. The assumption that time plus matter plus chance could produce intelligence is mythological. Things don't just come by chance. The idea of chance is meaningless and has no rational or factual support, hence it is logically fallacious. Chance can never be a causal agent for anything. It is not an entity, nor is it a being but a conceptual ambiguity which has no real existence, therefore it is not capable of producing anything.

Even a passionate atheist like Richard Dawkins admits, "The more statistically improbable a thing is, the less we can believe that it just happened by blind chance. Superficially, the obvious alternative to chance is an intelligent designer."[56] Philosopher Norman Geisler (1932–) concludes, "There may be some theoretical chance that wind and rain erosion could produce the faces of four presidents on the side of a mountain, but it is still far more reasonable to assume that an intelligent sculptor created Mount Rushmore."[57] Theologian Clark Pinnock (1937–2010) affirms, "The adaptive harmony we see in the world is meant to be a signal to us about the existence of a Creator."[58]

Some skeptics, including Professor Stephen Hawking (1942–)[59] who should know better, try an argument like: "We should not be surprised that we do not observe features of the universe incompatible with our own existence, for if features were incompatible, we would not be here to notice it, so no explanation is needed."

54. Taylor, R., *Metaphysics*, Prentice-Hall, Englewood Cliffs, NJ, pp. 99–102, 1983.
55. Cicero, M.T., *De Natura Deorum* (*On the Nature of the Gods*), 45 BC.
56. Dawkins, R., The necessity of Darwinism, *New Scientist* **94**:130, 15 April 1982.
57. Geisler, N., *False Gods of Our Time*, Harvest House, Eugene, OR, p. 52, 1985.
58. Pinnock, C.H., *Reason Enough: A Case for the Christian Faith*, InterVarsity Press, Downers Grove, p. 60, 1980.
59. Sarfati, J., Hawking atheopathy: famous physicist goes beyond the evidence: A review of *The Grand Design* by Stephen Hawking and Leonard Mlodinow, *J. Creation* **25**(1): 25–29, 2010; creation.com/hawking.

But William Lane Craig pointed out:

1. If you were dragged before a trained firing squad, and they fired and missed:
   a. it is true that you should not be surprised to observe that you are not dead, but
   b. it is equally true that you should be surprised to observe that you are alive.
2. If you were asked, "How did you survive?", it would be inadequate to answer, "If I didn't, I would not be here to answer you."[60]

Although critics have frequently argued that the teleological argument has been conclusively refuted by Hume and Kant, a careful study of their work proves otherwise. Philosophers of the calibre of Thomas Reid, F.R. Tennant, A.E. Taylor, Stewart Hackett, Frederick Copleston, Charles H. Malik, Hugo Meynell and others have cogently responded to Hume's skepticism. It is worth noting that Hume and Kant were not unbiased minds looking at the facts objectively. Their objections are often based on systems which are generally refuted and rejected by many modern philosophers. As Lebanese philosopher and diplomat Charles H. Malik (1906–1987) observes, "Hume and Kant did not *conclude* their scepticism and criticism from their rational investigations"[61] but from philosophical presuppositions, which are highly questionable, and which if accepted would undermine their own philosophical conclusions. Furthermore, few philosophers share their presuppositions.

It is worth noting that while Hume is often perceived as a skeptic, his comment on the famous *Dialogues* suggests otherwise. In the *Dialogues* Philo is the skeptic, Demea the pantheist and Cleanthes a theist who argues in favour of the teleological evidence. Hume gives his own verdict on the matter, "I confess that, upon a serious review of the whole, I cannot but think that Philo's principles are more probable than Demea's; but that those of Cleanthes approach still nearer to the truth."[62] The evidence of design in the universe provides adequate ground to affirm the existence of an intelligent Creator.

After returning from his unforgettable flight around the moon with *Apollo 8*, astronaut Frank Borman (1928–) was closely

60. Barrow, J. and Tipler, F., *The Anthropic Cosmological Principle*, Clarendon, 1986, use this objection to evade the implications of a Designer. However, Craig points out the fallacy in "Barrow and Tipler on the Anthropic Principle vs Divine Design", *Brit. J. Phil. Sci.* **38**:389–395, 1988. Once this fallacy is removed, the book becomes a compendium of data of modern science which point to design in nature inexplicable in natural terms and therefore pointing to a Divine Designer. However, some of the alleged design features presuppose the erroneous big bang, so are not considered here.
61. Malik, C.H., *The Wonder of Being*, Word, Waco, TX, p. 33, 1974.
62. Quoted in Geisler, N.L., *Philosophy of Religion*, Zondervan, Grand Rapids, p. 116, 1974.

questioned by the press. One reporter reminded him of the Soviet cosmonaut who stated that on his earlier space flight, he had "not seen angels or God". "Did Mr Borman see God?" was the question. The astronaut gave a brilliant response, "No, I did not see Him either, but I saw His evidence."

David correctly states, "In the beginning you laid the foundations of the earth, and the heavens are the work of your hands" (Psalm 102:25).

Design of Life

Living creatures have long impressed people with their intricate designs. Even the arch-atheist, Oxford biologist Richard Dawkins (1941–), had to concede the force of this:

> *"Biology is the study of complicated things that give the appearance of having been designed for a purpose."*[63]

The discoveries of modern molecular biology have greatly reinforced this already powerful argument, by showing microscopic design that Darwin couldn't have dreamed of.

Dawkins and Darwin claim that a Designer is not necessary, because they suppose natural selection could be a 'blind watchmaker'. But Dawkins agreed that if this doesn't work, atheism can't really respond to the design argument:

> *"An atheist before Darwin could have said, following Hume: 'I have no explanation for complex biological design. All I know is that God isn't a good explanation, so we must wait and hope that somebody comes up with a better one.' I can't help feeling that such a position, though logically sound, would have left one feeling pretty unsatisfied, and that although atheism might have been logically tenable before Darwin, Darwin made it possible to be an intellectually fulfilled atheist."*[64]

But unlike Dawkins above, we argue that things look designed because they *are*, and that this design inference is not limited to appearances, but extends to deep analogy with things we *know* have been designed.[65]

There are enormous problems with natural selection as an explanation for all living things, although they are outside the scope of this book.[66] Suffice it to say, natural selection *culls* from the genes *already* available; it doesn't create new genes with new information.[67] In this book, we will concentrate on a glaring weakness: natural selection can work only with the

63. Dawkins, R., *The Blind Watchmaker: Why the evidence of evolution reveals a universe without design*, W.W. Norton & Company, New York, p. 6, 1986.
64. Dawkins, ref. 63, p. 6.
65. Sarfati, ref. 49.
66. See Sarfati, J., *The Greatest Hoax On Earth? Refuting Dawkins on Evolution*, ch. 3, Creation Book Publishers, 2010.
67. See for example Wieland, C., Muddy Waters: Clarifying the confusion about natural selection, *Creation* **23**(3):26–29, 2001; creation.com/muddy. For how this could work with Darwin's iconic finches, see Cosner, L. and Sarfati, J., The birds of the Galápagos, *Creation* **31**(3):28–31, June 2009; creation.com/galapagos-birds.

pre-existence of *entities that can pass on any information selected*. It's pointless to talk about selection between two runners if both are dead on the starting line!

The famous philosopher Antony Flew (1923–2010) pointed out the problem, directly addressing Dawkins' claims:

> *"It seems to me that Richard Dawkins constantly overlooks the fact that Darwin himself, in the fourteenth chapter of* The Origin of Species, *pointed out that his whole argument began with a being which already possessed reproductive powers. This is the creature the evolution of which a truly comprehensive theory of evolution must give some account. Darwin himself was well aware that he had not produced such an account. It now seems to me that the findings of more than fifty years of DNA research have provided materials for a new and enormously powerful argument to design."*[68]

This is especially notable because Dr Flew was, until recently, known as a leading proponent of atheism, and you will see a lot more from him in the Atheism chapter (3). But he abandoned this belief prior to his death, to the consternation of the atheistic community.[69] One major factor in his decision was the enormous complexity of even the simplest self-reproducing cell.

Similarly, in 2011, evolutionist John Horgan wrote an article[70] in *Scientific American*[71] entitled "Pssst! Don't tell the creationists, but scientists don't have a clue how life began." Actually, creationists—including Ph.D. scientists—have known this for decades.

Cell machines

For example, for creatures to live at all, they need energy. This energy is supplied by a molecule called *ATP*.[72] In fact, the human body generates—and consumes—about its own weight of ATP every day. Nowadays we know that ATP is produced by the world's tiniest motor, *ATP synthase*.[73] This is only 10 nm across by 8 nm high—so tiny that 1,017 would fill the volume of a pinhead. Even the atheistic journal *Nature* called these motors "Real engines of

68. My pilgrimage from atheism to theism: An exclusive interview with former British atheist Professor Antony Flew, by Gary Habermas, *Philosophia Christi* **6**(2):197–212, Winter 2004; biola.edu/antonyflew/flew-interview.pdf.
69. See Flew, A. with Varghese, R., *There is No a God: How the world's most notorious atheist changed his mind*, Harper Collins, NY, 2007; and detailed review by Cosner, L., *J. Creation* **22**(3):21–24, 2008; creation.com/flew.
70. Horgan, J., Pssst! Don't tell the creationists, but scientists don't have a clue how life began, *Scientific American* blogs, blogs.scientificamerican.com, 28 February 2011.
71. See Sarfati, J., 15 ways to refute materialistic bigotry: A point by point response to *Scientific American*, creation.com/sciam, 20 June 2002.
72. Bergman, J., ATP: The perfect energy currency for the cell, *Creation Res. Soc. Q.* **36**(1):2–10, 1999; creationresearch.org/crsq/articles/36/36_1/atp.html.
73. Updated from Sarfati, J., Design in living organisms (motors), *J. Creation* **12**(1):3–5, 1998; creation.com/motor, written not long after the original discovery of the motor was published, and the Nobel Prize was awarded to the discoverers. A more up-to-date layman's article is Thomas, B., ATP synthase: Majestic molecular machine made by a Mastermind, *Creation* **31**(4):21–23, 2009. The web version creation.com/atp-synthase links to an animation made by CMI.

creation".[74] Recent work shows that it's also the most efficient motor in the world—in fact as efficient as the laws of physics allow. The researchers conclude:

> *"Our results suggested a 100% free-energy transduction efficiency and a tight mechanochemical coupling of F_1-ATPase."[75]*

There are many more nano-machines, for example, the kinesin linear motor that 'walks' along miniature highways in the cell, called microtubules. In 8-nm steps (125,000 per millimetre), at a rate of 100 steps per second, it delivers protein packages to the right place in the cell. It knows where to go because of address labels on the packages! Kinesin is powered by ATP: one molecule per step.[76]

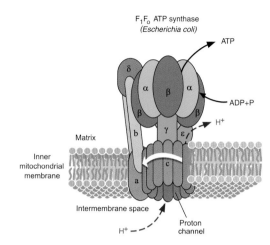

ATP synthase, after John Walker, one of the 1997 Nobel laureates, creation.com/atp-synthase.

Information

Not only do living things contain enormously complex machines, they also contain the 'instruction manual' to build them—a sort of 'recipe book' programmed on DNA, the famous 'double helix' molecule (**d**eoxyribo**n**ucleic **a**cid). This is a very complicated molecule, and actually a very unstable molecule. One article reported:

> *"'There is a general belief that DNA is "rock solid"—extremely stable,' says Brandt Eichman, associate professor of biological sciences at Vanderbilt, who directed the project. 'Actually DNA is highly reactive. On a good day about one million bases in the DNA in a human cell are damaged.'"[77]*

Fortunately, in our cells, we have many elaborate repair machines to undo this chemical damage.[78] But most skeptics believe that life evolved in a primordial soup,[79] which would

---

74. Block, S., Real engines of creation, *Nature* **386**(6622):217–219, 1997; Comment on Noji, H. *et al.*, Direct observation of the rotation of F_1-ATPase, same issue, pp. 299–302.
75. Toyabe, S. *et al.*, Thermodynamic efficiency and mechanochemical coupling of F_1-ATPase, *PNAS* **108**(44):17951–17956, 2011.
76. A lucid lay explanation is Smith, C., Fantastic voyage, *Creation* **30**(1): 20–23, 2007. The online version creation.com/voyage links to animations of both kinesin and ATP synthase motors.
77. Newly Discovered DNA Repair Mechanism, *Science News*, sciencedaily.com, 5 October 2010.
78. Sarfati, J., New DNA repair enzyme discovered, creation.com/DNA-repair-enzyme, 13 January 2010.
79. For problems with materialistic ideas that life evolved from non-living chemicals, see creation.com/origin and Sarfati, J., *By Design* (ref. 49), ch. 11.

have lacked such machines (not to mention, lacking any evidence that it existed at all[80]). So even if DNA managed to form spontaneously somehow, it would not have survived long.[81]

But even more important than the chemistry is the *enormous information content* of the 'recipe' stored on this DNA. This is transmitted from one generation to the next, so that living things reproduce "after their kinds" (cf. Genesis 1). Dawkins himself admits:

> "[T]here is enough information capacity in a single human cell to store the Encyclopaedia Britannica, all 30 volumes of it, three or four times over."[82]

Nowadays we would say that each of our cells—and there are about a hundred trillion in the human body—contains about *three gigabytes* of information. Even the simplest living creature, the tiny germ *Mycoplasma*, has about 600 kilobytes.[83]

To return to the *Britannica*, the information is in the form of ink molecules on paper. But *nothing in the ink molecules themselves* made them form into the letters, words, phrases, sentences, and paragraphs of the *Encyclopaedia*. It certainly wasn't produced by an ink spill. Rather, the information was imposed on the ink by an outside intelligent source (or a program ultimately programmed by an intelligent mind).

But here is the connection with living things. There is likewise *nothing in the chemistry of DNA's building blocks themselves* that would make them join up in predetermined ways, any more than forces between ink molecules make them join up into letters and words. Michael Polanyi (1891–1976), a former chairman of physical chemistry at the University of Manchester (UK) who turned to philosophy, confirmed this:

> "As the arrangement of a printed page is extraneous to the chemistry of the printed page, so is the base sequence in a DNA molecule extraneous to the chemical forces at work in the DNA molecule. It is this physical indeterminacy of the sequence that produces the improbability of any particular sequence and thereby enables it to have a meaning—a meaning that has a mathematically determinate information content."[84]

Just as the *Britannica* had intelligent writers to produce its information, so it is *scientific* to

80. If such a soup produced all the nitrogen-rich compounds required for life, then why is there no trace of them in the 'earliest' rocks? Cf. Brooks, J. and Shaw, G., *Origins and Development of Living Systems*, Academic Press, London and New York, 1973.

81. Many skeptics believe that life started with a similar molecule called RNA (ribonucleic acid). But this is even less stable than DNA, and so are its building blocks such as the sugar ribose. John Horgan (ref. 70) admits, "But the 'RNA-world' hypothesis remains problematic. RNA and its components are difficult to synthesize under the best of circumstances, in a laboratory, let alone under plausible prebiotic conditions. ... The RNA world is so dissatisfying that some frustrated scientists are resorting to much more far out—literally—speculation." For those interested in chemistry, more chemical problems with 'RNA World' ideas can be found at creation.com/rna.

82. Dawkins, ref. 64., p. 115.

83. Fraser, C.M. *et al.*, The minimal gene complement of *Mycoplasma genitalium*, *Science* **270**(5235):397–403, 1995; perspective by Goffeau, A., Life with 482 Genes, same issue, pp. 445–446. They reported 582,000 DNA bases or 'letters'. Other reports have a different number, but all within the same ball park.

84. Polanyi, M., Life's irreducible structure, *Science* **160**(3834):1313–1318, 21 June 1968; p. 1308.

believe that the information in the living world likewise had an original Writer.[85]

Alex Williams, who was Australian representative to a United Nations' International Atomic Energy Agency coordinated research program, explained this further in applying this to the cell machinery:

> *"Polanyi pointed to the machine-like structures that exist in living organisms. … Just as the structure and function of these common machine components cannot be explained in terms of the metal they are made of, so the structure and function of the parallel components in life cannot be reduced to the properties of the carbon, hydrogen, oxygen, nitrogen, phosphorus, sulphur and trace elements that they are made of. There are endless examples of such irreducible structures in living systems, but they all work under a unifying principle called 'autopoiesis'."[86]*

Decoding the information

Information is meaningless unless we understand its *language*. The *Britannica* is little use unless we know English. For example, 'gift' in English means a present, but in German it means poison. The wrong convention can mean the wrong message. One German friend said that the first time he came to an English-speaking country, he thought we were stark raving mad for having 'poison shops' everywhere.

The DNA code is also a language: three DNA 'letters' code for one protein 'letter'. This language requires many different decoding machines to read it, including the ribosome.[87] However, the instructions to build this decoding machinery are themselves stored on the DNA, thus producing a vicious circle, or chicken-and-egg problem. Furthermore, most of these processes use energy, supplied by ATP, produced by the nano-motor ATP synthase. But the ATP synthase motor can't be produced without instructions in the DNA, read by decoding machinery using ATP … a three-way circle, or perhaps an egg-nymph-grasshopper problem.

Multiple languages in DNA

In fact, there is more than one language involved.

Recently, another code was discovered: the 'splicing code' that controls how different parts of the DNA are chopped out and spliced together.[88] This enables a single gene to encode multiple proteins, and explains why humans have only about 20,000 genes yet make over 100,000 proteins, which surprised those who decoded the human genome. But thanks

---

85. See also Sarfati, J., DNA: marvellous messages or mostly mess? *Creation* **25**(2):26–31, 2003; creation.com/message.
86. Williams, A., Life's irreducible structure—Part 1: autopoiesis, *J. Creation* **21**(1), 2007; creation.com/autopoiesis.
87. Sarfati, ref. 85. The online version creation.com/message links to animations of a number of DNA decoding machines, including RNA polymerase, the ribosome, the t-RNA 'adaptor' and the chaperonin folding machine; as well as the ATP synthase motor.
88. Barash, Y. *et al.*, Deciphering the splicing code, *Nature* **465**(7294):53–59, 2010.

to the information decoded by the splicing code, "three neurexin genes can generate over 3,000 genetic messages that help control the wiring of the brain", according to co-discoverer Brendan Frey.[89,90] This also involves a complex machine called a *spliceosome*. One paper was tellingly entitled:, "Mechanical devices of the spliceosome: motors, clocks, springs, and things."[91]

Multiple codes are an even bigger problem for evolution, as geneticist John Sanford (1950–), the inventor of the gene gun, pointed out:

> *"Most DNA sequences are* poly-functional *and so must also be* poly-constrained. *This means that DNA sequences have meaning on several different levels (poly-functional) and each level of meaning limits possible future change (poly-constrained). For example, imagine a sentence which has a very specific message in its normal form but with an equally coherent message when read backwards. Now let's suppose that it also has a third message when reading every other letter, and a fourth message when a simple encryption program is used to translate it. Such a message would be poly-functional and poly-constrained. We know that misspellings in a normal sentence will not normally improve the message, but at least this would be* possible. *However, a poly-constrained message is fascinating, in that it cannot be improved. It can* only *degenerate. Any misspellings which might possibly improve the normal sentence will be disruptive to the other levels of information.* Any change at all *will diminish total information with absolute certainty.*
>
> ...
>
> *"The poly-constrained nature of DNA serves as strong evidence that higher genomes cannot evolve via mutation/selection except on a trivial level."*[92]

Atheist conundrum

The origin of the cell's *information*, and its decoding machinery, is thus a huge problem for atheists. Astrophysicist and evolutionist Paul Davies (1946–) says:

> *"We now know that the secret of life lies not with the chemical ingredients as such, but with the logical structure and organisational arrangement of the molecules. ... Like a supercomputer, life is an information processing system, ... It is the [software] of the living cell that is the real mystery, not the hardware".*

But he does nothing to solve this mystery. Instead he asks, "How did stupid atoms spontaneously write their own software?", and answers, "Nobody knows ..." and admits "there is no known law of physics able to create information from nothing".

89. Researchers crack 'Splicing Code', solve a mystery underlying biological complexity, sciencedaily.com, 5 May 2010.
90. Geneticist Dr Robert Carter explains this lucidly in "Splicing and dicing the human genome: Scientists begin to unravel the splicing code", creation.com/splicing, 1 July 2010.
91. Staley J.P. and Guthrie, C., *Cell* **92**(3):315–326, 1998.
92. Sanford, J., *Genetic Entropy & the Mystery of the Genome*, 3rd edition, FMS Publications, p. 131–133, 2008.

IV. CONSCIOUS MORAL EVIDENCE

A remarkable evidence that points to the existence of God is our moral experience. Morality is an essential part of our humanity. At the conclusion of his famous work, *Critique of Practical Reason*, Immanuel Kant (1724–1804) proposed a new argument for the existence of God called the 'moral argument'.[93] Kant declares, "Two things fill the mind with ever new and increasing admiration and awe, … the starry heavens above me and the moral law within me."[94] Long before Kant, Plato (424/423–348/347 BC) argued that the concept of goodness makes good sense only in relation to the greater or the ultimate good.[95,96]

If God exists, it would be natural to expect His created beings experiencing moral convictions. No human existence is possible without subscribing to moral values. Every day we observe politicians, doctors, lawyers, psychologists, judges, sociologists, editors, police, and ordinary citizens argue for justice, fairness, equality, tolerance, honesty, responsibility, duty, accountability, civil rights, human rights, women's rights, etc. We believe it is right to treat all people with equality. We condemn racism, rape, violence, child abuse, war, corruption, murder, treason, betrayal, abortion, and other such behaviour as evil and wrong. The reality of our moral commitment and conscience is unavoidable; we live in a moral universe.

Every individual appeals to a moral law by which he or she makes moral judgements. Our moral standards provide a basis for our thinking and behaviour. But what about the relativist who insists there are no absolutes and argues everything is relative? Those who reject absolute moral law and advocate relativism engage in promoting a belief which is logically self-contradictory, subjective, and arbitrary. The rejection of absolutes is, in an important sense, the death of morals. In this state the individual becomes morally paralysed and unable to make a distinction between good and evil, right and wrong.

The suggestion that there are no absolutes is in fact an absolute position! It is self-contradictory for someone to say, "I am absolutely sure that there are no absolutes!" It does not remove absolutes but seductively substitutes itself as the guiding principle. For example, consider the statements: there are no rules; trust no authority; everything is relative; all beliefs are false. Each such affirmation becomes an absolute in itself, which is what the person wishes to deny. Hence the argument is not only self-refuting but also arbitrary and meaningless.

93. For further discussion on the Moral Argument, see Adams, R.M., *The Virtue of Faith*, Oxford University Press, NY, 1987, "Moral Arguments for Theistic Belief" in Delaney, C.F. (Ed.), *Rationality and Religious Belief*, University of Notre Dame Press, 1979), Green, R.M., *Religious Reason: The Rational and Moral Basis of Religious Belief*, Oxford University Press, NY, 1978), Helm, P. (Ed.), *Divine Commands and Morality*, Oxford University Press, NY, 1981, Lewis, C.S., *Mere Christianity*, Macmillan, NY, 1943, Kant, I., *Critique of Practical Reason*, Bobbs–Merrill, Indianapolis, 1956, Mitchel, B., *Morality: Religious and Secular*, Clarendon, Oxford, 1980 and Owen, H.P., *The Moral Argument for Christian Theism*, Allen & Unwin, London, 1965.
94. Kant, I., *Critique of Practical Reason*, translated by Beck, Lewis White, Library of Liberal Arts, Indianapolis, IN, p. 166, 1956.
95. See *Republic* **6**:507b.
96. See also Sarfati, J., What is 'good'? (Answering the Euthyphro Dilemma), creation.com/euthyphro, 5 May 2007.

Like the old Greek philosopher who said, "Every statement is a lie!" or the Zen Buddhist aphorism, "All statements are absurd!" To reject moral absolutes is in essence to affirm that there are no essential differences between Mother Theresa and Hitler.

Relativism may appear impressive on the surface but it is philosophically false. It is logically contradictory, morally inadequate and existentially unliveable.[97] Consider the true story of a philosophy student who wrote an ethics paper arguing that there are no absolutes and everything is relative. Judged by the research, documentation, and scholarship, the paper deserved an 'A'. The professor however gave it an 'F' with a note explaining, "I do not like blue covers!" When the student received his paper, he was so upset that he stormed into the professor's office protesting, "This is not fair! This is not just! I shouldn't be graded on the colour of the cover but on the content of my paper." The professor looked the student in the eye and asked, "Was this the paper which argued that there are no objective moral principles such as fairness and justice and that everything is relative to one's taste?" "Yes! Yes! That's the one," replied the student. "Well then," said the professor. "I do not like blue covers. The grade will remain an 'F'!" Suddenly the young man understood that moral absolutes are unavoidable and that, in fact, he also believed in moral principles such as fairness and justice. Furthermore he was expecting them to be applied in his case.

97. For a critique of relativism, see Finnis, J., *Natural Law and Natural Rights*, Oxford, 1980, Geisler, N., *Options in Contemporary Christian Ethics*, Baker, Grand Rapids, 1981, Lewis, C.S., *Miracles*, Macmillan, NY, 1960, Lutzer, E., *The Necessity of Ethical Absolutes*, Zondervan, Grand Rapids, 1981 and Trigg, R., *Reason and Commitment*, Cambridge University Press, London, 1973.

The Cambridge scholar C.S. Lewis writes, "If no set of moral ideas were truer or better than any other, there would be no sense in preferring civilised morality to savage morality, or Christian morality to Nazi morality." Thus he says:

> *"The moment you say that one set of moral ideas can be better than another, you are, in fact, measuring them both by a standard, saying that one of them conforms to that standard more nearly than the other."*[98]

The reality of this universal law is very much part of the fabric of human society. We are not merely mechanical beings. Our moral convictions are essential to our existence; without them we would hardly qualify to be human, as Henry M. Morris explains:

> *"Each individual, however benighted, recognises something in him that tells him that he ought to do the thing that is right morally and ought to shun the wrong—even though individual standards as to what constitutes right and wrong seem to vary somewhat with time and place."*[99]

Are our moral values merely sociological conventions similar to driving on the left rather than the right side of the road, or like the subjective utterances that we produce when we order our meals in a restaurant? If morality is merely social convention then it is neither objective nor absolute. In this case the logical question would be, why follow the subjective opinions of society? Why should anyone sacrifice for another's well being? What if society approves cannibalism, ritual human sacrifice, or racism? After all, German 'society' in the 1930s and '40s gave rise to the Holocaust.

Morals cannot be the basis of instinct, for there is a law within us that judges between our instincts and decides which (of our instincts) we should obey. Philosopher C. Stephen Evans notes, "Morality is not simply a law of nature like the law of gravity. It doesn't describe how things in nature go on, but how human behaviour ought to go on."[100]

The moral law is not descriptive (state of being) but prescriptive, 'ought' (something we should do). It is not something physical but metaphysical. Moral philosophers have correctly argued that the prescriptive 'ought' can never be derived from a descriptive 'is'. The brilliant philosopher Ludwig Wittgenstein pointed out that the basis of morality and ethics comes from outside the human situation. "Ethics, if it is anything," he wrote, "is supernatural."[101] In essence morality is transcendental. If our universe affirms the reality of a moral law and we are creatures with moral capacities, then it is logical to assume that God must exist as a moral Being capable of ensuring justice. The English idealist and philosopher Hasting Rashdall's insight into the problem is remarkable. He concludes:

98. Lewis, C.S., "The Case for Christianity" in *The Best of C.S. Lewis*, Iversen, New York, p. 409, 1969.
99. Morris, H.M., *Many Infallible Proofs*, Creation-Life Publishers, San Diego, p. 117, 1974.
100. Evans, ref. 19, p. 45.
101. "Wittgenstein's Lectures on Ethics", *Philosophical Review* **47**:7, 1965.

"A moral ideal can exist nowhere and nohow but in a Mind; an absolute moral ideal can exist only in a Mind from which all Reality is derived. Our moral ideal can only claim objective validity in so far as it can rationally be regarded as the revelation of a moral ideal eternally existing in the mind of God."[102]

If the moral law is not from God then one must conclude that it evolved from non-moral matter. But the concept of an evolving morality is just tautology. Morality cannot simply evolve or change. People's idea of morality may change but morality itself is unchangeable, like the laws of logic and mathematics. It is a law of reality. Some things are always either right or wrong, good or evil. It is never right to kill an innocent person. It is always wrong to abuse a child, whether today or twenty years from now.

It would be unreasonable to argue as the lady who wrote to C.S. Lewis, declaring, "I don't worry if there is a shortage of bread in our town, because in our home we only eat toast." It is equally irrational to think that we could have objective moral law without an objective moral lawgiver. If there is no God there is no logical ground for our morality. The humanist philosopher Paul Kurtz argues correctly when he states, "The central question about moral and ethical principles concerns this ontological foundation. If they are neither derived from God nor anchored in some transcendent ground, are they purely ephemeral?"[103] Kurtz concedes that if ethics are not theistic they are transient, ephemeral, and temporal. The rejection of God logically implies the elimination of absolute morality. Richard Taylor, an eminent ethicist from New York, observes, "The modern age, more or less repudiating the idea of a divine lawgiver, has nevertheless tried to retain the ideas of moral right and wrong, not noticing that, in casting God aside, they have also abolished the conditions of meaningfulness for moral right and wrong as well."[104]

IT NEEDS BREAD

The point of the argument is that our moral experience points to a transcendent God who is the source and ground of our morality. If this is not the case, then the alternative is devastating, as the British theologian D.M. Baillie rightly suggests, "Either our moral values

102. Rashdall, H., *The Theory of Good and Evil*, Clarendon Press, Oxford, p. 212, 1907.
103. Krutz, P., *Forbidden Fruit*, Prometheus Books, Buffalo, NY, p. 65, 1988.
104. Taylor, R., *Ethics, Faith, and Reason*, Prentice-Hall, Englewood Cliffs, NJ, pp. 2–3, 1985.

tell us something about the nature and purpose of reality … or they are subjective and therefore meaningless."[105] This conclusion is logically sound. If our morality is not grounded in God then it is hopelessly subjective. But to reject moral values as meaningless is logically impossible and existentially inadequate. Those who argue that morality is simply descriptive rather than prescriptive miss the point. If morality is nothing more than what humans have invented then our moral behaviour is simply arbitrary and has no ultimate meaning, significance or value. Very few can live meaningful and consistent lives on this assumption.

More recently, the Jewish libertarian columnist Jeff Jacoby gave a lucid summary of the argument:

> "Can people be decent and moral without believing in a God who commands us to be good? Sure. There have always been kind and ethical nonbelievers. But how many of them reason their way to kindness and ethics, and how many simply reflect the moral expectations of the society in which they were raised?

> "In our culture, even the most passionate atheist cannot help having been influenced by the Judeo-Christian worldview that shaped Western civilization. …

> "For in a world without God, there is no obvious difference between good and evil. There is no way to prove that murder is wrong if there is no Creator who decrees 'Thou shalt not murder.' It certainly cannot be proved wrong by reason alone. One might reason instead—as Lenin and Stalin and Mao reasoned—that there is nothing wrong with murdering human beings by the millions if doing so advances the Marxist cause. Or one might reason from observing nature that the way of the world is for the strong to devour the weak—or that natural selection favors the survival of the fittest by any means necessary, including the killing of the less fit.

> "It may seem obvious to us today that human life is precious and that the weakest among us deserve special protection. Would we think so absent a moral tradition stretching back to Sinai? It seemed obvious in classical antiquity that sickly babies should be killed. …

> "Reason is not enough. Only if there is a God who forbids murder is murder definitively evil."[106]

An excellent case in point is the French atheistic existentialist Jean-Paul Sartre (1905–1980), who rejected morality as meaningless but could not live on the basis of that rejection. He said, "If God does not exist, we find no values or commands to turn to which legitimize our conduct. So, in the bright realm of values, we have no excuse behind us, nor justification before us. We are alone, with no excuses."[107] After denying the objectivity of morality, Sartre went against his view by signing the Algerian Manifesto (1960), which declared that the Algerian

105. Baillie, D.M., *Faith in God and Its Christian Consummation*, T. & T. Clark, Edinburgh, p. 173, 1927.
106. Jacoby, J., Created by God to Be Good, *Patriot Post*, patriotpost.us, 15 November 2010.
107. Sartre, J-P, "Existentialism," translated by Frechtman, B., in *Existentialism and Human Emotions*, Philosophical Library, New York, p. 22, 1957.

war was wrong. In other words Sartre could not live with his atheistic existentialism. If there is an objective moral law then there must be a moral lawgiver. David Elton Trueblood puts it as, "the recognition of an objective moral law drives us to the belief in God".[108]

And if we doubt this, we should remember the day of infamy of 20 April 1999: Two students, Eric Harris and Dylan Klebold, embarked on a massacre at their Columbine High School in Colorado, killing 12 students and a teacher, as well as wounding 23 others, before committing suicide. And on 7 November 2007, 18-year-old Pekka-Eric Auvinen killed nine people at his Jokela High School in Finland. What drove them to these atrocities?

For one thing, they all ardently believed that we are just rearranged pond scum who evolved by random mutation and natural selection. Harris and Klebold loved the Nazi application of evolution[109]—even choosing Hitler's 110th birthday for the massacre. Harris wore a T-shirt with "Natural Selection" inscribed.[110] and loved the Nazi application of evolution—even choosing Hitler's 110th birthday for the massacre. Auvinen likewise declared his atheistic evolutionary belief: "Human life is not sacred. … Death is not a tragedy, it happens in nature all the time between all species."[111]

Another example of the problem of denying God is that two evolutionists wrote a book claiming that rape had evolved as a device for men to perpetuate their genes[112]— *one of the authors tied himself in knots trying to explain why rape was still wrong under his own philosophy.*[113]

Our moral reality provides a crucial clue as to the meaning of the universe. In the words of the famous New York scholar Peter Berger, our moral factors are *"signals of transcendence within the … human condition"*.[114] The Apostle Paul, writing to the Christians in Rome, confirms the reality of the moral evidence, "Since they show that the requirements of the law are written on their hearts, their conscience also bearing witness, and their thoughts now accusing, now even defending them" (Romans 2:15).

V. CONCRETE CHRISTOLOGICAL EVIDENCE

A number of contemporary scholars insist that one of the greatest evidences for the existence of God is the reality of Jesus Christ. There is something truly remarkable in the

108. Trueblood, D.E., *Philosophy of Religion*, Harper, New York, p. 115, 1957.
109. See also Weikart, R., *From Darwin to Hitler: Evolutionary Ethics, Eugenics, and Racism in Germany*, Palgrave Macmillan, New York, 2004; creation.com/weikart.
110. Catchpoole, D., How to build a bomb in the public school system, *Creation* **22**(1):17, 1999; creation.com/bomb.
111. Catchpoole, D., Inside the mind of a killer; creation.com/killer, 9 November 2007.
112. Thornhill, R. and Palmer, C.T., *A Natural History of Rape: Biological Bases of Sexual Coercion*, The MIT Press, Massachusetts, 2000.
113. Lofton, J., Rape and evolution (interview with Craig Palmer, co-author of ref. 112), *Creation* **23**(4):50–53, 2001; creation.com/rape.
114. Berger, P., *A Rumor of Angels*, Doubleday, Garden City, NY, p. 52, 1970.

life and actions of Jesus. The noted theoretical physicist Dr John Polkinghorne, a former colleague of Stephen Hawking and a scholar known for brilliance in his field, after looking at the evidence for Christ observes, "The reason why I take my stand within the Christian community lies in certain events which took place in Palestine nearly two thousand years ago."[115]

The Christological evidence cannot be simply dismissed as religious fabrication. To do so is to pre-judge the case. A sensible approach would be to examine the facts, weigh the evidence, ask some tough questions, and then reach a reasonable conclusion in the light of existing evidence. A number of skeptics including Frank Morison, C.S. Lewis, John Warwick Montgomery, Josh McDowell and Simon Greenleaf have taken this approach and were overwhelmed by the evidence.[116]

The French philosopher Jean-Jacques Rousseau (1712–1778), no friend of Christianity, wrote, "Yes, if the life and death of Socrates are those of a philosopher, the life and death of Jesus Christ are those of a God."[117] As we approach this evidence, it is worth noting that we are moving from the ideal to the real, from the abstract to the concrete, from the invisible to the visible. It is absolutely impossible to explain Jesus apart from the fact that He was from God. The American theologian Loraine Boettner (1901–1990) puts it well:

> *"Nothing is more clear than that Christ cannot be explained by any humanistic system. He does not fit into any theory of natural evolution, for in that case the perfect flower of humanity should have appeared at the end of human history and not in the middle of it."[118]*

According to Arnold Toynbee, the famous English historian, "Jesus Christ will still be important for mankind two or three thousand years hence."[119] Jesus is a fact of history. To ignore Him is to ignore history. H.G. Wells, the Oxford historian, in his popular book *The Outline of History*, remarks, "Here was a man. This part of the tale could not have been invented."[120] And we cannot escape the logic of St Anselm, "Jesus is either God or he is not good." C.S. Lewis argues along the same line:

> *"The discrepancy between the depth and sanity … of His moral teaching and the rampant megalomania which must lie behind His theological teaching unless He is indeed God, has never been satisfactorily explained. Hence the non-Christian hypotheses succeed one another with the restless fertility of bewilderment."[121]*

The biblical evidence indicates that Christ claimed to be the Son of God, God in human

115. Polkinghorne, J., *The Way the World Is*, SPCK, London, p. 33, 1983.
116. See Frank Morison, C.S. Lewis, Simon Greenleaf, Josh McDowell, and others.
117. Quoted in Ballard, F., *The Miracles of Unbelief*, Clark, Edinburgh, p. 251, 1913.
118. Boettner, L., *Studies in Theology*, Presbyterian & Reformed, Philadelphia, p. 266, 1970.
119. Toynbee, A., *Civilization on Trial*, Oxford, New York, p. 218, 1948.
120. Wells, H.G., *The Outline of History*, Volume **I**, Doubleday, New York, p. 240, 1971.
121. Lewis, C.S., *Miracles*, MacMillan, New York, p. 113, 1947.

form, equal to God, sinless as God, with authority to forgive sin, to grant eternal life, to be worthy of worship and to be the truth. John Warwick Montgomery declares, "We may not like the Jesus of the historical documents; but like him or not, we meet him there as a divine being on whom our personal destiny depends."[122]

The claims of Christ are unique among the claims of all the religious founders of the world. Mohammed never claimed to be God; Buddha remained silent on the question of God; Confucius refused to discuss the idea of God; Moses merely claimed to be a prophet of God. Only Jesus claimed to *be* God incarnate.[123]

When one considers the claims of Christ, there are several points worth reflecting upon:

- His claims are consistent with His life.
- His claims are consistent with the entire revelation of God—general and special (written).
- His claims are consistent with the reality in which man lives.
- His claims are consistent with our religious experience.
- His claims are consistent with His resurrection.

If we reject the claims of Christ, then how do we account for His resurrection? One of Christ's biographers, the great historian and physician Luke, writes, "After his suffering, he showed himself to these men and gave many convincing proofs that he was alive. He appeared to them over a period of forty days and spoke about the kingdom of God" (Acts 1:3). The Apostle Paul, writing to the Romans, reveals a significant truth about Christ. He states that Christ "was declared with power to be the Son of God by his resurrection from the dead: Jesus Christ our Lord" (Romans 1:4).

The resurrection of Christ convincingly (in a remarkable way) demonstrates the deity of Christ. In essence the resurrection is the foundation of Christianity. Without it Christianity has no ground for belief. The significant question is, "Did the resurrection really happen?" It is reasonable to conclude that if the resurrection took place Jesus Christ is by far the most important person in history. There are three major evidences that support the historicity of the resurrection:

1. The Empty Tomb

The disciples of Jesus observed that the tomb was empty after the resurrection. The Gospels affirm that at least six of Christ's followers saw the empty tomb: Mary Magdalene (Matthew 28:1–10); Mary (the mother of James) and Salome (Mark 16:1–8); Joanna (Luke 24:10);

122. Montgomery, J.W., *History and Christianity*, InterVarsity, Downers Grove, p. 58, 1965.
123. See Sarfati, J., The Incarnation: Why did God become Man? creation.com/incarnation, 23 December 2010.

Peter and John (John 20:2–8). The Roman guards also saw the empty tomb (Matthew 28:2,11–15). The Jews never denied it and Peter proclaimed it to 3,000 people who could have refuted it. It is difficult to dismiss the evidence of the empty tomb.

According to D.H. Van Daalen, "It is extremely difficult to object to the empty tomb on historical grounds; those who deny it do so on the basis of theological or philosophical assumptions."[124] There are more than fifty reputable scholars in relevant specialist fields who accept the evidence for the empty tomb.[125]

The liberal Anglican bishop and New Testament scholar J.A.T. Robinson (1919–1983) states, "The recent mythological view fails to do justice to the scriptural evidence. Many in fact will continue to find it easier to believe that the empty tomb produced the disciples' faith than that the disciples' faith produced the empty tomb."[126] Of course: the disciples had basically lost their faith when their beloved Leader was crucified. Only seeing the Risen Christ after finding the empty tomb restored their faith. It turned them from beaten, frightened men cowering for fear of their lives into bold men who turned the world upside down. This leads to the next section.

2. The Appearances of Christ

Luke writes, "He showed himself to these men and gave many convincing proofs that he was alive. He appeared to them over a period of forty days and spoke about the kingdom of God" (Acts 1:3). The belief in the resurrection is not simply based on an empty tomb but on a living encounter with a risen Lord. The disciples of Christ persisted in their remarkable claim, that they saw the living Christ, even under persecution, torture and death. We cannot dismiss the resurrection experience on the basis of vision or hallucination for they are insufficient to explain the disciples' revolutionary transformation. This significant fact is vital to the case for the resurrection. Their unique testimony is powerful evidence that their message is trustworthy.

The facts demonstrate that on several occasions different individuals and groups saw Jesus alive after His death. He was seen not only by believers but also by skeptics, unbelievers and even enemies. The New Testament records twelve separate post-resurrection appearances of Christ. He appeared to: Mary Magdalene (John 20:11); the other women (Matthew 28:9–10); Peter (Luke 24:34); the two disciples (Luke 24:13–32); the ten Apostles (Luke 24:33–49); Thomas and the other Apostles (John 20:26–30); the seven Apostles (John 21);

124. Van Daalen, D.H., *The Real Resurrection*, Collins, London, p. 41, 1972.
125. See Blomberg, C., *The Historical Reliability of the Gospels*, InterVarsity, Downers Grove, 1987, Brown, R.E., *The Virginal Conception and Bodily Resurrection of Jesus*, Paulist, NY, 1973, Craig, W., *The Son Rises*, Moody, Chicago, 1981, Dunn, J.D.G., *The Evidence for Jesus*, Westminster, Philadelphia, 1985, France, R.T., *The Evidence for Jesus*, InterVarsity, Downers Grove, 1986, Jeremias, J., *New Testament Theology*, translated by Bowden, J., Scribner's & Macmillan, NY, 1971 and Marshall, I.H., *I Believe in the Historical Jesus*, Eerdmans, Grand Rapids, 1979).
126. Quoted in Buttrick, G.A. (Ed.), *The Interpreter's Dictionary of the Bible*, New York, 1962.

all the Apostles (Matthew 28:16–20 & Acts 1:4–9); the 500 brethren (1 Corinthians 15:6); James (1 Corinthians 15:7); and Paul (1 Corinthians 15:8). Dr Yandall Woodfin offers a pertinent note:

> "If the early followers had made up the stories, they had little to gain but outward persecution and a lifelong battle with guilt. It seems more reasonable to believe, rather, that hypocrites do not become good martyrs and that the resurrection happened."[127]

The question which we must face if we reject their testimony, is why would the disciples lie and what would they gain by lying about the event? That so many would so willingly die for a lie (which they knew to be so) would be an even greater miracle than the resurrection itself.

3. The Origin of the Christian Faith

The origin of the church proves the resurrection. What gave birth to the church? Why and how did the church come into being? What persuaded the early Jewish believers to put their faith in Jesus Christ? How did the Church grow from about 1,000 Christians in the Roman Empire by AD 40 to 32 million (or 53% of the population) by AD 350, as estimated by Rodney Stark of Baylor University in his new book *The Triumph of Christianity*?[128] Especially without wielding the power of the sword—in contrast to Islam (see chapters 6 and 8).

---

127. Woodfin, Y., *With All Your Mind: A Christian Philosophy*, Abingdon, Nashville, 1980.
128. Stark, R., *The Triumph of Christianity: How the Jesus Movement Became the World's Largest Religion*, HarperOne, 2011.

Scholars agree that Christianity came into being because the disciples believed that God had raised Jesus from the dead. Something dramatic took place in Jerusalem, which has altered human history. What caused the disciples to believe and preach the resurrection? It was the fact of the resurrection. (Acts 2:32,36; 13:26–39; 17:22–34; Romans 1:4; 14:9; 1 Thessalonians 4:14). In fact, there were at least 17 factors against it in that ancient culture that meant Christianity could not have succeeded in the ancient world, unless it were backed up with irrefutable proof of the Resurrection.[129]

The Apostle Paul clearly states, "And if Christ has not been raised, our preaching is useless and so is your faith" (1 Corinthians 15:14). If the resurrection is not true there is no eternal life and all who trusted in Christ are in fact lost. To deny the evidence of the resurrection would require far greater faith than to believe it. Outside of the resurrection there is no logical explanation for the origin of the Christian church. The objections against the resurrection have been adequately answered by a number of scholars including Charles Anderson, Raymond Brown, William Lane Craig, James D.G. Dunn, F.X. Durrwell, M. Green, Gary Habermas, Murray Harris, G.E. Ladd, F. Morison, James Orr, Grant Osborne, Wolfhart Pannenberg, W.J. Sparrow-Simpson, John W. Wenham and others.

C.F.D. Moule (1908–2007), who was Lady Margaret's Professor of Divinity at the University of Cambridge for 25 years, insists that the origin of Christianity must "remain an unsolved enigma for any historian who refuses to take seriously the only explanation offered by the Church itself".[130] According to Professor Moule, nothing can adequately explain the origin of Christianity outside the resurrection event. If the resurrection is true then we don't have to speculate on the meaning of life. We have something concrete on which to base our trust and hope. In the resurrection of Christ, God has demonstrated to the world that there is a purpose to life and ultimate hope for our existence beyond the grave. The resurrection reveals that God is not a cosmic executive gone away on a long distance trip, but a gracious loving Father compassionately seeking for His lost people.

Thomas Arnold (1795–1842), who held the chair of Modern History at Oxford University and was noted for his famous three-volume *History of Rome* (1838) (and for being headmaster of Rugby School for 13 years), declares:

> *"I know of no one fact in the history of mankind which is proved by better and fuller evidence of every sort, to the understanding of a fair inquirer, than the great sign which God has given us that Christ died and rose again from the dead."*[131]

No theory has ever been formed which could logically refute the reality of the resurrection while carefully observing all the evidence. The fact of the Resurrection is so important that

129. Holding, J.P., *The Impossible Faith*, Xulon Press, Florida, 2007; tektonics.org/lp/nowayjose.html.
130. Moule, C.F.D., *The Phenomenon of the New Testament*, SCM, London, p. 13, 1967.
131. Quoted in Riss, R., *The Evidence for the Resurrection of Jesus Christ*, Bethany, Minneapolis, p. 17, 1977.

we revisit it in chapter 8, p. 191, since it is vital to answering the claims of Islam. The bottom line is: Christians believe in a Saviour who conquered death itself, while Muslims have a prophet, Muhammad, who was conquered by death.

All the above evidences confirm that God really exists. There is more than enough evidence for a man who wants to believe, but there is no evidence for a man who refuses to believe. The conclusion of the great mathematician Blaise Pascal (1623–1662)[132] is most appropriate, "The evidence of God's existence and His gift is more than compelling, but those who insist that they have no need of Him or it will always find ways to discount the offer."[133]

A teacher once asked her students to produce a painting. Nearly all the pictures were vaguely human except the one produced by a boy named Tommy. "What's that?" enquired the teacher, observing a peculiar mass of colour. "It's God!" replied the youngster. "But no one knows what God is like," said the teacher. The boy looked up with an air of confidence and a sense of triumph, "Now they do!" This is precisely what the disciples said about Jesus Christ. "No one has ever seen God, but God the only Son, who is at the Father's side, has made him known" (John 1:18). By the light of the sun we see the world but by the brilliance of Christ we see God. In the ocean of darkness, Christ shines as a beacon of light. The Apostle Paul understood this truth when he wrote, "For God, who said, 'Let light shine out of darkness,' made his light shine in our hearts to give us the light of the knowledge of the glory of God in the face of Christ" (2 Corinthians 4:6).

132. Lamont, A., Great creation scientist: Blaise Pascal (1623–1662): Outstanding scientist and committed Christian, *Creation* **20**(1):38–39, 1997; creation.com/pascal.
133. Pascal, B., *Pensées* 430, translated by Stewart, H.F., Random House, New York.

RECOMMENDED READING

- Farrer, Austin, *Finite and the Infinite*, The Seabury Press, New York, 1979.

- Geisler, Norman L. and Turek, Frank, *I Don't Have Enough Faith to Be an Atheist*, Crossway Books, 2004.

- God Questions and Answers, creation.com/god. Hick, John (Ed.), *Arguments for the Existence of God*, Herder, New York, 1971.

- Holding, James Patrick, *The Impossible Faith*, Florida, 2007; tektonics.org/lp/nowayjose.html.

- Licona, Mike, *The Resurrection of Jesus: A New Historiographical Approach*, IVP Academic, 2010.

- Mascall, Eric, *He Who Is*, Longmans, Green, New York, 1943.

- Mavrodes, George (Ed.), *The Rationality of Belief in God*, Prentice-Hall, Englewood Cliffs, 1970.

- Reichenbach, Bruce, *The Cosmological Argument: A Reassessment*, Charles C. Thomas, Springfield, 1972.

- Sarfati, Jonathan, *By Design: Evidence for nature's Intelligent Designer—the God of the Bible*, Creation Book Publishers, 2008.

- Sarfati, Jonathan, *The Greatest Hoax On Earth? Refuting Dawkins on Evolution*, Creation Book Publishers, 2010.

- Sillem, Edward, *Ways of Thinking About God*, Darton, Longman and Todd, London, 1961.

- Stark, Rodney, *The Triumph of Christianity: How the Jesus Movement Became the World's Largest Religion*, HarperOne, 2011.

- Strobel, Lee, *The Case for Christ: A Journalist's Personal Investigation of the Evidence for Jesus*, Zondervan, Grand Rapids, MI, 1998.

- Strobel, Lee, *The Case for Faith: A Journalist Investigates the Toughest Objections to Christianity*, Zondervan, Grand Rapids, MI, 2000.

- Strobel, Lee, *The Case for a Creator: A Journalist Investigates Scientific Evidence That Points Toward God*, Zondervan, Grand Rapids, MI, 2005.

- Strobel, Lee, *The Case for the Resurrection: A First-Century Investigative Reporter Probes History's Pivotal Event*, Zondervan, Grand Rapids, MI, 2010.

- Swinburne, Richard, *The Existence of God*, Clarendon Press, Oxford, England, 1979.

- Wright, N.T. (Tom), *The Resurrection of the Son of God*, Fortress Press, 2003.

- Zacharias, Ravi, *Can Man Live without God?* Thomas Nelson, 1994.

If there is no God it would be necessary to invent him.
 — VOLTAIRE

*God whispers to us in our pleasures, speaks in our conscience,
but shouts in our pains: it is His megaphone to rouse a deaf
world.*
 — C.S. LEWIS

*The world is all the richer for having a Devil in it, so long as we
keep our foot upon his neck.*
 — WILLIAM JAMES

2

....

IF THERE IS A LOVING GOD, THEN WHY IS THERE EVIL?

Nothing disturbs our existence more than the tragic reality of evil. Indeed, the trouble that troubles humanity is trouble. No one escapes it or can ignore it. The reality of evil touches every level of our lives. Its existence staggers our mind and moves our hearts. Pain, cruelty, calamities, injustices, and death disturb us and leave us helpless. How frequently one hears statements like, "I believed in God until my child was killed in an accident." "Why do the innocent suffer?" "Why are babies born blind and many maimed for life?"

If there is a God, why did He allow Hitler, Stalin, Mao Zedong, Idi Amin, and Pol Pot to murder the innocent? If God exists how could He allow these tragic wars? These are pressing questions which every reflective and sensitive mind frequently ponders—questions which we must face both intellectually and existentially.

Various philosophers have debated over the question of evil; theologians have proposed a variety of solutions and skeptics frequently rely on it to advance their unbelief. Disturbed by its reality, Stendhal declares, "God's only excuse is that he does not exist."[134] Thomas Huxley was even more adamant, "If our hearing were sufficiently acute to catch every note of pain, we would be deafened by one continuous scream."[135] Particularly striking are the remarks of the British philosopher Bertrand Russell (1872–1970):

> "I would invite any Christian to accompany me to the children's ward of a hospital, to watch the suffering that is there being endured, and then to persist in the assertion that those children are so morally abandoned as to deserve what they are suffering."[136]

....

134. Hick, J., *Christianity at the Centre*, SCM Press, London, p. 82, 1968.
135. Quoted in *Oliphant–Smith Debate*, Gospel Advocate Co., Nashville, p. 28, 1929.
136. Russell, B., *Why I Am Not a Christian*, ed. Paul Edwards, George Allen & Unwin, London, p. 22, 1957.

According to Russell, no-one could sit beside a dying child and still believe in the existence of God. However, a Christian minister, who actually sat with dying children regularly, asked in turn what Professor Russell would say to such a child instead—what sort of comfort would atheism provide?

After wrestling with the reality of evil, Nobel Prize winner Albert Camus (1913–1960) concluded, "The final philosophical question is the question of suicide."[137]

In his famous novel, *The Plague*, Camus has a striking scene where a priest, an unbeliever, and a doctor surround the bed of a little boy dying of bubonic plague. As the boy suffers in pain, the priest asks God for help, "God, spare the child." But tragically the boy dies. Later, in the hospital garden, the priest declares, "That sort of thing is revolting because it passes human understanding, but perhaps we should try to love what we cannot understand." The doctor, hearing this, shouts, "No Father! I have a very different idea of love and until my dying day I refuse to believe in a God who lets a child die like that."[138]

In an important public debate several years ago, the atheist Charles Smith passionately illustrated the problem for those who believe in the existence of a good God:

"A few years ago in Arizona a mother and child were left alone on a ranch. The father had gone away. A rattlesnake bit the mother. She tried to get help, but was far distant from the nearest human being. What could she do? She saw she was going to die and that the children would starve, as the father would not return for a week. She killed her babies and herself. How can you explain such an event if God exists?"[139]

The existence of evil is indeed one of the greatest perceived obstacles to belief in God. It is without a doubt the most intellectually challenging of all objections. Evangelical philosopher Elton Trueblood notes, "It is a problem which no theist can avoid and no honest thinker will try to avoid."[140] James Orr insists, "The problem of evil is one of the most crucial protests raised by unbelievers against the fact of God."[141] The process philosopher Alfred North Whitehead writes, "All simplifications of religious dogma are shipwrecked upon the rock

137. Camus, A., *The Myth of Sisyphus and Other Essays*, translated by O'Brien, J., Vintage Books, New York, p. 40, 1955.
138. Camus, A., *The Plague*, translated by Gilbert, S., Modern Library, New York, p. 196, 1948.
139. Smith, ref. 2, p. 32.
140. Trueblood, D.E., *General Philosophy*, Baker, Grand Rapids, p. 226, 1976.
141. Orr, J.E., *The Faith That Persuades*, Harper & Row, New York, p. 80, 1977.

of the problem of evil."[142] The British writer, John W. Wenham, was not exaggerating when he said, "Evil constitutes the biggest single argument against the existence of an almighty, loving God."[143] Hugh Silvester looks at the problem from another angle, "If God knew that certain of His creatures were destined to an eternal sentence in hell, we may ask why He created them at all."[144] In the light of this problem, the modern poet Robert Hale concludes, "If you give me a choice between voting for 'God is dead' or 'Everything (including evil) is God's will,' I would have to abstain."[145]

The reality of evil confronts every philosophy of life and the burden of explaining its origin and existence lies equally upon all. It is not a problem unique to the Christian faith, as R.C. Sproul Sr has so aptly observed, "Indeed, every philosophical theory has to deal with it in some way."[146] However, in theological circles the problem is treated very poorly, as the American philosopher Brand Blanshard (1892–1987) states in his extremely significant volume *Reason and Belief*, "The treatment of evil by theology seems to me an intellectual disgrace."[147] Ed. L. Miller insists, "The theologian's inability to supply the skeptic with a straightforward and satisfying answer to this challenge has made evil, no doubt, the biggest single stumbling block to belief in a God of love",[148] although this may be an overstatement, as there are excellent insights one could gain from the reflections of theologians.

What are we to make of evil? How shall we respond to this pressing problem? Does pain and suffering contradict the existence of God? Does He care for the suffering of mankind? Is He interested in our pain and grief? In what sense is the problem of evil incompatible with the existence of God? If there is a God, why is there evil? These are important questions and they deserve our deepest reflection. If we avoid these questions, then we have nothing to say to a troubled world!

There are a number of approaches to the problem but space will not allow us to treat all the attempted solutions. We will limit our discussion to a number of fundamental factors. From a contemporary point of view there are generally three main responses to this problem: Atheism, Eastern Religion and Christianity.

I.   ATHEISTIC CONFUSION

Atheists frequently argue that the presence of evil in the world is incompatible with the nature of God's existence. Atheists, such as George H. Smith, Woolsey Teller, Kai Nielson, Michael

142. Whitehead, A.N., *Religion in the Making*, Cambridge University Press, p. 77, 1936.
143. Wenham, J.W., "Response," in Geisler, N.L., *The Roots of Evil*, Zondervan, Grand Rapids, p. 89, 1978.
144. Silvester, H., *Arguing with God*, InterVarsity, Downers Grove, p. 36, 1971.
145. Hale, R., quoted in Cassels, L., *The Reality of God*, Herald Press, Scottdale, PA, p. 31, 1972.
146. Sproul, R.C., *Objections Answered*, G/L Pub., Glendale, CA, p. 131, 1978.
147. Blanshard, B., *Reason and Belief*, London, p. 546, 1962.
148. Miller, E.L., *God and Reason: A Historical Approach to Philosophical Theology*, Macmillan, New York, p. 139, 1972.

Martin, Richard R. LaCroix and Antony Flew (in his long career before his conversion to theism) and others, offer several arguments from the problem of evil against the existence of God.

The most famous version of the argument comes from the Greek philosopher Epicurus who sums up the indictment as, "Either He is not good, or else He is not almighty." David Hume, the skeptical philosopher, states the same argument with much clarity:

> *"Is he (God) willing to prevent evil, but not able? then he is impotent. Is he able, but not willing? then he is malevolent. Is he both able and willing? whence then is evil?"[149]*

Epicurus (341–270 BC) first stated this problem and later was quoted by Lactanitus (AD 260–340). The problem could be expressed in the following logical diagram:

Theists believe (A) God is good and (B) God is powerful but the problem is how do we explain (C) in the light of A and B? There are a number of possible explanations why evil exists.[150] Christian thinkers provide the following reasons:

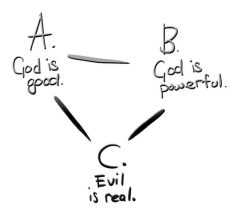

- The existence of Satan, who is often responsible for evil actions.

- The eschatological explanation that God will finally defeat evil.

- The concept of punishment and retribution provide further reason for the existence of evil.

- The idea of discipline for wrongdoing provides insight into the meaning of evil.

- The concept of probation also makes some sense in the light of evil.

- The idea that suffering can be a means of revelation to understand God.

- The concept of redemption makes sense in the light of evil.

- Death and suffering in the world is ultimately due to *sin*, starting with the first man, Adam.

149. Hume, D., *Dialogues Concerning Natural Religion*, ed. Henry D. Aiken, Hafner, New York, p. 66, 1948.
150. For further insight see Bush, L.R., *A Handbook for Christian Philosophy*, Zondervan, Grand Rapids, 1991.

The Scriptures clearly declare that in the final equation it is not evil which is ultimate but God. Jesus said, "Be of good cheer. I have overcome the world" (John 16:33 KJV).

Thomas Aquinas, the brilliant medieval philosopher, recognized the problem of evil and offered the following response:

> *"For because we have proven that every agent acts insofar as it acts through God's power, with God being thus the cause of all effects and acts, and since we proved that evil and defects in beings directed by divine providence come from the condition of the secondary causes, which themselves may be defective, it is obvious that evil actions, understood as defective, do not originate from God but from their defective proximate causes."*[151]

Several Christian philosophers have adequately responded to this dilemma. The works of C.S. Lewis, Alvin C. Plantinga, John Hick, M.B. Ahern, Norman L. Geisler, Austin Farrer, Nelson Pike, Michael L. Peterson and others, offer excellent replies to the charges of atheists.

The popular arguments of the atheist carry little weight and are self-refuting. The argument could be stated as follows:

1. There is evil in the world.

2. Evil is incompatible with God.

3. Therefore God does not exist.

C.S. Lewis, a former atheist who rejected the existence of God on the basis of the existence of evil, asserts, "My argument against God was that the universe seemed so cruel and unjust."[152] The objection is logically fallacious. It misses the truth at several points. Firstly, the skeptics presuppose subjectively—without proof—that evil is incompatible with the existence of God. This premise is presumed, not proven. The skeptic must prove his assumption in order to validate his argument. Secondly, it is still logically possible that God in His wisdom may allow evil for a very good purpose and for some wise reason He has not disclosed that truth. Unless the skeptic has all the reason on the matter and is able to offer good reason that it is the case, the skeptic is indeed rather premature to conclude that the existence of evil is incompatible with God. A logical response to the atheistic argument is:

151. Aquinas, T., *Compendium of Theology*, Chapter 141.
152. Lewis, C.S., *The Best of C.S. Lewis*, Iversen, New York, p. 429, 1969.

1. God is omnipotent.

2. God is benevolent.

3. Since God is not *yet* finished with the world,

4. He *will* eliminate evil one day.

American theologian William Dyrness is right, "Many people who do not believe in God seem to bear a great resentment against Christians and against God for a problem which on their own assumptions does not exist at all."[153] The fact of evil in no way eliminates the reality of God. Through His infinite knowledge, God may permit evil for a very good reason—unknown to His finite creatures.

Thus, as Arlie J. Hoover, professor of history at Abilene Christian University (Texas), rightly points out, "If we don't know his reason for evil this is very interesting philosophically and psychologically, but hardly a contradiction."[154] To charge this as a contradiction, Hoover says:

> *"You would have to know everything to truly assert that evil is a serious contradiction to Christian theism. You'd need to know that all proposed harmonies are false. You'd have to establish propositions like, 'God would never allow suffering,' or 'God would have created only blessed men.' Can any man really prove such propositions as these? How? How would one know so much about what God could or would do?"[21]*

The obvious fallacy in the argument from evil is that of 'begging the question.' In 'begging the question' the person does not prove his point but merely moves in a circle and states the same point twice. This fallacy fails to support the very question at issue, for example a circular definition would be, "A morally good man is one who acts virtuously." Another common one is, "It is better to be idle than to do nothing." Atheists argue from a premise, which their philosophy denies. Jean-Paul Sartre poignantly suggests the atheistic position, "The existentialist (atheist) finds it extremely embarrassing that God does not exist, for there disappears with Him all possibility of finding value in an intelligible heaven."[155]

In his work, *Existentialism and Humanism*, Sartre agrees with the great Russian novelist Fyodor

153. Dyrness, W., *Christian Apologetics in a World Community*, InterVarsity, Downers Grove, IL, p. 155, 1983.
154. Hoover, A.J., *Fallacies of Unbelief*, Biblical Research Press, Abilene, TX, p. 41, 1975.
155. Sartre, J-P., *Existentialism and Humanism*, Methuen, London, p. 33, 1948.

Dostoyevsky (1821–1881) that, "If God did not exist, everything would be permitted."[156] Strictly from an atheistic context there are no absolutes, everything is relative, there is no ultimate law of morals, everything is subjective. If there is no God, there is no absolute moral standard by which to determine what is good or evil. C.S. Lewis effectively points out the difficulty of maintaining absolute standards and principles in a human society:

> *"Unless we take our own standard of goodness to be valid in principle (however fallible our particular applications of it) we cannot mean anything by calling waste and cruelty evils. And unless we take our own standard to be something more than ours, to be in fact an objective principle to which we are responding, we cannot regard that standard as valid. In a word, unless we all consider ultimate reality to be moral, we cannot morally condemn it."[157]*

Philosopher David Freeman argues rightly, "The point is that unless moral standards have the approval and sanction of God, unless God is the moral law-giver, there are no unchanging moral standards."[158] In the same vein, British neo-Thomistic philosopher Eric Mascall observes:

> *"If there is no God, then there is no problem of reconciling the existence of pain and sin with his love and power; and, while the atheist may with reason urge against theism that it has set itself a problem which it cannot solve, he has no business to feel evil as constituting a problem for him, except in the purely intellectual sense of causing him to wonder where it came from."[159]*

C.S. Lewis argues with irrefutable logic in his popular volume *Mere Christianity* the fallacy of arguing against God on the basis of evil. He writes:

> *"Thus in the very act of trying to prove that God did not exist—in other words, that the whole of reality was senseless—I found I was forced to assume that one part of reality—namely my idea of justice—was full of sense. Consequently atheism turns out to be too simple."[160]*

Atheists stand on a moral principle and charge God for breaking this principle. The point is, where did this principle come from? Not from society, for what is a society but a group of individuals, and we don't get principles and values just by approaching them. We don't determine truth by counting noses. If society can produce absolute moral standards then who could argue against Hitler's society for killing the Jews? Philosopher Richard Purtill correctly observes:

156. Sartre, ref. 155, p. 33.
157. Lewis, C.S., quoted in Hooper, W. (Ed.), *Christian Reflection*, Eerdmans, Grand Rapids, MI, p. 70, 1967.
158. Freeman, D.H., *A Philosophical Study of Religion*, Craig Press, Nutley, NJ, p. 223, 1964.
159. Mascall, E.L., *He Who Is*, Longmans, Green & Co., London, p. 183, 1943.
160. Lewis, C.S., *Mere Christianity*, Collins, London, pp. 429–430, 1960.

"If our rationality and morality do not come from God they come from chance permutations of some basic stuff or from the working of mindless forces. In either case, they have no validity."[161]

The atheistic view of evil is totally inadequate in the light of reality. It is subjective, arbitrary, and meaningless. For this important reason the former atheistic philosopher C.E.M. Joad abandoned his faith in atheism and became a Christian. Professor Joad writes:

"To me, at any rate, the view of evil implied by Marxism, expressed by Shaw and maintained by modern psychotherapy, a view which regards evil as the by-product of circumstances which circumstances can, therefore, alter and even eliminate, has come to seem intolerably shallow."[162]

What is most interesting is that atheists appear to be very resentful toward the reality of evil even though, according to their worldview, there is no-one to be resentful against. Mascall points out, "This is very mysterious, and almost leads one to suspect that the atheists have been indulging in a little surreptitious theism on the quiet."[163] Thus, the fact of human moral experience points to the reality of God—not to its negation. Australian lawyer and lay

161. Purtill, R.L., *Reason to Believe*, Eerdmans, Grand Rapids, p. 96, 1974.
162. Joad, C.E.M., *The Recovery of Belief*, Faber & Faber, London, p. 63, 1952.
163. Mascall, ref. 159, p. 183.

theologian Frank J. Sheed (1897–1937) says:

> "*Suffering would be altogether intolerable if there were no God ... Atheism answers that the fact of suffering proves that there is no God. But this does not reduce the world's sufferings by one hair-breadth, it only takes away hope.*"[164]

Cardinal John Henry Newman (1801–1890) was speaking on this point when he wrote, "I think if this life is the end, and there is no God to wipe away all tears from all eyes, why, I could go mad."[165] Our discussion should not escape the splendid insight of philosopher Ed. L. Miller:

> "*Why is it any easier to account for goodness without God than it is to account for evil with him? That the problem of evil generates more fury than the problem of goodness may be more a matter of psychology than philosophy.*"[166]

The most serious fallacy in the atheistic argument is what logicians call 'the diversion'. The fallacy here is to move away from the central issue to a secondary issue. The point of the matter is that evil has nothing to do with the existence of God. In reality, the problem of evil questions God's character but not His existence. Agreeing to this notion the British scientist A.E. Wilder-Smith observes with splendid insight:

> "*For the atheist maintains that he sees nothing but contradictions in nature. He, therefore, rejects from his world of ideas any thought of a creator behind nature. However, we dare not forget that even the tiniest island of order in the largest sea of chaos demands a creator of that small remaining order.*"[167]

There is no logical necessity to conclude that God does not exist simply on the ground that evil exists. In his brilliant work *God, Freedom and Evil*, philosopher Alvin Plantinga provides an excellent response to the atheistic confusion:

> "*Why suppose that if God* does *have a good reason for permitting evil, the theist would be the first to know? Perhaps God has a good reason, but that reason is too complicated for us to understand.*"[168]

II. PANTHEISTIC ILLUSION

Eastern religions such as Hinduism and Buddhism respond to the problem of evil by

164. Quoted in Mascall, ref. 159, p. 184.
165. Flew, A., *God and Philosophy*, Hutchinson & Harcourt, London, p. 106, 1966.
166. Miller, ref. 148, p. 143.
167. Wilder-Smith, A.E., *Why Does God Allow It?* Master Books, San Diego, pp. 25–26, 1980.
168. Plantinga, A., *God, Freedom, and Evil*, Eerdmans, Grand Rapids, p. 10, 1974.

denying its actual existence. With its concept of monism, that all diversity is mere illusion and ultimate reality is both One and Good, eastern religion denies the reality of evil. Following the East, Christian Science likewise rejects the existence of evil as illusory. Its founder Mary Baker Eddy, in *Science and Health*, states, "Evil is but an illusion, and it has no real basis. Evil is a false belief."[169]

This mode of thinking is apparent in the works of Shakespeare when he wrote, "There is nothing either good or bad, but thinking makes it so."[170] To say there are no evils—only how you feel about it matters—is unrealistic in a world of real pain. At a university meeting some years ago, a pantheistic student challenged me on my views on evil. He objected very strongly to my presentation that evil is real. I gently asked him if it was wrong for me to teach that evil was real. He responded, "Yes!" I then asked, "Is it evil to teach that evil is real?" He had no answer, he was in a dilemma. If he accepted my statement he would have to agree to the reality of evil. If he rejected my statement then he would have to deny his basic premise. His only solution was to reject me as an illusion!

The eastern approach to evil does not solve the problem of evil but rather creates a new one. It is not an answer but an escape from reason. If evil, which is so obvious and evident to our minds, is an illusion, what are we to think of the arguments for the illusion of evil? Should we not also consider them as illusions? If we grant the premise that evil is an illusion, what are we to think of the fact that people consider evil to be real? What about the illusion itself, is that not a genuine evil? Since people are deceived into thinking that evil is real, should not this constitute a serious problem, in which case, a real evil?

This view does not explain the origin of the illusion. It offers no explanation to the apparent reality of evil. Its denial does not remove the presence of evil in the world. To accept this theory is to reject the fact of experience. As Christian apologist Norman L. Geisler logically affirms, "Accepting the illusionist's position demands that one admit that all of life as he

169. Eddy, M.B., *Science and Health with Key to the Scriptures*, The First Church of Christ, Scientist, Boston, p. 480, 1994.
170. Shakespeare, W., *Hamlet*, Act 2, Scene 3, line 255.

experiences it is deceiving him."[171] The eastern poet effectively illustrates the dilemma, "Though evil is an illusion, yet when I sit on a pin and it punctures my skin, I dislike what I fancy I feel." It is one thing to believe that evil is an illusion but quite a different matter to live consistently on this premise. As Dr Geisler correctly points out:

"Those who believe that evil and the world are illusions do not actually function as if this were so. They may maintain that all is an illusion, but if one were to push them in front of an oncoming bus, they would quickly 'warm up' to the reality idea!"[172]

Sigmund Freud is right, "It would be nice if it were true that no evil existed, but the very fact that men wish it to be so makes this belief highly suspect."[173] Along the same line, Elton Trueblood argues, "If all evil, whether moral, natural or intellectual, is truly illusory, we are foolish indeed to fight it; it would be far preferable to forget it."[174]

If evil is an illusion it is pointless to try to improve the problem of life. Hence the destitute would be left to starve, the sick left to die, and there would be no need to have hospitals, schools, and universities. Learning would cease and a new dark age would descend upon the earth. Thus, we reject this view as inhuman, impossible, and irrational. "It is a Christian conviction," writes William Dyrness, "that evil is permitted by a sovereign God in some way that is ultimately compatible with his goodness."[175] But how do we go about justifying the goodness of God in a world of suffering, pain, and evil?

III. THEISTIC SOLUTION

The Christian answer to the problem of evil (theodicy) is the only adequate solution to the reality of evil in the world. The Christian answer differs significantly from all other belief systems. Biblical revelation shines considerable light on the subject and the Christian need not sink into the depths of despair and 'kiss his brain good-bye' on this issue.

171. Geisler, N.L., *Philosophy of Religion*, Zondervan, Grand Rapids, p. 312, 1974.
172. Geisler, N.L., *The Roots of Evil*, Zondervan, Grand Rapids, p. 18, 1978.
173. Geisler, ref. 171, p. 312.
174. Trueblood, ref. 140, p. 237.
175. Dyrness, ref. 153, p. 156.

Since the fact of God's existence is overwhelming it is indeed foolish to deny His existence on the basis of evil. To reject God on the basis of evil is like rejecting your parents because they act in a certain way. A scientist does not give up science because he or she encounters a particular puzzle or a difficult problem. The Christian, says David Elton Trueblood:

> *"Has abundant reason to believe in God in the full theistic sense. If, then, he runs into some difficulty, even a difficulty as great as the problem of evil, he does not, for that reason, give up his faith. The reasons for his faith are so great that they can weather a few storms."* [176]

Evil is commonly spoken of in two senses: natural evil and moral evil. J. Edwin Orr's analogy is useful at this point:

> *"A wayfarer takes shelter under a great rock which, loosened by the rain, comes tumbling down, killing him. That is natural evil. A wayfarer takes shelter in a little hut, but a wicked robber stabs him to death. That is moral evil."* [177]

Historically, evil is understood in terms of the Latin word *negatio*. Evil is defined in negative terms, e.g. ungodly, unrighteous, unhappy, etc. To know what is ungodly we have to understand 'godly'. C.S. Lewis suggests, "Goodness is, so to speak, itself: badness is only spoiled goodness. And there must be something good first before it can be spoiled." Lewis adds, "Evil is a parasite, not an original thing." [178] Evil is meaningful only with the good; it is contingent and dependent, an absence of good; not a positive quality but a negative. Evil is not a being but a parasite of being. Hence, evil is a bad relationship existing between good

176. Trueblood, ref. 140, p. 244.
177. Orr, ref. 141, p. 81.
178. Lewis, ref. 160, pp. 46–47.

things. Norman L. Geisler makes an important point:

> *"Darkness is not nothing; it is the absence of light. Likewise, sickness is the absence of health, and death is the absence of life which belongs to a being. All of these are real lacks. Similarly, evil is just as real, although it has no more being of its own than does darkness or sickness."*[179]

Death and suffering are the result of sin

God created human beings with the potential and the capacity to choose good or evil. He created the possibility of evil but not its reality. Thus, God is not the author of evil. As E.J. Carnell (1919–1967), President of Fuller Theological Seminary, observes, "God is the author of the author of sin, but He cannot be the author of sin itself, for sin is the result of a rebellion against God. Can God rebel against Himself?"[180] In essence, sin is the abuse of free will, the misuse of what is good. As Augustine reminds us:

> *"The will … commits sin when it turns away from immutable and common good, toward its private good, either something external to itself or lower than itself. It turns to its own private good when it desires to be its own master."*[181]

The Bible reveals where evil on Earth came from.[182] According to Genesis, the first book in the Bible, God originally created a perfect world, described by God as "very good" (Genesis 1:31). This means there was no violence or pain in the original creation. In fact, people and animals ate plants, not other animals (Genesis 1:29–30).

But this paradise was destroyed when it was marred by the rebellion of the first man, Adam (Acts 17:26, 1 Corinthians 15:46). His sin brought an intruder into the world—death. God had to judge sin with death, as He warned Adam He would (Genesis 2:17, cf. 3:19).

The Bible tells us that Adam was the head of the human race (Genesis 1:26–27), representing each one of us, who are his descendants. Paul says in Romans 5:12–19 that we sin "in Adam", after the likeness of Adam. So when Adam rebelled, all humanity rebelled with him. That is, all of us collectively said, "We want life without God."

Putting it another way, we inherit Adam's sin nature, right from conception. This is expressed when we sin by thought, word or deed. If any of us had been in the Garden of Eden, we would have done just the same as Adam. So there is no suffering of the truly innocent in the sense

179. Geisler, ref. 171, p. 347.
180. Carnell, E.J., *An Introduction to Christian Apologetics*, Eerdmans, Grand Rapids, p. 302, 1948.
181. St. Augustine, *On Free Choice of the Will*, **2**:18, translated by Benjamin, A.S. and Hackstaff, L.H., Library of Liberal Arts, Indianapolis, IN, 1964.
182. Sarfati, J., *Why would a loving God allow death and suffering?* Creation Book Publishers, 2012; creation.com/death.

of sinless. There is really no undeserved suffering. Instead of asking, "Why me?", we should ask, "Why not me?"

Furthermore, as Adam was the 'federal head' of the whole creation (Genesis 1:28), his sin brought the whole creation into bondage. As Romans 8:22 says, "the whole creation groans and labors with birth pangs"—because God Himself subjected the creation to processes of decay (v. 20). When Adam rebelled against God, all human beings, represented by Adam, effectively said that they wanted life without God. So God may have withdrawn some of His sustaining power—Colossians 1:16–17 tells us that all things are held together, right now, by the power of the Creator, the Lord Jesus Christ (see ch. 4). Fortunately for us, in His mercy, he didn't withdraw all of His sustaining power, or else the creation would cease to exist.

The first reflection of these changed conditions was when God slew an animal to make coats of skin for Adam and Eve (Genesis 3:21). Ever since, as a result of God's judgment on the world, God has given us a taste of life without Him—a world that is running down—a world full of death and suffering. But this first animal death provided a clue for the ultimate solution (explained more on p. 65): God would Himself take human nature in the form of Jesus Christ (see chapter 4), die for our sins, and conquer death (see the Resurrection, p. 41).

Norman Geisler summarizes:

> "God did not create animals to be eaten in paradise, and animals weren't eating each other. The prophet Isaiah said someday God will 'create a new heavens and a new earth' where 'the wolf and the lamb will feed together and the lion will eat straw like an ox.' In other words, there's not going to be the same kind of killing that goes on now."[183]

> "In sum, everything God created was good. What changed things was the Fall. When God was told, in effect, to shove off, he partially did. Romans 8 says all creation was affected—that includes plant life, human beings, animals, everything. There were fundamental genetic changes; we see, for instance, how life spans rapidly decreased after the Fall [sic—actually after the Flood; see Genesis 11[184]]. God's plan was not designed to be this way; it's only this way because of sin. Ultimately it will be remedied."[185]

Individual suffering does not entail individual sin

We must avoid a common error. Yes, death and suffering is the result of Adam's sin, and all

183. For explanations of the origin of carnivorous behaviour in animals, and disease-causing properties of germs, see Batten, D. (Ed.), Catchpoole, D., Sarfati, J. and Wieland, C., *The Creation Answers Book*, ch. 6., Creation Book Publishers, 2007; creation.com/cab. See also the articles under creation.com/carnivory.
184. For some explanations, see Wieland, C., Living for 900 years, *Creation* **20**(4):10–13, 1998; creation.com/900.
185. Cited in Strobel, L., *The Case for Faith*, Zondervan, Grand Rapids, MI, pp. 176–177, 2000 .

of us are sinners as well. But this doesn't mean that the most sinful people have the most suffering, or that a particular tragedy is proof of a serious sin in a person's life. The Bible is clear on this:[186]

The Bible tells us of the most righteous man of his day, Job, who suffered intensely—losing all his children, servants and possessions in a single day; then he was struck by a painful illness. Yet he refused to curse God.

And when Jesus and His disciples encountered a man born blind, the disciples asked Him whether the man's blindness from birth was due to his own sin or the sin of his parents. Jesus explained that neither was the case. The man was born blind so that God could demonstrate His power (when Jesus healed him, John 9:1–7).

Jesus also discussed a tragedy that His hearers would have understood, and which can be applied to victims of tragedies today—certainly those of natural evil: "Those eighteen who died when the tower in Siloam fell on them—do you think they were sinners above all the others living in Jerusalem? I tell you, no!" (Luke 13:4). Thus sufferers of tragedies are not usually those who commit the worst sins.

Evil and choice

The question, which comes immediately to our mind when we start to think along this line, is, "Why can't God make men who will not do evil?" But here the power of God is called into question. What one fails to understand on this point is that God could only do that which is logically possible and not the logically absurd, such as create square circles or married bachelors. This limitation in no way questions God's power. God's power, says C.S. Lewis:

> "Means power to do all that is intrinsically possible, not to do the intrinsically impossible. You may attribute miracles to Him, but not nonsense. This is no limit to His power ... It remains true that all things are possible with God: the intrinsic impossibilities are not things but nonentities."[187]

Along the same line Ed. L. Miller writes:

> "Even an omnipotent God cannot do that which is logically impossible; he cannot make a rock so big that he cannot lift it, he cannot make four-sided triangles, he cannot make things both to be and not to be at the same time and in the same respect, and he cannot create something that possesses the full power of being that he himself possesses."[188]

Can God make free, man who is not free? No! Man who is not free, is not man. If man is free then he is free to choose but choice logically implies the existence of things to choose

---

186. Sarfati, ref. 182.
187. Lewis, C.S., *The Problem of Pain*, Whitefriars Press, London, p. 16, 1950.
188. Miller, ref. 148, p. 144. See also creation.com/omnipotence.

between. We agree with Cherbonnier, "Only if man can do evil is there any meaning in doing good." William Dyrness remarks rightly:

> *"It is a Christian conviction that evil can be used in a higher purpose, that suffering produces saintliness. If this is true, then it is possible that God's unwillingness to create a world in which evil is impossible reflects neither on his goodness nor on his power, but flows from his eternal and unchanging purposes."*

He further adds, "Perhaps when we view creation in its totality, we will see evil as a necessary element in the meaning of the whole."[189]

How much evil and suffering is allowable?

To the question, "Why doesn't God stop evil?" we ask, "How much evil do you want God to stop? If God started stopping evil do you think you will survive till midnight?" No one desires God to interfere with his or her actions. How many of us would like a headache each time we think against God? Which robber wants God to prevent him from stealing? The reformed scholar John Gerstner suggests:

> *"While we do not believe that personal freedom is the ultimate explanation of the origin of evil, we do believe that freedom was the means by which sin did come into the world."*[190]

In the same vein John W. Montgomery adds:

> *"To create only those who 'must' (in any sense) choose good is to create automata; and to whisk away evil effects as they are produced is to whisk away evil itself, for an act and its consequences are bound together."*[191]

A world where nothing could go wrong would in fact be a world without freedom. As Anglican clergyman and social commentator V.A. Demant (1893–1983) put it, "It would be a kind of infallible clockwork—or it would be a world in which God left no independence of His control at all."[192] It is because of this reality that former atheists, like Lewis, Schelling, Joad and others have come to believe in the Christian faith.

The same sort of argument can be applied to suffering: 'How much suffering do you want God to stop?' Christian medical doctor Carl Wieland, who has both seen and

189. Dyrness, ref. 153, p. 162.
190. Gerstner, J.H., *Reasons For Faith*, Baker, Grand Rapids, p. 19, 1967.
191. Montgomery, J.W., *The Suicide of Christian Theology*, Bethany, Minneapolis, MN, p. 259, 1975.
192. Demant, V.A., *Difficulties*, Mowbray, London, p. 137, 1958.

experienced terrible suffering, writes about a horrible tragedy where a collapsing slagheap suffocated many children in a Welsh mining town:

> *"There was a worldwide outpouring of not just grief, but a railing against God's 'unfairness' because of their young ages. … But think on this. Is it any 'fairer' for an old person to die than a young one? It is somehow seen as more reasonable, or more natural; he or she has had a more of a 'fair go' at life. But is death at any age 'natural'? … Let's be honest, if you were a sprightly seventy, and found out that you were (medically or judicially) condemned to die tomorrow, would you shrug your shoulders and just casually accept it on account of your age? If you could have some special advanced genetic engineering done, and keep living a healthy life for many hundreds of years, would you not eagerly seize the opportunity? I suggest that, deep down, we all realize that death at any age is an abomination, not the way things were meant to be. …*

> *"To put it another way, let's say that you have concluded that it is 'unfair' of God to permit the deaths of the school children in Wales … So that means you are saying that to be 'fair', God should have prevented the deaths of those Welsh children. But then, to be really 'fair', He should prevent all deaths of school-age children in accidents, anywhere. If he were to have done that, we would then conclude that it was 'unfair' for Him to allow childhood deaths from disease. So let's assume that He chose to prevent all deaths in children, anywhere, anytime. But if He chose to define childhood as ending at 18, why would it now be 'fair' to allow a 19-year-old to die, while preventing all death under that age? I hope this abstract 'thought experiment' makes it clear that, logically, we could not be satisfied with the situation's 'fairness' until death had been eliminated altogether.*

> *"Which brings us back to the point that death is an intruder, an outrage. When Jesus was at the tomb of His recently dead friend Lazarus, He wept."*[193]

The presence of evil has some good purposes, as C.S. Lewis points out, "God whispers to us in our pleasures, speaks in our conscience, but shouts in our pains: it is His megaphone to rouse a deaf world."[194] G.K. Chesterton (1874–1936), the brilliant British novelist, apologist and debater,[195] provides an eloquent description of human existence defaced by sin and suffering. He states:

> *"According to Christianity, in making it (the world), He set it free. God had written, not so much a poem, but rather a play; a play he had planned as perfect, but which had necessarily been left to human actors and stage-managers, who had since made a great mess of it."*[196]

193. Wieland, W., *Beyond the Shadows: making sense of personal tragedy*, Creation Book Publishers, pp. 72–74, 2011.

194. Lewis, ref. 187, p. 81,

195. See Cosner, L., "G.K. Chesterton: Darwinism is 'An attack upon thought itself'" *J. Creation* **23**(1):119–122, 2009; creation.com/chesterton.

196. Chesterton, G.K., *Orthodoxy*, Doubleday, Garden City, NJ, p. 79, 1959.

Christ: the ultimate solution

In the Christian faith we have a God of amazing love who enters fully into our human anguish and pain, then in the Resurrection He gives us a pledge that He will one day finally overcome evil:

> "Now the dwelling of God is with men, and he will live with them. They will be his people, and God himself will be with them and be their God. He will wipe every tear from their eyes. There will be no more death or mourning or crying or pain, for the old order of things has passed away (Revelation 21:3–4)."

What is the ultimate answer to the problem of suffering? Christianity says the answer is the Cross! It is the greatest of all answers to the greatest of all questions. The Christian message affirms that God did not avoid pain and suffering but endured it. A skeptic once challenged a minister with a provoking question, "Where was your God when my son was dying?" The minister thoughtfully replied, "Exactly where He was, when His Son was dying." Dorothy L. Sayers' eloquent remarks on the subject are worthy of our reflection:

> "For whatever reason God chose to make man as he is—limited and suffering and subject to sorrows and death—He had the honesty and the courage to take His own medicine. Whatever game He is playing with His creation, He has kept His own rules and played fair. He can exact nothing from man that He has not exacted from Himself. He has Himself gone through the whole of human experience, from the trivial irritations of family life and the cramping restrictions of hard work and lack of money to the worst horrors of pain and humiliation, defeat, despair, and death. When He was a man, He played the man. He was born in poverty and died in disgrace and thought it well worthwhile."[197]

"At the heart of the story stands the cross of Christ," writes Anglican Bible scholar John W. Wenham (1913–1996), "where evil did its worst and met its match."[198] Along the same line Canon W.H.T. Gairdner (1873–1928) of Oxford writes, "Against the dark background of

197. Sayers, D.L., *Christian Letters to a Post-Christian World*, Eerdmans, Grand Rapids, p. 14, 1969.
198. Quoted in Wenham, ref. 143, p. 90.

man's failure and sin, the Cross shows us the measure of God's passion against evil and the measure of God's passion to redeem His sinful children." He eloquently concludes, "Therefore in the Cross holiness and love, wrath and pity, justice and mercy, meet together, and kiss one another."[199]

E.J. Carnell put this delightfully, "The cross of Christ is God's final answer to the problem of evil because the problem of evil is in the cross itself."[200] It is here that we see what God has done about evil. He has taken evil at its most brutal and senseless level and transformed it for our eternal redemption. God Himself, in the person of Jesus Christ, went through pain, suffering, and death to redeem us from our eternal suffering. Christ not only endured evil but triumphed over it, as Dorothy Sayers so eloquently puts it, "He did not stop the crucifixion; He rose from the dead."[201]

Dr Wieland concludes about the ultimate answer to evil:

> "Bottom line—the only way that God can be truly 'fair' is to do exactly what He will do—create another perfect world (by restoring or recreating this one), a world in which there can be no more death and suffering of any kind, at all.

> "But it is not possible for us to enter that perfect new creation carrying our sin natures, or we would soon ruin it too. He had to make a way to take our sin away forever, through the perfect sacrifice of the Lord Jesus Christ, God the Son, God's sinless lamb bearing the penalty of God's wrath on our behalf."[202]

In the light of this reality, life has purpose and meaning, the cosmos is not chaos. There is ultimate significance; God who created the universe is also able to redeem the universe. Job, who suffered greatly, also understood deeply when he said:

> "I know that my Redeemer lives, and that in the end he will stand upon the earth. And after my skin has been destroyed, yet in my flesh I will see God" (Job 19:25–26).

199. Quoted in Storrs, C.E., *Many Creeds: One Cross*, SCM, London, p. 80, 1945.
200. Carnell, E.J., *Christian Commitment: An Apologetic*, Macmillan, New York, p. 281, 1957.
201. Sayers, D.L., *Creed or Chaos?* Harcourt, Brace & Co., New York, p. 4, 1949.
202. Wieland, ref. 193, pp. 74–75.

RECOMMENDED READING

- Alcorn, Randy, *If God Is Good: Faith in the Midst of Suffering and Evil*, Multnomah Books, 2009.

- Death and Suffering Questions and Answers, creation.com/curse.

- Geisler, Norman L., *Roots of Evil*, Zondervan, Grand Rapids, MI, 1978.

- Hick, John, *Evil and the God of Love*, Macmillan, New York, 1966.

- Lewis, C.S., *The Problem of Pain*, Macmillan, New York, 1948.

- Pike, Nelson (Ed.), *God and Evil*, Prentice-Hall, Englewood Cliffs, NJ, 1964.

- Plantinga, Alvin, *God, Freedom and Evil*, Eerdmans, Grand Rapids, 1974.

- Wenham, John W., *The Goodness of God*, InterVarsity Press, Downers Grove, 1974.

- Wieland, Carl, *Beyond the Shadows: making sense of personal tragedy*, Creation Book Publishers, 2011.

A little philosophy leads to atheism, depth in philosophy leads to God.
— FRANCIS BACON

Atheism is a disease of the soul before it is an error of the mind.
— PLATO

3

IS ATHEISM RATIONAL?

If there is a God, why are there atheists? Why do people call themselves atheists? What makes atheism so fashionable these days? There was a time when the numbers of atheists were few and fleeting but today atheism is massively popular in terms of media attention and book sales.

Philosopher Patrick Masterson (1936–), in his popular book *Atheism and Alienation*, asserts:

"For today, on an ever increasing scale, people proclaim themselves to be atheists, not so much because of objections to alleged proofs for the existence of God, but rather because they consider that to affirm the existence of God is to set men at odds within themselves and with one another."[203]

Atheism is an interesting subject for study. Why are the atheists so passionate and obsessed with the non-being of God? Why do many of them devote a lifetime of religious zeal and commitment to the ideals of atheism? Recent studies on atheism provide fascinating insights.[204]

Atheism does not rest on a proven belief but rather on the unsupported assumption that there is no God. Boris Pasternak, who wrote the famous novel *Dr Zhivago*, once declared, "I am an atheist who has lost his faith."[205] Atheism is a belief based on an idea. It is a particular conceptual approach to life and the universe.[206]

203. Masterson, P., *Atheism and Alienation*, Penguin, Middlesex, pp. 13–14, 1971.
204. See Borne, E., *Atheism*, Hawthorn, New York, 1961, Collins, J., *God in Modern Philosophy*, Regnery, Chicago, 1959, Fabro, C., *God in Exile*, Newman, New York, 1968 and Sproul, R.C., *Psychology of Atheism*, Bethany, Minneapolis, 1974.
205. Quoted in McGrath, A., *Bridge-Building*, Inter-Varsity Press, Leicester, p. 116, 1992.
206. See Morey, R.A., *The New Atheism and the Erosion of Freedom*, Bethany, Minneapolis, 1986.

I. THE ASSUMPTIONS OF ATHEISM

Who is an atheist? An atheist is one who rejects any belief in God. The word 'atheism' comes from the Greek word *atheos*, meaning 'without God' (Ephesians 2:12). Atheism is an *active* belief that God doesn't exist, *not* merely a lack of belief in God. Consider the following:

> *"According to the atheistic philosopher Paul Edwards, 'An "atheist" is a person who maintains that there is no God, that is, that the sentence "God exists" expresses a false proposition.'"*[207]

The article "Atheism" in *Encyclopaedia Britannica* **1**:666, 1992, reflecting the usual definition in philosophy, begins:

> *"Atheism, the critique or denial of metaphysical beliefs in God or spiritual beings. As such, it is the opposite of theism, which affirms the reality of the divine and seeks to demonstrate its existence. Atheism is to be distinguished from agnosticism, which leaves open the question of whether there is a god or not, professing to find the question unanswered or unanswerable; for the atheist, the nonexistence of God is a certainty."*

The entry on atheism in the *Routledge Encyclopedia of Philosophy*, probably the preeminent reference tool for philosophy, begins, "Atheism is the position that affirms the nonexistence of God. It proposes positive disbelief rather than mere suspension of belief."[208] It goes on to say that this is the most commonly understood form of atheism, also called 'positive atheism', in contrast to 'negative atheism' which is just non-belief in God.

Some atheists explain their view as follows. Ludwig Feuerbach says, "The personality of God is nothing else than the projected personality of man."[209] The atheistic philosopher Michael Scriven states:

> *"The atheist may believe there is no God because he thinks the concept is essentially self-contradictory, or meaningless, or because he thinks it is wholly superfluous, or because he thinks it is factually false."*[210]

Elton Trueblood writes,

> *"The honest atheist is simply a person who has looked out upon the world and has come to believe either that there is no adequate evidence that God is or that there is good evidence that God is not."*[211]

In her book *What on Earth is an Atheist?*, activist Madalyn Murray O'Hair (1919–1995) states, "I am an atheist and this means at least: I do not believe there is a god, or any gods,

207. Edwards, P., *Encyclopedia of Philosophy* **I**:175, Macmillan, New York, 1967.
208. Rowe, W.L., "Atheism", in: Craig, E. (Ed.), *Routledge Encyclopedia of Philosophy* **1**:530, Routledge, London, 1998.
209. Feuerbach, L., *The Essence of Christianity*, Harper Torchbooks, New York, p. 226, 1957.
210. Scriven, M., *Primary Philosophy*, McGraw-Hill, New York, p. 88, 1966.
211. Trueblood, E., *Philosophy of Religion*, Harper, New York, p. 82, 1957.

personal or in nature, or manifesting himself, herself, or itself in any way."[212]

Robert Blatchford (1851–1943), an English atheist, patriot and socialist campaigner, states a position that is typical of atheists:

"I claim that the heavenly Father is a myth; that in the face of a knowledge of life and the world, we cannot reasonably believe in Him. There is no heavenly Father watching tenderly over us, His children. He is the baseless shadow of a wistful human dream.

"I do not believe in a God. The belief in a God is still generally accepted … But, in the light of scientific discoveries and demonstrations, such a belief is unfounded and utterly untenable today."[213]

The American theologian Harold O.J. Brown suggests, "Atheism as we know it in the West is not merely lack of belief in, but rather an attack on God; only where God has been seen as real and personal can much energy be generated in the cause of rebellion against Him."[214]

Theologian Alan Richardson (1905–1975), Dean of York, affirms, "Atheism in the sense of the denial of God's existence is a modern phenomenon, intelligible only in a theistic context; it made its appearance in a serious sense during the period of the Enlightenment."[215] Before that, the great scientist Sir Isaac Newton could say, "Opposition to godliness is atheism in profession and idolatry in practice. Atheism is so senseless and odious to mankind that it never had many professors."[216]

There are many forms of atheism in the philosophical jungles of the twentieth century. There is the mythological atheist, dialectical atheist, semantical atheist, and the traditional atheist. The most common of these would be the traditional atheist whose views pose a serious challenge to all who believe in God.

212. O'Hair, M.M., *What On Earth is an Atheist?* Arno Press, New York, p. 38, 1972.
213. Quoted in Grounds, V.C., *The Reason for Our Hope*, Moody, Chicago, p. 18, 1945.
214. Brown, H.O.J., "The Conservative Option," in Gundry, S.N. and Johnson, A.F. (Eds.), *Tension in Contemporary Theology*, Moody, Chicago, pp. 334–335, 1976.
215. Richardson, A. (Ed.), "Atheism," in *A Dictionary of Christian Theology*, Westminster Press, Philadelphia, p. 18, 1969.
216. *A Short Scheme of the True Religion*, manuscript quoted in *Memoirs of the Life, Writings and Discoveries of Sir Isaac Newton* by Sir David Brewster, Edinburgh, 1850; cited in: Thayer, H.S. (Ed.), *Newton's Philosophy of Nature: Selections from his writings*, Hafner Library of Classics, NY, p. 42, 1953.

THE DOGMAS OF ATHEISM
There is no God.
There is no objective Truth.
There is no ground for Reason.
There are no absolute Morals.
There is no ultimate Value.
There is no ultimate Meaning.
There is no eternal Hope.

II. THE APOSTLES OF ATHEISM

Every religion has its apostles and prophets, and atheism is no exception. Its high priests, preachers, and prophets are all actively preaching the faith of atheism in every country around the world. The evangelists of atheism are constantly seeking for converts to their denomination. Richard Dawkins, former Professor for Public Understanding of Science at Oxford, has been described as 'Darwin's Rottweiler' and a 'fundamentalist' in the service of the cause of atheism. He champions the 'coming out' of atheists, and urges those who hold to a naturalistic worldview to now describe themselves by the title 'brights' (although even some atheists object to such self-adulation). While secularism has long dominated our institutions and centres of culture, it has never been more popular to be an atheist than today.

The most brilliant of all atheists was likely Friedrich Nietzsche (1844–1900), who took great pains to express that 'God is Dead'.[217] His works include: *The AntiChrist, Thus Spoke Zarathustra, Beyond Good and Evil, Ecce Homo,* and *The Genealogy of Morals.* In his book, *The Joyful Wisdom,* Nietzsche states:

> *"The most important of more recent events—that 'god is dead,' that the belief in the Christian God has become unworthy of belief—already begins to cast its first shadows over Europe … In fact, we philosophers and 'free spirits' feel ourselves irradiated as by a new dawn by the report that the 'old God is dead'; our hearts overflow with gratitude, astonishment, presentiment and expectation. At last the horizon seems open once more, granting even that it is not bright; our ships can at last put out to sea in face of every danger; every hazard is again permitted to the discerner; the sea, our sea, again lies open before us; perhaps never before did such an 'open sea' exist."[218]*

For Nietzsche the 'death of God' means the death of all absolutes, values, and morals.

217. See Grigg, R., Nietzsche, the man who took on God and lost! *J. Creation* **24**(1):106–112, 2010.
218. Brown, C., *Philosophy and the Christian Faith*, Tyndale Press, London, p. 139, 1971.

He believed that man can create meaning and significance without any reference to a Transcendent Being. Man is sovereign and self-sufficient to produce his own kingdom. In one of his popular works Nietzsche projects himself as the madman; the death of God leads to madness. In his final existential rejection Nietzsche declares, "But we do not at all want to enter the kingdom of heaven: we have become men—so we want the kingdom of earth."[219]

The German philosopher Ludwig Feuerbach (1804–1872) did much to discredit the existence of God through many of his works and especially through his *The Essence of Christianity*, which is still widely read in academic circles. Religious ideas, according to Feuerbach, are merely the projection of human needs and desires. God is simply personified human wishes. He argues:

> *"Man first of all sees his nature as if out of himself, before he finds it in himself. His own nature is in the first instance contemplated by him as that of another being … Hence the historical progress of religion consists in this: that what by an earlier religion was regarded as objective, is now recognized as subjective; that is, what was formerly contemplated and worshipped as God is now perceived to be something human."[220]*

Two individuals who picked up Feuerbach's atheistic ideas are Sigmund Freud (1856–1939) and Karl Marx (1818–1883). Freud applied Feuerbach's ideas in the field of psychology. His work *The Future of an Illusion* asserts that the idea of God is nothing but wish fulfilment, an infantile neurosis for a cosmic comforter. God is an illusory projection of the human mind, removed from truth and reality, hence the enlightened person will abandon the idea of God and live without any commitment to a deity beyond man. Freud argues:

> *"We say to ourselves, it would indeed be very nice if there were a God, who was both creator of the world and a benevolent providence, if there were a moral world order and a future life, but at the same time it is very odd that this is all just as we should wish it ourselves."[221]*

Karl Marx is undoubtedly one of the most influential figures of modern time. He applied Feuerbach's arguments on political science, and argued that man "looked for the superman in the fantastic reality of heaven and found nothing there but the reflexion of himself."[222] His grandfather was a Jewish rabbi and when Marx was six years old his father joined the Lutheran Church. He went to Berlin to study philosophy where he came under the influence of a liberal theological lecturer, Bruno Bauer (1809–1882), who was promoting the view that the Gospels are not reliable historically but are simply man's imaginative ideas and desires. Jesus of Nazareth was nothing more than a mythological figure invented by the religious mind. The *Encyclopaedia Britannica* notes:

219. Nietzsche, F., *Thus Spoke Zarathustra*, Random House, New York, p. 355, 1983–1985.
220. Feuerbach, ref. 209.
221. Quoted in Trueblood, ref. 211, p. 186.
222. Marx, K. and Engels, F., *On Religion*, Schocken, New York, p. 41, 1964.

"Marx enrolled in a course of lectures given by Bauer on the prophet Isaiah. Bauer taught that a new social catastrophe 'more tremendous' than that of the advent of Christianity was in the making. The Young Hegelians[223] began moving rapidly towards atheism and also talked vaguely of political action."[224]

Thinking that Feuerbach had spoken the last word on religion, Marx uncritically accepted his critique on religion and moved passionately into politics to solve the plight of man. Believing religion is the enemy of man Marx argues:

"Man makes religion, religion does not make man. Religion is indeed man's self-consciousness and self-awareness as long as he has not found his feet in the universe. But man is not an abstract being, squatting outside the world. Man is the world of men, the State, and society. This State, this society, produce religion which is an inverted world consciousness, because they are an inverted world … Religious suffering is at the same time an expression of real suffering and a protest against real suffering. Religion is the sigh of the oppressed creature, the sentiment of a heartless world, and the soul of soulless conditions. It is the opium of the people. The abolition of religion, as the illusory happiness of men, is a demand for their real happiness."[225]

Arthur Schopenhauer (1788–1860) rejected all the traditional arguments of God's existence and advocated atheistic pessimism in place of theism. His influence on Friedrich Nietzsche is profound and the miserable condition of human existence led him to affirm suicide as a possible remedy. It is believed that he slept at night with loaded pistols beside his bed. He trusted no barber in Germany to shave him with a razor. He lived thirty years in a two-room boarding house and had no companion but a dog. His father committed suicide and his mother died insane.

223. Followers of leading German philosopher Georg Wilhelm Friedrich Hegel, (1770–1831). While a lot of atheists were influenced by him, he was a lifelong Lutheran, albeit a somewhat unorthodox one. Hegel accepted the superiority of Christianity, as well as the Deity and Resurrection of Christ—see *Vorlesungen über die Philosophie der Religion* (*Lectures on the Philosophy of Religion*) **3**.
224. "Marx and Marxism" in *The New Encyclopaedia Britannica* **13**:573–574, Encyclopaedia Britannica, Chicago, 1986.
225. Marx, K., Critique of Hegel's Philosophy of Right, *Deutsch-Französische Jahrbücher*, 7 and 10 February 1844.

Auguste Comte (1798–1857), the French atheistic philosopher, rejected God at the age of thirteen and replaced him with the credo, 'All is relative'. Comte rejected God on cultural and sociological grounds. He grew up in a Catholic home where there was constant conflict and controversy. Unable to bear the pressure he left his family declaring himself an atheist. He formulated the philosophy of positivism on the basic assumption of atheism. He attempted to popularize positivism as a substitute for religion. Colin Brown notes:

> *"Much to the disgust of thoroughgoing atheists like Nietzsche, Comte proposed a religion of humanity in which God was dethroned and humanity, 'the great being', put in his place. He even adapted Catholic worship, priests and sacraments to his secular purposes."*[226]

His writings indicate an absence of theistic understanding and arguments.

Imagine no religion...

Bertrand Russell (1872–1970) is one of the few philosophers who is frequently quoted by atheists. *The Oxford Companion to Philosophy* notes that Russell is, "The most widely read British philosopher of the twentieth century."[227] His writings have influenced a large number of people including the famous musician John Lennon. Although Russell maintained an agnostic position it would be fair to include him as an atheist on account of a number of his writings and his general attitude to God and religion. Russell, who had a Christian background, rejected God at the age of eighteen after reflecting on the cosmological argument. In his work *Why I Am Not a Christian*, Russell suggests his reason for rejecting the arguments for God's existence:

> *"I may say that when I was a young man and was debating these questions very seriously in my mind, I for a long time accepted the argument of the First Cause, until one day, at the age of eighteen, I read John Stuart Mill's* Autobiography, *and I there found this sentence: 'My father taught me that the question, "Who made me?" cannot be answered, since it immediately suggests the further question, "Who made God?"' That very simple sentence showed me, as I still think, the fallacy in the argument of the First Cause."*[228]

But as we showed in chapter 1, p. 19, this is easily refuted: only things that *have a beginning* need a cause.[229]

Jean-Paul Sartre (1905–1981), the French Existentialist and the winner of the Nobel Prize for literature, advocated an atheism based on Nietzsche's Existentialism. According to Sartre the fundamental axiom in philosophy is not essence but existence. "If God exists," argues Sartre,

226. Brown, ref. 214, p. 142.
227. Honderich, T. (Ed.), *The Oxford Companion to Philosophy*, Oxford University Press, p. 116, 1995.
228. Russell, B., *Why I Am Not a Christian*, Simon & Schuster, New York, pp. 3–4, 1957.
229. For a recent lucid refutation of Russell's argument, see Batten, D., Who created God? It's an illogical question, *Creation* **32**(4):18–20, 2010; creation.com/whocreatedgod.

"man cannot be free. But man is free, therefore God cannot exist. Since God does not exist all things are morally permissible." Hence, man is "an empty bubble on the sea of nothingness."[230] Most of his life Sartre believed that, "All existing things are born for no reason, continue through weakness and die by accident … It is meaningless that we are born; it is meaningless that we die."[231] Sartre admitted that he once believed in God and later abandoned his religious convictions:

> "Only once did I have the feeling that He existed. I had been playing with matches and burned a small rug. I was in the process of covering up my crime when suddenly God saw me. I felt His gaze inside my head and on my hands … I flew into a rage against so crude an indiscretion, I blasphemed … He never looked at me again."[232]

The New Atheists

As early as Epicurus, there have been attempts to debunk the supernatural, but since the early twenty-first century a new pattern of atheism has emerged. Departing from their skeptical forebears, the New Atheists espouse a dogma that differs in both tone and content. Religion is said to be not only wrong, but evil. They do not just denounce belief in God but respect for belief in God.

The prominent figures who have come to embody New Atheism are Daniel Dennett, philosophy professor at Tufts University and author of *Breaking the Spell: Religion as Natural Phenomenon*, Christopher Hitchens, a journalist and author of *God is not Great: How Religion Poisons Everything*, and Sam Harris, author of *The End of Faith* and *Letter to a Christian Nation*. However, the most famous of the 'four horsemen' is British ethologist[233] and evolutionary biologist Richard Dawkins. His book *The God Delusion* (2006) was on the *New York Times* best seller list for fifty-one weeks and has sold more than 1.5 million copies.[234]

230. Sartre, J-P., *Being and Nothingness*, Part 4, Chapter 1, 1943.
231. Sartre, J-P., *La nausée* (*Nausea*), 1938.
232. Sartre, J-P., *Words*, George Braziller, New York, p. 102, 1964.
233. One who studies animal behaviour.
234. See detailed refutation by former cancer researcher Philip Bell, Atheist with a Mission, *J. Creation* **21**(2):28–34, 2007; creation.com/delusion.

The popularity of New Atheism has been a direct result of the terrorist threat following 9/11. In the fertile soil of fear, the New Atheists' hostility towards not merely fundamentalists but moderates has captured massive attention. After the 11 September 2001 terrorist attack, Dawkins argued:

> *"Many of us saw religion as harmless nonsense. Beliefs might lack all supporting evidence but, we thought, if people needed a crutch for consolation, where's the harm? September 11th changed all that. Revealed faith is not harmless nonsense; it can be lethally dangerous nonsense. Dangerous, because it gives people unshakeable confidence in their own righteousness. Dangerous, because it gives them false courage to kill themselves, which automatically removes normal barriers to killing others. Dangerous, because it teaches enmity to others labelled only by a difference of inherited tradition. And, dangerous, because we have all bought into a weird respect, which uniquely protects religion from normal criticism. Let's now stop being so damned respectful!"[235]*

Dawkins somehow overlooked the record-breaking tens of millions killed by atheistic/ evolutionary regimes last century. This has been thoroughly documented by Rudolph Rummel (1932–), Professor Emeritus of Political Science at the University of Hawaii, who coined the term *democide* for murder by government:[236] 77 million in Communist China, 62 million in the Soviet Gulag State, 21 million non-battle killings by the Nazis, 2 million murdered in the Khmer Rouge killing fields. This is many times more deaths than all 'religious' wars put together in all centuries of human history.

Not surprisingly, the substance of the neo-atheists' arguments has been criticized by both theist and atheist alike. One atheist who was scathing of Dawkins is Terry Eagleton, professor of cultural theory at the National University of Ireland. In the *London Review of Books*, he writes:

> *"Imagine someone holding forth on biology whose only knowledge of the subject is the Book of British Birds, and you have a rough idea of what it feels like to read Richard Dawkins on theology. Card-carrying rationalists like Dawkins, who is the nearest thing to a professional atheist we have had since Bertrand Russell, are in one sense the least well equipped to understand what they castigate, since they don't believe there is anything there to be understood, or at least anything worth understanding. This is why they invariably come up with vulgar caricatures of religious faith that would make a first-year theology student wince."[237]*

Michael Ruse, atheist philosopher of biology at Florida State University, is equally critical of both the arguments and academic credentials of the New Atheists:

> *"Let me say that I believe the new atheists do the side of science a grave disservice. I*

235. Multiple contributors, Has the world changed? *The Guardian* (UK), 11 September 2001.
236. Rummel, R.J., *Death by Government*, Transaction Publishers, New Brunswick, NJ, 1994; hawaii.edu/powerkills/NOTE1.HTM.
237. Eagleton, T., *London Review of Books* **28**(20):32–34, 19 October 2006.

will defend to the death the right of them to say what they do—as one who is English-born one of the things I admire most about the USA is the First Amendment. But I think first that these people do a disservice to scholarship. Their treatment of the religious viewpoint is pathetic to the point of non-being. Richard Dawkins in The God Delusion *would fail any introductory philosophy or religion course. Proudly he criticizes that whereof he knows nothing. As I have said elsewhere, for the first time in my life, I felt sorry for the ontological argument. If we criticized gene theory with as little knowledge as Dawkins has of religion and philosophy, he would be rightly indignant. (He was just this when, thirty years ago, Mary Midgeley went after the selfish gene concept without the slightest knowledge of genetics.) Conversely, I am indignant at the poor quality of the argumentation in Dawkins, Dennett, Hitchens, and all of the others in that group."[238]*

Evolutionary geneticist and Professor of Biology at the University of Rochester, H. Allen Orr, is blunt:

"Despite my admiration for much of Dawkins's work, I'm afraid that I'm among those scientists who must part company with him here. Indeed, The God Delusion *seems to me badly flawed. Though I once labeled Dawkins a professional atheist, I'm forced, after reading his new book, to conclude he's actually more an amateur."[239]*

III. THE ARGUMENTS OF ATHEISM

Although a large number of atheists accept atheism without reason, a good number of them affirm atheism on the basis of several arguments. These arguments differ one from another but they are the standard arguments employed by the atheistic apologists:

1. The existence of God is incompatible with the existence of evil (Mackie).[240]

2. God is a projection of man's imagination (Feuerbach).[241]

3. Since God cannot be scientifically demonstrated, God cannot exist (Flew).[242]

4. People believe in God because they are culturally conditioned (Freud).[243]

5. The idea of God is nonsensical like the idea of square circles (Matson).[244]

6. If God made the world who made God? (Russell).[245]

7. Since there is no evidence of God's existence, God does not exist (Kaufmann).[246]

238. Ruse, M., Why I think the New Atheists are a bloody disaster, blog.beliefnet.com, 14 August 2009.
239. Orr, H.A., *New York Review of Books* **54**(1), 11 January 2007.
240. Mackie, J.L., *The Miracle of Theism*, Clarendon, Oxford, 1982.
241. Feuerbach, ref. 209.
242. Antony G.N. Flew (decades before his conversion to theism), *God and Philosophy*, Hutchinson & Co., London, 1966.
243. Freud, S., *The Future of an Illusion*, translated by Robson-Scott, W.D., Doubleday & Co., New York, 1957.
244. Matson, W., *The Existence of God*, Cornell University, 1965.
245. Honderich, ref. 227.
246. Kaufmann, W., *Critique of Religion and Philosophy*, Doubleday, New York, 1961.

On the strength of these arguments, atheists deny the existence of God. These objections, however, have been adequately answered by a great number of Christian philosophers. We will briefly respond to the above arguments in the order they are raised, but for a fuller response please consult the works suggested in the footnote.[247]

1. The existence of God is incompatible with the existence of evil. This objection does not logically deny the existence of God but merely questions or challenges God's character or means of operation. The existence of evil is not incompatible with the existence of God. There is no logical contradiction. In order to make a contradiction the atheist must introduce new premises or assumptions. The atheist presumes a worldview because of a prior assumption which he entertains which is "Evil should not exist with God." This assumption 'begs the question' (see Chapter 2).

2. God is a projection of man's imagination. This objection invented by Feuerbach and popularized by Freud is without substance. The argument is guilty of committing the 'genetic fallacy'. In the genetic fallacy one seeks to discredit a view by merely going to its origin. One does not disprove a belief by merely going back and describing how that belief originated. You do not refute a belief by simply dating it or explaining its origin. By comparison, Kekulé thought up the (correct) ring structure of the benzene (C_6H_6) molecule after a dream of a snake grasping its tail, but chemists don't need to worry about correct ophiology to analyse benzene![248] The psychological objection is not a logical explanation but a logical fallacy.[249]

3. Since God cannot be scientifically demonstrated, God cannot exist. The person who seeks to refute God on the basis of science commits the fallacy of reductionism or scientism. To test God on the basis of science is to use a false criterion. Science is useful in testing a number of phenomena but to suggest that God must fit the scientific dress is arbitrary and wrongheaded. Science is useful for testing some things but not all things. This objection is also guilty of committing the categorical fallacy e.g., "Tell me what is the taste of blue?" The person who argues all things must be tested by science is not able to test the assertion "All things must be tested by science." How does one test love, values,

247. Brown, C., *Miracles and the Critical Mind*, Eerdmans, Grand Rapids, 1984, Collins, J., *God in Modern Philosophy*, Craig, W.L., *The Kalam Cosmological Argument*, Macmillan, NY, 1979, Craig, W.L., *Knowing the Truth About the Resurrection*, Servant, Ann Arbor, MI, 1988, Davis, S.T., *Logic and the Nature of God*, Eerdmans, Grand Rapids, 1983, Geisler, N.L., *Miracles and Modern Thought*, Zondervan, Grand Rapids, 1982, Geisler, N.L. and Corduan, W., *Philosophy of Religion*, Baker, Grand Rapids, 1989, Jaki, S.L., *The Origin of Science and the Science of its Origin*, Regnery/Gateway, South Bend, IN, 1978, Miethe, T.L. (Ed.), *Did Jesus Rise From the Dead? The Resurrection Debate*, Harper & Row, San Francisco, 1987, Mitchell, B., *Morality: Religious and Secular*, Clarendon, Oxford, 1980, Moreland, J.P., *Scaling the Secular City*, Baker, Grand Rapids, 1987, Morris, T.V. (Ed.), *The Concept of God*, Oxford University Press, 1987, Nash, R.H., *The Concept of God*, Zondervan, Grand Rapids, 1983, Nash, R.H., *Faith and Reason*, Zondervan, Grand Rapids, 1988, Owen, H.P., *The Moral Argument for Christian Theism*, Allen & Unwin, London, 1965, Plantinga, A., *God, Freedom, and Evil*, Harper & Row, NY, 1974, Swinburne, R., *The Coherence of Theism*, Clarendon, Oxford, 1977, Swinburne, R., *The Concept of Miracle*, St. Martin's Press, NY, 1970, Swinburne, R., *The Existence of God*, Clarendon, Oxford, 1979, Tennant, F.R., *Philosophical Theology* Vol. **2**, Cambridge University Press, 1956, Thaxton, C.B., Bradley, W.L. and Olsen, R.L., *The Mystery of Life's Origin: Reassessing Current Theories*, Philosophical Library, New York, 1984, Yandell, K.E., *Christianity and Philosophy*, Eerdmans, Grand Rapids, 1984.
248. See Sarfati, J., Loving God with all your mind: logic and creation, *J. Creation* **12**(2):142–151, 1998; creation.com/logic#genetic.
249. See Purtill, R., *Reason to Believe*, Eerdmans, Grand Rapids, 1974, Sproul, R.C., *Psychology of Atheism* and Trueblood, D.E., *Philosophy of Religion*.

morals, logic, beauty, etc. scientifically?[250]

4. People believe in God because they are culturally conditioned. This argument if taken to its logical conclusion would not only refute Christianity but also the atheistic beliefs. The person who advocates this assumption must also be prepared to be judged by this principle. If all beliefs are conditioned, then the unbeliever is also conditioned not to believe. This is a two-edged sword, which will not only kill your enemy but will also kill you. The atheists cannot claim special privileges and escape philosophical scrutiny. To suggest that only religious people have hang-ups is to propose a false psychology, a questionable sociology, and an unverified scientific theory.[251]

English doctor and insightful social commentator Theodore Dalrymple (not a Christian) shows up the problem in a refutation of New Atheist Daniel Dennett:

> *"Dennett argues that religion is explicable in evolutionary terms—for example, by our inborn human propensity, at one time valuable for our survival on the African savannahs, to attribute animate agency to threatening events.*
>
> *"For Dennett, to prove the biological origin of belief in God is to show its irrationality, to break its spell. But of course it is a necessary part of the argument that all possible human beliefs, including belief in evolution, must be explicable in precisely the same way; or else why single out religion for this treatment? Either we test ideas according to arguments in their favor, independent of their origins, thus making the argument from evolution irrelevant, or all possible beliefs come under the same suspicion of being only evolutionary adaptations— and thus biologically contingent rather than true or false. We find ourselves facing a version of the paradox of the Cretan liar: all beliefs, including this one, are the products of evolution, and all beliefs that are products of evolution cannot be known to be true."*[252]

5. The idea of God is nonsensical like the idea of square circles. This is a straw

250. See Clark, G.H., *The Philosophy of Science and Belief in God*, 1964, Jaki, S.L., *The Roads of Science and the Ways to God*, University of Chicago Press, 1978 and Moreland, J.P., *Scaling the Secular City*.

251. See Buswell, J.O., *A Systematic Theology of the Christian Religion*, Christian Life, Singapore, 1994, Craig, W.L., *Reasonable Faith*, Crossway Books, Wheaton, IL, 1994, Hackett, S., *The Resurrection of Theism*, Baker, Grand Rapids, 1982 and Thompson, S.M., *A Modern Philosophy of Religion*, Regnery, Chicago, 1955.

252. Dalrymple, T., What the New Atheists don't see: to regret religion is to regret Western civilization, *City Journal*, Autumn 2007; city-journal.org.

man argument. The person defines God arbitrarily and subjectively, claiming that God is equivalent to a square circle. Such a move is really in essence building a straw man in which case you define your opponent's position conveniently in order to shoot him down. To suggest that God is like a square circle is arbitrary. The atheist has no logical or epistemological ground for making this assumption.[253]

6. If God made the world who made God? This objection presupposes that God had a beginning. The argument "Everything has a cause, God is a thing, therefore God must have a cause" is a simple version of a 'straw man argument'. Here the atheist subjectively and arbitrarily equates God to the order of the created and finite thing. By setting God up on the level of the created, the atheist insists that God must have a cause too. From a logical point of view "Everything that begins has a cause" but not as the atheists irrationally argue, "Everything must have a cause." Only finite beings and effects need causes, God by definition and essence is not an effect or something made. God is the unmade eternal Creator of the universe. To argue that an unmade being is a contradiction the atheist must explain how they could maintain the concept of an 'uncaused universe'. What is sauce for the goose is sauce for the gander.

7. Since there is no evidence of God's existence, God does not exist. The logical response to this objection is to first examine the nature of evidence—what constitutes evidence. Since there is a great amount of dispute as to what is legitimate evidence we must first settle the issue of evidence. Since the nature and existence of God is unlike any other issue or category, therefore one must approach God's existence axiomatically. If God is the basic ground of reality then the issue of God's existence is not on the same plane as finite elements like humans and potatoes. For example take the nature of air; to debate the existence of God is in a sense like debating the existence of air while breathing. If God is the Creator of the universe then He is the necessary pre-condition for all of reality. If God exists He is the essential element for all existence (see Chapter 1).

In reality atheists deny not the God of the Bible but an caricature of their own imagination.

IV. THE ABSURDITY OF ATHEISM

Is atheism logical? Can one really be an atheist on logical grounds? How does an atheist know with certainty that there is no God? On what ground is atheism believable? What proof is there for atheism? These are questions one must answer if one wishes to be an atheist.

It is fallacious to argue as some atheists, such as Gordon Stein, George Smith, Michael Martin, and Michael Scriven[254] do, insisting on the 'presumption of atheism'.[255] Philosopher L. Russ Bush explains, "Atheism is like 'innocence' in English law. It is to be presumed until 'guilt' (theism) is proven beyond reasonable doubt."[256] To suggest that the atheist

253. See Chesterton, G.K., *Orthodoxy*, Fontana, London, 1961 and Nash, R., *Christianity and the Hellenistic World*, Zondervan, Grand Rapids, 1984.
254. This approach is challenged by philosophers such as Alvin Plantinga and Nicholas Wolterstorff in *Faith and Rationality: Reason and Belief in God*, University of Notre Dame Press, London, 1986.
255. This was the title of a 1976 book by Antony Flew when he was still very much an atheist.
256. Bush, L.R., *A Handbook for Christian Philosophy*, Zondervan, Grand Rapids, p. 225, 1991.

does not have the burden of proof is in a sense refusing to take part in playing the game but nevertheless insisting on getting the prize at the end of the game. The atheist is in fact begging the question and becomes philosophically self-righteous. Evangelical philosopher William Lane Craig rightly notes, "Atheism is a claim to know something ('There is no God') just as much as theism ('There is a God'). Therefore, it can claim no presumption when the evidence is equal."[257]

Such atheists are using the tactic of throwing the burden of proof on those asserting an affirmative proposition, e.g. "God exists" as opposed to the negative proposition "God does not exist". But then an example of self-refutation occurs—the proposition: "The burden of proof falls on the affirmative position" is *itself* an affirmative proposition, so requires proof in itself![258] Furthermore, atheists assert many affirmative statements without proof, e.g. that the universe is either eternal or came into existence uncaused, non-living matter evolved into living cells by pure undirected chemistry, complex specified information arose without intelligence, design features arose without a designer, moral sensibilities arose out of amoral matter, etc.[258]

Atheism takes all the above on faith—but a blind faith; it takes greater faith to be an atheist.

Atheism is a religion without God, a faith without reason and a journey without a destination. An atheist is not a person without beliefs but one who upholds a variety of beliefs. What Mark

257. Craig, W.L., *The Existence of God and the Beginning of the Universe*, Here's Life Publishers, San Bernardino, p. 32, 1979.
258. Sarfati, J., Atheism is more rational? creation.com/atheism_rational, 5 September 2000.

Twain said equally applies to the atheist, "It is amazing what a man will believe as long as it is not in the Bible." To be an atheist you must accept the impossible, believe the ridiculous, and trust the absurd. From a logical point of view it is impossible to disprove God:

PREMISE 1.	The statement "God does not exist" is a universal negative.
PREMISE 2.	But in principle it is impossible to prove a universal negative.
CONCLUSION:	Therefore atheism is unprovable.

Observe the irrationality of the atheistic premise. An atheist is someone who, after studying Philosophy, Theology, History, Religion, Psychology, Biology, Archaeology, Anthropology, Sociology, etc., and searching every space of the universe, thinks he has found conclusive evidence that God does not exist. He has inspected the heavenly throne and found it to be empty!

The only way for the atheist to be absolutely certain that there is no God, is for the atheist to know everything about reality. In order to maintain the premise, 'there is no God' the atheist must have total knowledge of all reality. He must know all facts and realities of existence. This would imply that an atheist must have a knowledge which only God could possess. He must possess infinite knowledge throughout time, be everywhere at the same time, and be absolutely sure of everything. In reality the atheist must be omniscient, omnipresent and omnipotent, in which case the atheist must become God in order to prove there is no God. In fact he has to become the very God he is seeking to disprove.

But the atheist says there is no God, so how could he argue his position? There is no way by which he could defend his case. Consider the analogy: in order for me to affirm that there is no pin in your room I must examine every space in your room, then conclude there is no pin in your room. It would be meaningless to assert there is no pin in your room when I only have a limited knowledge of your room, therefore the assertion there is no pin in your room cannot be made without total knowledge of your room. Atheism is ultimately self-refuting. Atheism falls into the category of what logicians call 'self-refuting statements' or

'arguments that commit suicide'.[259] Philosopher J.P. Moreland (1948–) points out:

"When a statement fails to satisfy itself (i.e., to conform to its own criteria of validity or acceptability), it is self-refuting. Such statements are necessarily false. The facts which falsify them are unavoidably given with the statement when it is uttered."[260]

He provides examples like, "I cannot say a word of English", which is self-refuted when uttered in English. He adds, "The claim 'there are no truths' is self-refuting. If it is false, then it is false. But if it is true, then it is false as well, for in that case there would be no truths, including the statement itself."[58] No-one knows enough to be an atheist. There is no logical ground for atheism. Atheism is logically impossible. The basis by which the atheist proclaims his faith is empty. He has no foundation, rationality, or an epistemology for his denial of God.

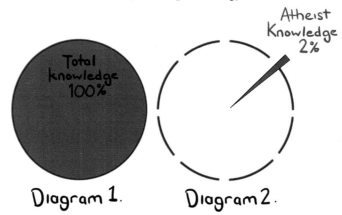

The above diagrams illustrate this truth. The first diagram represents total knowledge of reality. It includes everything there is to know; hence it has one hundred percent knowledge. The logical question we must ask is, "How much of this knowledge does the atheist possess?" Very little! Einstein said he knew less than half of one percent. Let us be generous and give the atheist two percent of the total knowledge. The second diagram represents the knowledge of the atheist in relation to total knowledge of reality. The next logical question: "Is it possible for God to exist outside of the knowledge the atheist possesses?" The answer, logically, is yes! Then how could the atheist say there is no God? He cannot logically say there is no God. Is it any wonder the Bible says, "The fool says in his heart, 'There is no God'" (Psalm 14:1).

Speaking at a university, I (SK) encountered a student who professed to be an atheist and who declared that there was no God. I asked, "Are you absolutely sure there is no God?" "Yes," he replied. Then I remarked, "You have absolute knowledge to be absolutely sure there is no God?" He replied, "No, I don't!" I responded, "Then you are not absolutely sure there is no God?"

259. Koukl, G., Arguments that commit suicide, *Clear Thinking*, Winter, 1999; part II, Spring, 1999.
260. Moreland, J.P., *Scaling the Secular City*, Baker, Grand Rapids, p. 92, 1987.

His response was, "I believe there is no God." Atheism is a belief based on faith. In *What I Believe*, Bertrand Russell, the famous philosopher admits, "I do not pretend to be able to prove that there is no God."[261] In fact, Nietzsche showed that he wasn't even interested in proof, by saying, in his work *AntiChrist*, "If one were to prove this God of the Christians to us, we should be even less able to believe in him."[262]

An atheist is not one who has no faith. He has no faith in God, but he puts his faith and trust in the belief that there is no God. No one lives in a vacuum. Every person believes in something. The atheist is committed to a set of beliefs. The atheist by faith believes that atheism is true. He offers no evidence for his belief but merely imagines there is no God, because God is outside of his frame of thinking.

The atheist mind-set is adequately illustrated in an analogy employed by the famous scientist Sir Arthur Eddington. He spoke of a fisherman who argued from his experience with a particular net that "No creature of the sea is less than two inches long." The people did not believe it. They affirmed that a great number of sea creatures were under two inches and they simply slipped through the holes in his net. But the fisherman was unconvinced. He insisted, "What my net can't catch ain't fish," and went on accusing his opponents of having a pre-scientific, medieval and metaphysical bias. The atheist commits the same fallacy. He confines God into a particular point of reference and defines Him out of existence. The net

261. Russell, B., *What I Believe*, Dutton & Co., New York, p. 13, 1925.
262. Nietzsche, F., "The AntiChrist" in *The Portable Nietzsche*, translated by Kaufmann, W., Viking Press, New York, p. 627, 1968.

which he habitually uses is hopelessly deficient—what I cannot see does not exist. Whatever does not fit into my view of reality (naturalism—the reductionistic view which insists that all reality is just matter in motion and excludes the supernatural) is meaningless. An atheist's blind faith in naturalism will not allow anything supernatural, transcendent or metaphysical. It is at this point that the atheist is letting fish slip through his atheistic net.

A clear example of this appeared in the classic debate between Bertrand Russell and Frederick Copleston. Russell, arguing from a naturalistic base, insisted that God was a meaningless proposition outside empirical verification. Copleston gave a fitting response that merits our attention:

> *"The proposition that metaphysical terms are meaningless seems to me to be a proposition based on an assumed philosophy. The dogmatic position behind it seems to be this: What will not go into my machine is non-existent, or it is meaningless."*[263]

The atheist in reality is engaged in explaining and defining God out of existence. Explaining God away does not necessarily disprove His existence. The problem is that naturalism is not an adequate net to catch the truth of all realities. It has too many holes in it to hold much truth. Naturalism fails to explain not only the great things of life but desperately fails to explain even the most simple facts of life.

To summarize, anyone who rejects the existence of God must believe the following creed:

- Matter is eternal.

- Matter without life created life.

- Matter without mind created mind.

- Matter without intelligence created intelligence.

- Matter without morals created morals.

- Matter without conscience created conscience.

- Matter without purpose created purpose and order.

Plato was right, "Atheism is a disease of the soul before it is an error of the mind."[264] Nietzsche boldly declared against his religious background, "But we do not at all want to enter into the kingdom of heaven: we have become men—so we want the kingdom of earth."[265] G.K. Chesterton's (paraphrased) dictum has much wisdom, "When people stop believing in God, they do not believe in nothing—they believe in anything." Atheism is rationally impossible. In order to be an atheist:

263. Hick, J., *The Existence of God*, Macmillan, New York, pp. 170–171, 1964.
264. Baisnée, J.A., ed., *Readings in Natural Theology*, Newman Press, Westminster, MD, p. 149, 1962.
265. Nietzsche, ref. 219.

- One must prove there is no God.

- Refute all the evidence for the existence of God.

- Explain away the reality of Christ.

- Remove the evidence for the resurrection of Christ.

- Disprove all the prophecies in the Bible.

- Demonstrate the Bible is a fraud.

- Establish the credibility of atheism.

Christian thinker, Alphonse Gratry, writes:

> *"The actual theory of atheism, … entails at the close of the argument a manifest absurdity; which must be so, since a correct train of reasoning must reduce to an absurdity the hypothesis that there is no God."*[266]

No wonder that the ideas of the atheist writer Camus contributed to the philosophy known as *absurdism.*

V. THE AGONY OF ATHEISM

Some time ago they buried an atheist dressed up in a beautiful tuxedo. After a tombstone was placed on his grave a cynic wrote the following words, "Here lies an atheist all dressed up and nowhere to go." Atheism is a journey without a destiny, a body without a soul, a religion without reason, life without meaning, a faith without hope, and a universe without God.

The truth of atheism is the death of truth. The absence of God logically means the absence of all that God implies. In Nietzschean terms, the death of God means the death of reason, morals, good, value, virtue and ultimately the Christian view of man. As one college cynic declared, "God is dead, Marx is dead and I'm not feeling too well myself."

Atheism is existentially unfulfilling. Sigmund Freud concluded, "The moment a man questions the meaning and value of life, he is sick, since objectively neither has any existence."[267]

266. Baisnée, ref. 264.
267. Freud, E.L. (Ed.), *Letters of Sigmund Freud*, Hogarth, London, p. 432, 1961.

Nietzsche found life unbearable without God and finally went mad. He wrote, "My life now consists in the wish that it might be otherwise with all things that I comprehend, and that somebody might make my 'truths' appear incredible to me."[268]

Jean-Paul Sartre admitted that it was distressing that God does not exist because it implies that man tragically stands alone in an empty space and a meaningless universe without a spiritual home.

Jackson Pollock struggled with the problem of not being able to live on the basis of atheism. He complained that there was no God, and denied any purpose or design in life. He became exhausted by his style of chance painting and committed suicide.

Albert Camus was insightful when he wrote, "To kill God is to become god oneself: it is to realize on this earth the eternal life of which the Gospel speaks."[269]

Bertrand Russell said, "I have to read at least one detective book a day to drug myself against the nuclear threat."[270]

John Cage advocated an atheistic universe which exists by blind chance and sought to live on the basis of his chance philosophy, but he couldn't live out his atheistic chance philosophy when he tried to apply it to his hobby of mushroom picking. He admits, "I became aware that if I approached mushrooms in the spirit of my chance operations, I would die shortly … So I decided that I would not approach them in this way."[271] In an important sense atheism proves the existence of God.

D.E. Roberts, Professor of Philosophy at New York University, speaking about atheists, suggests that, "They offer us the strongest possible argument FOR God that can possibly be conceived."[272]

With great agony the Nobel Prize winner Samuel Beckett describes his atheistic condition:

"How am I, an a-temporal being imprisoned in time and space, to escape from my imprisonment, when I know that outside space and time lies nothing, and that I, in the ultimate depths of my reality, am nothing also?"[273]

268. Nietzsche, F., *The Portable Nietzsche*, ed. Walter Kaufmann, Princeton University Press, p. 441, 1968.
269. Camus, A., *The Myth of Sisyphus & Other Essays*, translated by O'Brien, J., Vintage Books, New York, p. 80, 1955.
270. Quoted in Mehta, V., *Fly and the Fly-Bottle: Encounters with British Intellectuals*, Weidenfeld & Nicolson, p. 41, 1963.
271. Schaeffer, F., *The God Who is There*, InterVarsity, Downers Grove, pp. 73–74, 1968.
272. Quoted in Badham, L., *Verdict on Jesus*, Hodder & Stoughton, London, p. 156, 1950.
273. Coe, R., *Samuel Beckett*, Grove, New York, p. 18, 1964.

Listen to the agonizing words of Bertrand Russell:

"That man is the product of causes which had no provision of the end they were achieving; that his origin, his growth, his hopes and fears, his loves and his beliefs, are but the outcome of accidental collections of atoms; that no fire, no heroism, no intensity of thought and feeling, can preserve an individual life beyond the grave; that all the labour of the ages, all the devotion, all the inspiration, all the noonday brightness of human genius, are destined to extinction in the vast death of the solar system, and that the whole temple of Man's achievement must inevitably be buried beneath the debris of a universe in ruins—all these things, if not quite beyond dispute, are yet so nearly certain, that no philosophy which rejects them can hope to stand. Only within the scaffolding of these truths, only on the firm foundation of unyielding despair, can the soul's habitation henceforth be safely built."[274]

Or hear the despair of 'Gerard', who called in to a radio show about depression:

"I think that some people may have an inability to cope, and maybe this might sound a bit extreme, but that might be Darwinian theory, the Darwin theory of survival of the fittest. Maybe some of us aren't meant to survive, maybe some of us are meant to kill ourselves …

"There's too many people in the world as it is. Maybe it is survival of the fittest, maybe some of us are meant to just give up, and maybe that would help the species."[275]

Indeed, atheism has had tragic consequences. One psychiatric study concluded:

"Religiously unaffiliated subjects had significantly more lifetime suicide attempts and more first-degree relatives who committed suicide than subjects who endorsed a religious affiliation. Unaffiliated subjects were younger, less often married, less often had children, and had less contact with family members.

"Furthermore, subjects with no religious affiliation perceived fewer reasons for living, particularly fewer moral objections to suicide. In terms of clinical characteristics, religiously unaffiliated subjects had more lifetime impulsivity, aggression, and past substance use disorder. No differences in the level of subjective and objective depression, hopelessness, or stressful life events were found."[276]

274. Russell, B., *A Free Man's Worship*, Thomas Mosher, Portland, MN, pp. 6–7, 1927.
275. ABC (Australia) radio, *Life Matters* with Norman Swan, 4 May 2000: "Black Dog Days—The Experience and Treatment of Depression"; Wieland, C., Darwin, Spurgeon and the 'black dog', *Creation* **22**(4):54–55, 2000, creation.com/suicide.
276. Dervic, K. *et al.*, Religious affiliation and suicide attempt, *American J. Psychiatry* **161**(12):2303–2308, December 2004.

It would not be off the mark to state an old maxim which touches the core of atheism, "God does not exist because his existence threatens my world view." Philosopher Thomas Nagel was explicit (bold emphases added):

> "*I want atheism to be true and am made uneasy by the fact that some of the most intelligent and well-informed people I know are religious believers. It isn't just that I don't believe in God and, naturally, hope that I'm right in my belief. It's that I hope there is no God! I don't want there to be a God; I don't want the universe to be like that.*"[277]

Atheism offers no answer to the fundamental metaphysical questions regarding the reality of the universe or the genesis of human personality. The testimony of Robert J. Dean, a scientist, provides a remarkable insight into the position of atheism:

> "*My father and mother were deeply religious. My brother and I had no time for religion. We thought that religion was all right for old people, but we were scientists and we thought we had found our way through what we were pleased to call scientific methods. Then my brother was killed. My father and mother had resources, and with their resources they could meet that shattering loss. But I had no one. I had no resources at all.*"[278]

When his confidence in atheism was shattered, this scientist decided to test the reality of God and found to his satisfaction that God is real. It is more reasonable to believe in God, for the existence of this life is an enigma without the supposition of God's existence.

The brilliant writer and Nobel Prize winner for literature, Alexandr Solzhenitsyn (1918–2008), came to the right conclusion after observing the consequences of atheism. In a speech before a group of students at Harvard University, Solzhenitsyn insisted:

> "*If I were asked today to formulate as concisely as possible the main cause of the ruinous revolution that swallowed up some 60 million of our people, I could not put it more accurately than to repeat: 'Men have forgotten God; that is why all this has happened.'*"

277. Nagel, T., *The Last Word*, pp. 130–131, 1997.
278. Dean, R.J., *How Can We Believe?* Broadman, Nashville, p. 25, 1978.

RECOMMENDED READING

- Berlinski, David, *The Devil's Delusion: Atheism and its Scientific Pretensions*, Basic Books, 2009.

- Borne, Etienne, *Atheism*, Hawthorn Books, New York, 1961.

- Collins, James, *God in Modern Philosophy*, Henry Regnery, Chicago, 1959.

- Copan, Paul and Craig, William (Eds.), *Contending with Christianity's Critics: Answering New Atheists and Other Objectors*, B&H Academic, 2009.

- Grisez, Germain, *Beyond the New Theism*, University of Notre Dame Press, Notre Dame, IN, 1975.

- Lepp, Ignace, *Atheism in Our Time*, Macmillan, New York, 1964.

- Mariano, *Atheism*; creation.com/atheism, 2009.

- Schilling, S. Paul, *God in an Age of Atheism*, Abingdon Press, Nashville, 1969.

- Spiegel, James S., *The Making of an Atheist: How Immorality Leads to Unbelief*, Moody Publishers, 2010.

- Strunk, Orlo, Jr, *The Choice Called Atheism*, Abingdon, Nashville, 1969.

- Zacharias, Ravi and Strobel, Lee, *Atheists*, Zondervan, 2008.

If ever God was man or man was God, Jesus Christ was both.
— LORD BYRON

If the life and death of Socrates are those of a philosopher, the life and death of Jesus Christ are those of a God.
— JEAN-JACQUES ROUSSEAU

I tell the Hindus that their lives will be imperfect if they do not also study reverently the teaching of Jesus.
— GANDHI

4

....

IS JESUS
TRULY GOD?

Why believe in Jesus Christ? What makes Him so different from Socrates, Buddha, Confucius and others? Can we be sure of His existence? What evidences support His claim to divinity? Is He relevant to modern man? Why do Christians believe in Him?

In an age of conflicting religious claims, no issue confronts the modern mind more than the founder of Christianity. Nearly 2,000 years ago in a province of the Roman Empire, there lived a man whose life altered the entire history of the Western world. Through the centuries, theologians have debated on His origin, skeptics have denounced His existence and philosophers have wrestled over His teachings. Today He is still the centre of discussion, a point for debate and a source of inspiration to many who follow His teachings. The Swiss church historian Philip Schaff (1819–1893) is on good ground when he states:

> *"Jesus of Nazareth, without money and arms, conquered more millions than Alexander, Caesar, Mohammed and Napoleon; without science and learning, He shed more light on things human and divine, than all the philosophers and scholars combined; without the eloquence of the school, He spoke words of life such as were never spoken before, nor since, and produced effects which lie beyond the reach of orator or poet; without writing a single line, He has set more pens in motion and furnished themes for more sermons, orations, discussions, works of art, learned volumes, and sweet songs of praise than the whole army of great men of ancient and modern times. Born in a manger and crucified as a malefactor, He now controls the destinies of the civilized world, and rules a spiritual empire which embraces one-third of the inhabitants of the globe."[279]*

Whatever assumptions we might entertain about Christ, we cannot dismiss Him from the facts of history. We may ignore Him but we cannot avoid Him. We may reject Him but we cannot escape Him. His name is written across every page of modern history. Every time

....

279. Schaff, P., *The Person of Christ*, American Tract Society, NY, pp. 33–34, 1913.

we write a letter we acknowledge His entrance to our planet. He is indeed a stubborn fact of history. Polish-born American Yiddish novelist, Sholem Asch (1880–1957) affirms, "Jesus Christ is the outstanding personality of all time ... every act and word of Jesus has value for all of us. He became the Light of the World. Why shouldn't I, a Jew, be proud of that?"[280]

Jesus of Nazareth is one of a kind; there is simply no comparison, as apologist and church historian John H. Gerstner (1914–1996) delightfully puts it:

> *"To the artist He is the one altogether lovely. To the educator He is the master teacher. To the philosopher He is the wisdom of God. To the lonely He is a brother; to the sorrowful, a comforter; to the bereaved, the resurrection and the life. And to the sinner He is the Lamb of God that taketh away the sin of the world."*[281]

I. THE CERTAINTY OF HIS EXISTENCE

One of the most amazing facts about contemporary skepticism regarding the existence of Christ is that it comes not from experts in ancient history who are trained in the historical studies and ancient historiography, but from non-specialists. Recent theories of Christology advocated by the Jesus Seminar people,[282] John Shelby Spong,[283] Barbara Thiering,[284] A.N. Wilson[285] and others, have not succeeded in replacing the historical view. These writers at best are sensational and have a fertile imagination. Their fanciful theories have been adequately refuted by a number of contemporary scholars.[286] Distinguished scholars in ancient history like A.N. Sherwin-White, Sir William Ramsay, B.W. Henderson, F.F. Bruce, C.F.D. Moule, Ethelbert Stauffer, and C.H. Dodd and many others, have accepted without question the historicity of Christ.

280. Asch, S., "I had to write these things", *Christian Herald*, cited in Mead, F. (Ed.), *Encyclopedia of Religious Quotations*, Fleming H. Revel Company, West Wood, NJ, p. 43, 1965.
281. Gerstner, J.H., *Reasons For Faith*, Baker, Grand Rapids, p. 80, 1967.
282. See for example Wright, N.T., *Jesus and the Victory of God*, Augsburg Fortress Pub, 1997. He points out how the Seminar presupposed many assumptions before starting, such as Premise 45, "Only a small proportion of the sayings attributed to Jesus in the Gospels was actually spoken by him." But the mass media present this as the conclusion of their research, yet when they start with that assumption, it would have been a miracle to reach any other conclusion.
283. For detailed refutation, see Bott, M. and Sarfati, J., What's wrong with Bishop Spong? Laymen rethink the scholarship of John Shelby Spong, *Apologia* **4**(1):3–27, 1995; creation.com/spong.
284. Sarfati, J., "Barbara Thiering: A short critique"; creation.com/thiering.
285. See Wright, N.T., *Who was Jesus?*, SPCK, Great Britain, p. 89, 1992. This book is an excellent critique by a New Testament scholar of the three recent anti-Christian books: 1) Thiering, B., *Jesus the Man: A New Interpretation from the Dead Sea Scrolls*; 2) Wilson, A.N., *Jesus*, Sinclair-Stevenson, London, 1992; 3) Spong, J.S., *Born of a Woman: A Bishop Rethinks the Birth of Jesus*, HarperSanFrancisco, 1992.
286. See Nash, R.H., *Christianity and the Hellenistic World*, Zondervan, Grand Rapids, 1984, Wilkins, M.J. and Moreland, J.P., *Jesus Under Fire*, Zondervan, Grand Rapids, 1995, Blomberg, C., *The Historical Reliability of the Gospels*, InterVarsity, Downers Grove, 1987, France, R.T., *The Evidence for Jesus*, InterVarsity, Downers Grove, 1986 and Wright, N.T., *Who Was Jesus?* Eerdmans, Grand Rapids, 1992.

The famous writer and agnostic H.G. Wells, in his popular work *The Outline of History*, referring to Jesus, affirms, "Here was a man. This part of the tale could not have been invented."[287] Will Durant, an equally famous agnostic and former professor of Philosophy of History at Columbia University, perhaps America's foremost historian, in his book *Caesar and Christ* declares:

> *"That a few simple men should in one generation have invented so powerful and appealing a personality, so lofty an ethic, and so inspiring a vision of human brotherhood, would be a miracle far more incredible than any recorded in the gospels."[288]*

Otto Betz points out, "No serious scholar has ventured to postulate the non-historicity of Jesus."[289] F.F. Bruce (1910–1990), Ryland professor of Biblical Criticism at the University of Manchester, writes:

> *"Some writers may toy with the fancy of a 'Christ-myth', but they do not do so on the ground of historical evidence. The historicity of Christ is as axiomatic for an unbiased historian as the historicity of Julius Caesar. It is not historians who propagate the 'Christ-myth' theories."[290]*

Indeed, the main proponent of the 'Christ Myth' idea was G.A. Wells (1926–), a professor of *German*, not a historian.[291] Yet the arch-neo-atheist Richard Dawkins claims that it's "possible to mount a serious, though not widely supported, historical case that Jesus never lived at all", and appeals to Wells.[292] This alone should be enough to shatter his intellectual credibility,[293] although there is much besides as shown in chapters one and three.

American Transcendentalist Theodore Parker's delightful aphorism ought not to escape us, "It takes a Newton to forge a Newton. What man could have fabricated a Jesus? None but a Jesus."[294] This is quite an admission from Parker (1810–1850), who was a Unitarian minister, i.e. he denied Christ's deity.

Even an unbelieving writer such as James Frazer (1854–1941) notes, "The doubts which have been cast on the historical reality of Jesus are, in my judgement, unworthy of serious attention."[295] He concludes, "The origin of a great religious and moral reform is inexplicable without the personal existence of a great reformer."[93]

287. Wells, H.G., *The Outline of History*, Volume **I**, The Macmillan Company, New York, p. 574, 1921.
288. Durant, W., "Caesar and Christ", *The Story of Civilization*, Volume **III**, Simon & Schuster, New York, p. 557, 1944.
289. Betz, O., *What Do We Know About Jesus?* S.C.M., London, p. 9, 1968.
290. Bruce, F.F., *The New Testament Documents: Are they Reliable?* Inter-Varsity, London, p. 119, 1968.
291. For thorough refutation of the 'Jesus didn't exist' nonsense, which has spread thanks to the internet, see Holding, J.P., *Shattering the Christ Myth*, Xulon Press, 2008; tektonics.org/jesusexisthub.html.
292. Dawkins, R., *The God Delusion*, Mariner Books, p. 122, 2008.
293. Holding, J.P., Dawkins' ironic hypocrisy; creation.com/dawk-hyp, 21 November 2008.
294. McGuiggan, J., *If God Came*, Montex Publishing, Lubbock, TX, p. 33, 1980.
295. Frazer, J., *The Golden Bough*, Volume **IX**, Studley Press, London, p. 412, 1951.

The case for Christianity depends on the historicity of Jesus Christ. In this sense, Christianity differs from all other religions. Prolific British Christian author Michael Green (1930–) is right, "Once disprove the historicity of Jesus Christ, and Christianity will collapse like a pack of cards."[296] The conviction of the British political philosopher John Stuart Mill (1806–1873) is worth noting:

> "It is of no use to say that Christ as exhibited in the gospels is not historical … Who among his disciples or among their proselytes was capable of inventing the sayings ascribed to Jesus, or of imagining the life and character revealed in the gospels? Certainly not the fishermen of Galilee, still less the early Christian writers."[297]

The evidence for the existence of Christ is simply so unbeatable that, if the critics wish to challenge His existence, they would be wise to heed the words of Australian educator W.H. Fitchett before doing so, "When any one undertakes to prove that Christ did not exist nineteen hundred years ago, he may well be asked to attempt a feat much nearer at hand. Let him prove that He does not exist to-day!"[298] The essence of the Christian message is the entrance of Jesus of Nazareth into space-time history. British historian Herbert Butterfield (1970–1979), rightly points out, "It would be a dangerous error to imagine that the characteristics of an historical religion would be maintained if the Christ of the theologians were divorced from the Jesus of history."[299]

It is on very good ground that the great genius of German literature, Johann Wolfgang von Goethe (1749–1832) declares:

> "I esteem the Gospels to be thoroughly genuine, for there shines forth from them the reflected splendour of a sublimity, proceeding from the person of Jesus Christ, and of as Divine a king as was ever manifested upon earth."[300]

The reliability of the Gospels is so important that we defend it in detail in ch. 5 on the Bible, under "III The manuscripts support it", p. 118.

II. THE SECULAR EVIDENCE

Secularists seldom pay serious attention to religious issues and one should not expect to find an abundance of evidences from secular sources. However, there are adequate evidences from secular writers to establish the historicity of Christ apart from the biblical narratives.

One of the most significant pieces of evidence comes from Pliny the Younger, the governor of Bithynia in Northern Turkey, in the year AD 112. In his correspondence to the Emperor

---

296. Green, M., *Runaway World*, Inter-Varsity, London, p. 2, 1968.
297. Mill, J.S., *Essays on Nature, the Utility of Religion and Theism*, Longmans, London, 1874.
298. Fitchett, W.H., *The Beliefs of Unbelief*, Cassell & Co., London, p. 178, 1908. Fitchett (1841–1928) was also a journalist, editor and minister, and founding president of the Methodist Ladies' College, Melbourne.
299. Butterfield, H., *Christianity and History*, George Bell, London, p. 129, 1950.
300. Ballard, F., *The Miracles of Unbelief*, Clark, Edinburgh, p. 251, 1904.

Trajan, Pliny makes reference to Christ, "They were in the habit of meeting on a certain fixed day before it was light, when they sang an anthem to Christ as God, and bound themselves by a solemn oath not to commit any wicked deed, …"[301]

A Syrian named Mara Bar-Serapion, sometime during the period 70–150 AD, wrote to his son, Serapion, a letter which is preserved in the British Museum. He acknowledges the existence of Jesus. Part of the letter reads, "What advantage did the Jews gain from executing their wise King? It was just after that their kingdom was abolished."[302] Cornelius Tacitus, the famous Roman historian, being governor of Asia Minor in AD 112, reveals his knowledge of the existence of Christ, "Christus, from whom they got their name, had been executed by sentence of the procurator Pontius Pilate, when Tiberius was emperor; …"[303] The Roman historian Suetonius (AD 120), in his book *The Life of Claudius*, makes an interesting reference to the fact of Christ's existence, "As the Jews were making constant disturbances at the instigation of Chrestus, he [Claudius] expelled them from Rome."[304]

III. THE JEWISH EVIDENCE

The Jewish historian Flavius Josephus, in his famous work *Antiquities of the Jews* (published AD 93), makes several references to familiar figures in the New Testament. They include, among many others, John the Baptist, Pilate, the Herods, Felix, Festus, Annas, Caiaphas and James "the brother of Jesus". His reference to Christ reads, "And there arose about this time Jesus, a wise man, if indeed we should call him a man: for he was a doer of marvellous deeds, a teacher of men …"[305] Even if the above passage is questionable, what are we to make of his second reference? "So he (Ananus) assembled a council of judges, and brought before it the brother of Jesus the so-called Christ, whose name was James …"[306] Professor Ethelbert

301. Bruce, ref. 290, p. 119.
302. Bruce, ref. 290, p. 114.
303. Bruce, ref. 290, p. 117.
304. Bruce, ref. 290, p. 118.
305. Josephus, F., *Antiquities of the Jews* XVIII.3.3, AD 93.
306. Josephus, ref. 305, XX.9.1.

Stauffer (1802–1979), of the University of Erlangen, in his *Jesus and His Story*, informs, "In AD 95 Rabbi Eliezer ben Hyrcanus of Lydda speaks of Jesus' magic arts."[307]

In the Jewish document *The Talmud*, one can find numerous allusions to Jesus. Rabbi Eliezer said, "Balaam looked forth and saw that there was a man, born of a woman, who would rise up and seek to make himself God, and cause the whole world to go astray."[308] Jewish historian, Joseph Klausner (1874–1958), in his work *Jesus of Nazareth*, provides ample Jewish evidence for the historicity of Christ.

We must agree with F.F. Bruce, "Whatever else may be thought of the evidence from early Jewish and Gentile writers … it does at least establish, for those who refuse the witness of Christian writings, the historical character of Jesus Himself."[309]

IV. THE CREDIBILITY OF HIS CLAIMS

What makes Christ so different from all other men of history? Why is He so special to the Christian? What is it about Him that is unique? Moses did not claim to be God; Paul was horrified when people tried to worship him as a god (Acts 14:11–18); Confucius was confused on the nature of God; Zoroaster was a follower of God, never God; Buddha never identifies himself as God; Mohammed did not claim to be Allah (Arabic for God), but Jesus Christ did—Jesus claimed to be God in the flesh. This very fact set Him apart from every other man. C.S. Lewis points out, with his usual brilliance, the radical differences between the claims of Christ and the claims of other religious leaders:

> *"There is no half-way house and there is no parallel in other religions. If you had gone to Buddha and asked him, 'Are you the son of Bramah?' he would have said, 'My son, you are still in the vale of illusion.' If you had gone to Socrates and asked, 'Are you Zeus?' he would have laughed at you. If you had gone to Mohammed and asked, 'Are you Allah?' he would first have rent his clothes and then cut your head off. If you had asked Confucius, 'Are you Heaven?' I think he would have probably replied, 'Remarks which are not in accordance with nature are in bad taste.'"[310]*

But when 'doubting Thomas' confessed to Jesus, "My Lord and my God!" (John 20:28), Jesus did *not* rebuke or contradict him; rather Jesus *blessed* Thomas.

John Gerstner writes:

> *"It is true that Bronson Alcott once said to a friend, 'Today I feel that I could say, as Christ did, I and the Father are one.' 'Yes,' the other replied, 'but the difference is this:*

307. Stauffer, E., *Jesus and His Story*, Alfred P. Knoph, New York, p. 9, 1959.
308. Green, ref. 296, p. 20.
309. Bruce, ref. 290, p. 119.
310. Lewis, C.S., "What are we to make of Jesus Christ?" in Hooper, W. (Ed.), *God in the Dock: Essays on Theology and Ethics*, Eerdmans, Grand Rapids, pp. 157–158, 1970.

Christ got the world to believe him.'[311]

Most of the world's religious founders stressed the importance of their teaching but Christ focused on Himself. He made it clear that man's eternal destiny depends on how we regard Him, "I told you that you would die in your sins; if you do not believe that I am the one I claim to be, you will indeed die in your sins" (John 8:24).

The claims of Christ are truly staggering. Very few leaders have made the kind of claims Christ has made. His claims have dazzled many of His disciples, muddled many religious leaders, and puzzled a great number of scholars. Henry J. Heydt, founder of Lancaster Bible College in Pennsylvania, said:

> *"No founder of any religion has dared to claim for himself one fraction of the assertions made by the Lord Jesus Christ about himself. No religion has claimed for its founder what Christianity has claimed for the Lord Jesus Christ. No founder of any religion has been as highly acclaimed by those of other faiths as has the Lord Jesus Christ."[312]*

311. Gerstner, ref. 281, p. 82.
312. Heydt, H.J., *A Comparison of World Religions*, Christian Literature Crusade, Fort Washington, PN, pp. 92–93, 1976.

His claim to divinity marks Him from every other claim. Jesus claimed the highest title which only God could have:

- To forgive sin, and His enemies got the point: "Only God can forgive sins"—Matthew 9:1–8.

- To judge the world—John 5:25,29.

- To give eternal life—John 3:16.

- To be sinless—John 8:46.

- To be the object of faith—John 8:24.

- To answer prayer—John 14:13.

- To be worthy of worship—Matthew 14:33.

- To be the Truth—John 14:6.

- To have all authority—Matthew 28:18.

- To be one in essence with God—John 10:30.

In Matthew 26:63 and John 5:25 the phrase "Son of God" is used but this does not mean that He is less than deity as some wrongly believe. Theologian J. Oliver Buswell (1895–1977), in his *A Systematic Theology of the Christian Religion*, points out:

"In Jewish usage the term 'son of …' did not generally imply any subordination, but rather equality and identity of nature. Thus Bar Kokba, who led the Jewish revolt AD 132–135 in the reign of Hadrian, was called by a name which means 'Son of the Star.' It is supposed that he took this name to identify himself as the very Star predicted in Numbers 24:17. The name Son of Consolation (Acts 4:36) doubtless means, 'The Consoler.' 'Sons of Thunder' (Mark 3:17) probably means 'Thunderous Men.' 'Son of Man,' especially as applied to Christ in Daniel 7:13 and constantly in the New Testament, essentially means 'The Representative Man.' Thus for Christ to say, 'I am the Son of God' (John 10:36) was understood by His contemporaries as identifying Himself as God, equal with the Father, in an unqualified sense."[313]

English Anglican theologian John R.W. Stott (1921–2011) writes:

"So close was His connection with God that He equated a man's attitude to Himself with the man's attitude to God. Thus, to know Him was to know God (John 8:19; 14:7). To see Him was to see God (12:45; 14:9). To believe in Him was to believe in God (12:44; 14:1). To receive Him was to receive God (Mark 9:37). To hate Him was to hate God (John 15:23). And to honor Him was to honor God (5:23)."[314]

313. Buswell, J.O., *A Systematic Theology of the Christian Religion*, Christian Life Publishers, Singapore, p. 105, 1994).
314. Stott, J.R.W., *Basic Christianity*, Inter-Varsity, Chicago, p. 26, 1964.

Any sensible person facing these claims is led to only four possible conclusions—a tetralemma:[315]

1. Jesus claimed to be God but knew He was not: Therefore He was a liar.

2. Jesus thought He was God but He was not: Therefore He was a lunatic.

3. Jesus never claimed to be God but His followers created the idea: Therefore it is a legend.

4. Jesus claimed to be God because He was God: Therefore He is Lord.

A serious reflection on the above propositions will lead any rational person to the fourth position. The ministry of Christ and His teaching goes against the nature of a lunatic. For example take His Sermon on the Mount, which is universally regarded as the highest ideal for living even by non-Christian writers.

Even many of those who deny His divinity assert that Christ was a great moral teacher. The overwhelming testimony of the world is that Jesus of Nazareth was a perfect man. When it comes to principles of morality the world knows of no superior principles than those of Christ. The famous historian W.E.H. Lecky, in his significant work *History of European Morals from Augustus to Charlemagne*, comments on the life of Christ, that "the simple record of three short years of active life has done more to regenerate and to soften mankind, than all the disquisitions of philosophers and than all the exhortations of moralists."[316] The fact is, how could He be a great moral teacher if He was lying about the nature of His true being? If Jesus is wrong on the crucial area of His life, He could hardly be a great moral teacher! Professor A.M. Hunter of Aberdeen University makes an important point:

> *"No mortal man makes such a claim, or we know him to be mad. We are driven back on the words of wise old 'Rabbi' Duncan: 'Christ either deceived mankind by conscious fraud, or He was Himself deluded, or He was divine. There is no getting out of this trilemma.'"[317]*

Jean-Jacques Rousseau asks, "Can the Person whose history the Gospels relate be himself a man? … Yes, if the life and death of Socrates are those of a philosopher, the life and death of Jesus Christ are those of a God."[318] If we accept Jesus as a perfect man we must also accept Him as God. But why should we? John Gerstner rightly answers:

> *"Because the perfect man says He is God. And if He is not God, then neither can He be a perfect man. We despise Father Divine as a man for claiming to be God, which we know he is not. If Jesus Christ is not God, we must despise Him also, for He claims far*

315. C.S. Lewis famously popularized a 'trilemma' argument, or "Liar, Lunatic or Lord", which presupposed that Jesus was reported accurately, i.e. rejecting option 3 as not even worth debating.

316. Lecky, W.E.H., *History of European Morals from Augustus to Charlemagne*, Volume **II**, Longmans Green, London, p. 88, 1869.

317. Young, J., *The Case Against Christ*, Church Pastoral Aid Society, London, p. 83, 1978.

318. Quoted in Ballard, ref. 300, p. 251.

more clearly than Father Divine that He is God. We must, therefore, either worship Christ as God or despise or pity Him as a man."[319]

As we observe the life of Christ, we see no evidence of mental illness or psychological disturbance. The facts will not permit us to conclude that He was schizophrenic or paranoid. C.S. Lewis sums up the real point of the argument:

> *"A man who was merely a man and said the sort of things Jesus said would not be a great moral teacher. He would either be a lunatic—on a level with the man who says he is a poached egg—or else he would be the Devil of Hell. You must make your choice. Either this man was, and is, the Son of God: or else a madman or something worse. You can shut Him up for a fool, you can spit at Him and kill Him as a demon; or you can fall at His feet and call Him Lord and God."*[320]

The deity of Christ, and the corollary of this, the Trinity, are vital doctrines of the Christian faith. They are so important that we revisit them in the chapter on Islam, since this is a crucial difference between the two most populous world religions (see p. 187).

V. THE CREDENTIALS OF HIS DEITY

Anyone could claim to be God but what proof do we have to back up that claim? Christ did not just make empty claims about His divinity but proved them with adequate evidence. Luke writes, "He showed himself to these men and gave many convincing proofs that he was alive" (Acts 1:3). The credential of Christ is His resurrection from the dead. It was the resurrection event that separates Jesus Christ from any other individual. In this important event we see Christ's unique demonstration of divinity. Clark Pinnock's remarks are worth noting, "If there is a God and if he wanted us to know that his authority was vested in the invitation of the gospel, he could scarcely have done a more appropriate thing than he has done in raising Christ."[321]

319. Gerstner, ref. 281, p. 81.
320. Lewis, C.S., *Mere Christianity*, Collins, London, pp. 52–53, 1960.
321. Pinnock, C.H., *Reason Enough: A Case for the Christian Faith*, InterVarsity, Downers Grove, p. 90, 1980.

Along the same line the brilliant American philosopher Richard L. Purtill (1931–) argues:

> *"If I claim to have authority in a certain organization, strong evidence of my authority would be an ability to suspend the rules or make exceptions to usual procedures. You might meditate on the problem of how a God who never interfered with the working of the universe could establish a message from Himself as authoritative."[322]*

The Scripture is very plain, "If Christ has not been raised our preaching is useless and so is your faith" (1 Corinthians 15:14). Paul E. Little (1928–1975), associate professor of evangelism at Trinity Evangelical Divinity School (Illinois) rightly affirms:

> *"Jesus' supreme credential to authenticate his claim to deity was his resurrection from the dead. Five times in the course of his life he predicted he would die. He also predicted how he would die and that three days later he would rise from the dead and appear to his disciples."[323]*

The Apostle Paul, writing to the Romans, says, "Who, through the Spirit of holiness was declared with power to be the Son of God by his resurrection from the dead: Jesus Christ our Lord" (Romans 1:4). Without the resurrection there would not be a Christianity— Christianity stands or falls with the resurrection and this single factor makes Christianity remarkably one of a kind. The brilliant scholar James Orr perceptively notes:

> *"No single example can be produced of belief in the resurrection of an historical personage such as Jesus was: none at least on which anything was ever founded … The Christian Resurrection is thus a fact without historical analogy."[324]*

B.B. Warfield asserts, "Christ Himself deliberately staked His whole claim to the credit of men upon His resurrection. When asked for a sign He pointed to this sign as His single and sufficient credential."[325] The critics of Christianity are fighting a losing battle. Christianity cannot be refuted, simply for one reason: we cannot explain away the resurrection. It is this fact which brought life and courage to the disappointed and disillusioned disciples. It is because of this event that Christianity

322. Purtill, R.L., *Thinking About Religion*, Prentice-Hall, Englewood Cliffs, NJ, p. 70, 1978. See also "Miracles and science", creation.com/miracles, 1 September 2006.
323. Little, P.E., *Know Why You Believe*, Scripture Union, London, p. 21, 1968.
324. Orr, J., *The Resurrection of Jesus*, College Press, Joplin, MO, p. 224, 1972.
325. Warfield, B.B., *The Person and Work of Christ*, Puritan Reformed, Philadelphia, p. 537, 1950.

spread across the Roman Empire and continues to influence our present world.

What evidences do we have for the resurrection? How can we be sure that Christ rose from the dead? Finally, why is this such an important issue?

Fact 1. Christ died on the Cross.

Fact 2. Christ was buried.

Fact 3. Christ's disciples were discouraged.

Fact 4. Christ's tomb was empty.

Fact 5. Christ appeared to the disciples.

Fact 6. The disciples were transformed.

Fact 7. The disciples proclaimed the resurrection.

The evidences for the resurrection are the three indisputable facts: the empty tomb, the resurrection appearances and the origin of Christianity, as discussed in ch. 1, p. 41. These provide solid evidence that Christ rose from the dead. If these facts are true and the alternative theories against the resurrection are inadequate, then we must accept the resurrection as a historical fact.

We agree with Richard Riss, "It is certainly the case that it takes more faith to believe, against the evidence, that the resurrection did not occur, than it does to believe that it has occurred."[326] Dr Thomas Arnold (1795–1842), the author of the famous three-volume *History of Rome* and Regius Professor of Modern History at Oxford, a scholar who was acquainted with historical evidence and an authority capable of weighing facts from fiction, after studying the evidence for Christ's resurrection stated, "I know of no one fact in the history of mankind which is proved by better and fuller evidence of every sort, to the understanding of a fair inquirer, than the great sign which God has given us that Christ died and rose again from the dead."[327]

C.S. Lewis' poignant analysis should move us:

> *"If the thing happened, it was the central event in the history of the Earth—the very thing that the whole story has been about. Since it happened only once, it is by Hume's standards infinitely improbable. But then the whole history of the Earth has also happened only once; is it therefore incredible? Hence the difficulty, which weighs upon Christian and atheist alike, of estimating the probability of the Incarnation. It is like asking whether the existence of Nature herself is intrinsically probable. That is why it is easier to argue, on historical grounds, that*

326. Riss, R., *The Evidence for the Resurrection of Jesus Christ*, Bethany Fellowship, Minneapolis, pp. 104–105, 1977.
327. Arnold, T., *Sermons on the Christian Life. Its Hopes, Its Fears, and Its Close*, 6th edition, T. Fellowes, London, p. 15–16, 1859.

the Incarnation actually occurred than to show, on philosophical grounds, the probability of its occurrence."[328]

Jesus Christ is the perfect revelation of God. In Christ we see what God is like. He is our clue to the existence of God, the meaning of life and the hope of our destiny. Philip Schaff, the Yale scholar, is right in stating that, "Standing on this rock, I feel safe against all the attacks of infidelity. The person of Christ is to me the greatest and surest of all facts; as certain as my own personal existence."[329]

That God should reveal Himself in our space and time is too great for our small hearts. This unique event is too wonderful to be true. It is simply incredible that the God of the universe should take such a humble step to communicate His infinite love to mankind. This is the meaning and the message of Christ. "No one has ever seen God, but God the only Son, who is at the Father's side, has made him known" (John 1:18).

328. Lewis, C.S., "Miracles," *The Best of C.S. Lewis*, Iversen, New York, pp. 306–307, 1969. See also creation.com/miracles.
329. Schaff, P., *The Person of Christ*, American Tract Society, NY, p. 8, 1913.

RECOMMENDED READING

- Anderson, J.N.D., *Christianity: the Witness of History*, Tyndale Press, London, 1970.

- France, R.T. *The Evidence for Jesus*, Inter-Varsity, Downers Grove, 1976.

- Jesus Christ Questions and Answers, creation.com/jesuschrist.

- Marshall, I. Howard, *I Believe in the Historical Jesus*, Eerdmans, Grand Rapids, 1977.

- Mitton, C. Leslie, *Jesus: The Fact Behind the Faith*, Eerdmans, Grand Rapids, 1977.

- Morison, Frank, *Who Moved the Stone*, Faber & Faber, London, 1958.

- Moule, C.F.D., *The Birth of the New Testament*, Harper & Row, San Francisco, 1981.

- Strobel, Lee, *The Case for Christ: A Journalist's Personal Investigation of the Evidence for Jesus*, Zondervan, Grand Rapids, MI, 1998.

- Wright, Tom, *Jesus and the Victory of God*, SPCK, 1993.

There is a book worth all other books in the world.
— PATRICK HENRY

A man has deprived himself of the best there is in the world who has deprived himself of a knowledge of the Bible.
— WOODROW WILSON

The existence of the Bible, as a book for the people, is the greatest benefit which the human race has ever experienced. Every attempt to belittle it is a crime against humanity.
— IMMANUEL KANT[330]

I know that some of the pleasantest recollections of my childhood are connected with the voluntary study of an ancient Bible belonging to my grandmother. ... I prize them as an evidence that a child of five or six years old, left to his own devices, may be deeply interested in the Bible and draw sound moral nourishment from it.
— T.H. HUXLEY[330]

330. Agnostics Kant and Huxley are cited as *hostile witnesses*.

5

....

IS THE BIBLE THE WORD OF GOD?

Is the Bible really the Word of God? Can we be sure that God has spoken through the Bible? How do we know that the Bible is really true? What makes the Bible more authoritative than the Koran and Bhagavad Gita? And how do we go about demonstrating its authenticity? These are pressing questions of concern to every thinking person. Here is a challenge which every Christian will face, and a challenge which cannot be ignored. It demands an answer.

In the age of science and technology, modern man cannot escape facing ultimate questions regarding existence, truth, authority, meaning and destiny. Remarkably, the Bible astonishes the modern mind as no other book. No other book has influenced man and history as has the Bible; its influence is reflected in the works of the artists, poets, statesmen, musicians, sculptors and scientists. From Shakespeare to Browning and Longfellow, the Bible shines through. No other ancient book has been copied and recopied over such a long period of time as this book. No other book has gone through such processes and yet has come through as remarkably accurate as the Bible.

The Bible is unlike any other book in the world. Its history is striking, its message is impeccable, its influence is incomparable, its unity is amazing and its accuracy is remarkable. How do we explain its uniqueness? Is it a collusion or just a coincidence? It is far too complex to accept those options! Speaking about the Bible, Jean-Jacques Rousseau, a French philosopher, declares, "I must confess to you that the majesty of the scriptures astonishes me; ... if it had been the invention of man, the invention would have been greater than the greatest heroes."[331] Consider the following:

---

331. Dehoff, G.W., *Why We Believe the Bible*, Dehoff Publications, Murfreesboro, TN, p. 14, 1974.

- The world's first printed book was a Bible: Gutenberg's Vulgate.

- The most expensive book in the world is a Bible: Gutenberg's Latin Vulgate.

- One of the most expensive manuscripts in the world is the Codex Sinaiticus, a 4th century Greek manuscript of the Bible.

- The longest telegram in history is the Revised Version of the New Testament sent from New York to Chicago.

- The largest first edition of any book in history was a Bible: the R.S.V., 1,000,000 copies.

- The Bible was written over a period of 1,500 years by more than forty different authors from different walks of life, and over forty generations: Moses, a political leader; Joshua, a general; Amos, a herdsman; David and Solomon, kings; Luke, a physician; Matthew, a tax collector; Peter and John, fishermen; Paul, a scholar.

- It was written on three continents: Asia, Africa and Europe. It was written in three languages: Hebrew, Aramaic and Greek. It was written in different places: Moses in the wilderness; Daniel in a palace; Jeremiah in a dungeon; Paul in a Roman prison; Luke while travelling. It was written at different times: David wrote in times of war; Solomon in times of peace. It was written in different moods: some passages were written from the heights of joy and others in the depths of sorrow.

The Holy Bible is an amazing book. When we consider its uniqueness, it is indeed a book of wonder; there is no other book which can come near it. Theologian and apologist Dr Bernard Ramm (1916–1992) pertinently observes that:

"A thousand times over, the death knell of the Bible has been sounded, the funeral procession formed, the inscription cut on the tombstone, and the committal read. But somehow the corpse never stays put.

...it has possibilities

No other book has been so chopped, knifed, sifted, scrutinized, and vilified. What book on philosophy or religion or psychology or belles lettres of classical or modern times has been subject to such a mass attack as the Bible? With such venom and skepticism? With such thoroughness and erudition? Upon every chapter, line and tenet?

The Bible is still loved by millions, read by millions, and studied by millions ... It still remains the most published and most read book in the world of literature."[332]

The Bible touches on a variety of controversial topics, such as the problem of man, the destiny of the universe, the nature of happiness, the way of redemption, the hope of the world, courtship and married love, etc. In spite of its diversity, there is one story, one theme, one solution and one plan of redemption for mankind. Apologist and author Don Stewart, after examining the uniqueness of the Bible, remarks:

"How can this be explained? By the fact that there is only one author behind all of the books of the Bible: God Himself. The unity of the Bible is only one unique feature that separates it from all other books ever written."[333]

Werner Keller, a former skeptic, had a hard time believing the Bible to be God's Word, but finally he came to believe it. In his best-selling book, *The Bible as History*, he concludes:

"In view of the overwhelming mass of authentic and well-attested evidence now available, as I thought of the sceptical criticism which from the eighteenth century onward would fain have demolished the Bible altogether, there kept hammering in my brain this one sentence: 'The Bible is right after all.'"[334]

The case for the Bible does not merely depend on its uniqueness but on five solid grounds which establish beyond reasonable doubt that the Bible is the Word of God.

I. REASON DEMANDS IT

It is reasonable to believe that the Bible is a divine revelation. Reason can lead the open-

332. Ramm, B., *Protestant Christian Evidences*, Moody, pp. 232–233, Chicago, 1953.
333. Stewart, D., *You Be The Judge*, Here's Life Publishers, San Bernardino, CA, p. 83, 1983.
334. Keller, W., *The Bible as History*, translated by Neil, W., William Morrow, New York, p. 45, 1956.

minded skeptic to the conclusion that the Bible is from God. As we approach the Bible we are logically limited to two alternatives. Either the Bible is a worthless fraud or the Bible is in truth the Word of God. It is either the words of man or a revelation from God. There is no other alternative. Every person has a basis of authority which becomes a ground for operations of his or her thinking and living. In some cases the basis of authority is highly complex, for it is made up of several things; and too often people are ignorant of the fact that they have such a thing as a basis of authority. But everyone, without exception, has one.

Through the centuries, man's greatest quest has always been to know, "Why am I here?" "Where did I come from?" and "Where am I going?" Only an infinite God can answer our greatest questions. Modern man is desperately struggling in darkness for the answers to the questions of life. Without divine revelation man's search for truth is a hopeless quest. Without a message from God, man's life is a fathomless riddle, man's existence a dark mystery and death a wicked joke. In his book, *Modern Man In Search of a Soul*, psychoanalyst Carl Jung (1875–1961) correctly points out, "Human thought cannot conceive any system of final truth that can give a patient what he needs in order to live."[335] Without a divine revelation one can never understand the lessons of the past, the meaning of the present, and the direction for the future. Logically speaking, if the Bible is not from God, we cannot rely on its content nor derive hope and comfort from its promise.

Man needs a divine revelation but only God can provide such a revelation. Nature is inadequate to act as a guide for the existence of man. It takes an infinite being to provide infinite truth. We need absolute truth to be absolutely sure, but man is finite and limited hence he cannot act as an authority on, nor possibly ascertain (through autonomous human reasoning alone) any notion of ultimate truth. If there is no absolute truth or ultimate authority to appeal to, we have no obligation to do anything!

Only God is in a position to speak with absolute knowledge to the needs of man. R.C. Sproul wisely asserts, "Only God can provide us with an eternal perspective and speak to us with absolute and final authority."[336] This sentiment is eloquently argued by no less an authority than Ludwig Wittgenstein, perhaps the most respected philosopher of the twentieth

335. Jung, C., *Modern Man In Search of a Soul*, translated by Dell and Bayress, Harcourt Brace, New York, p. 264, 1933.
336. Sproul, R.C., *Knowing Scripture*, InterVarsity, Downers Grove, p. 23, 1978.

century, in his remarkable work *Tractatus Logico-Philosophicus*, "If there is any value that does have value, it must lie outside the whole sphere of what happens and is the case. For all that happens and is the case is accidental." He further adds, "It is clear that ethics cannot be put into words. Ethics is transcendental."[337] This apt statement evokes the following comment from John W. Montgomery:

> *"The plain consequence is that the only possible answer to modern man's quest for the ultimate meaning of history and for an absolute ethical standard would have to lie in a revelation from outside the world. If such a revelation does not exist, man will of logical (not merely practical) necessity remain forever bound to his cultural relativities, forever ignorant of life's meaning. But if such a revelation should exist, it would explode the world—turn it, as men said the early Christians did, upside down (Acts 17:6)."[338]*

Where can we turn to solve the question of truth, the meaning of life and the problem of man? With all his wisdom man has never been able to provide an absolute answer to the question of his existence nor offer a meaning to his life, nor chart a course through the fog of unhappiness, uncertainties and untold misery of human existence. As Sproul so aptly states:

> *"The world's best geographer cannot show us the way to God, and the world's best psychiatrist cannot give us a final answer to the problem of our guilt. There are matters contained in Holy Writ that 'unveil' for us that which is not exposed to the natural course of human investigation."[339]*

From a logical point of view, if man is to know the truth of God, it is essential that God reveal His truth to man. Since only God has absolute truth and all things are possible with God, it is logically conceivable that God could communicate His truth to man. If God exists, He can speak to man; since man needs God's truth, it would be reasonable for God to provide man with His truth. God has met man's need in every other dimension of existence; what would prevent God from meeting our ultimate need? There is nothing in reason which denies the possibility for a divine revelation.

337. Wittgenstein, L., *Tractatus Logico-Philosophicus*, translated by Pears, D.F. and McGuinness, B.F., Routledge & Kegan Paul, London, pp. 145, 147, 1969.
338. Montgomery, J.W., *The Suicide of Christian Theology*, Bethany Fellowship, Minneapolis, MN, p. 366, 1975.
339. Sproul, ref. 336, p. 24.

Since man cannot know God's will without God's revelation, it is necessary that God reveals His revelation to man. God, being infinite in power, is able to communicate with man, and, since revelation is both possible and necessary, it is therefore reasonable that God should give man a revelation. There is nothing in reason which denies the possibility for such a revelation.

II. HISTORY VERIFIES IT

If the Bible is really the Word of God we would expect to find it historically reliable. Unlike all other religious writings of world religions, the Bible is historically verifiable. Historian after historian has accepted the trustworthiness of the Scriptures. The reliability of biblical documents are well argued in such standard texts as James Martin's *The Reliability of the Gospel*, F.F. Bruce's *The New Testament Documents: Are They Reliable?* and *The Defense of the Gospel in the New Testament*. The late Dr Clark Pinnock, Professor of Interpretation at McMasters University in Canada, rightly observes:

> *"There exists no document from the ancient world witnessed by so excellent a set of textual and historical testimonies, and offering so superb an array of historical data on which an intelligent decision may be made. An honest man cannot dismiss a source of this kind. Skepticism regarding the historical credentials of Christianity is based upon an irrational bias."[340]*

The wonder of the Bible does not simply stand on its ethical teachings but its historical facts. The Bible contains many facts of history. In Luke, chapter three, verse one, we have fifteen historical references all in one verse:

> *"In the fifteenth year (one) of the reign of Tiberius Caesar (two) when Pontius Pilate (three) was governor (four) of Judea (five), Herod (six) tetrarch (seven) of Galilee (eight), his brother Philip (nine) tetrarch (ten) of Iturea (eleven) and Trachonitis, (twelve) and Lysanias (thirteen) tetrarch (fourteen) of Abilene (fifteen)."*

Any classical historian could check out the historical accuracy of the above references. This implies that the Bible is historically verifiable. Historian Will Durant, in his momentous work *The Story of Civilization*, makes comments on the gospel writers that should be noted:

> *"They record many incidents that mere inventors would have concealed—the competition of the apostles for high places in the Kingdom, their flight after Jesus' arrest, Peter's denial, the failure of Christ to work miracles in Galilee, the references of some auditors to his possible insanity, ... no one reading these scenes can doubt the reality of the figure behind them."[341]*

340. Pinnock, C., *Set Forth Your Case*, Moody, Chicago, p. 85, 1971.
341. Durant, W., "Caesar and Christ" *The Story of Civilization*, Volume **III**, Simon & Schuster, New York, p. 557, 1944.

H.G. Wells, the famous agnostic[342] historian and science fiction writer, acknowledged the gospels as historical documents in his popular work, *The Outline of History*:

"Almost our only sources of information about the personality of Jesus are derived from the four gospels, all of which were certainly in existence a few decades after his death. … Here was a man. This part of the tale could not have been invented."[343]

The Bible is historically reliable; it provides facts for our faith. Modern man need not speculate aimlessly on the nature of Christ's existence. The Bible offers modern man some hard facts about life. "Christianity", writes evangelist Richard Riss, "claims to be based upon something more than mere speculation, and if its claims are true, the implications are overwhelming."[344]

The historical reality of the Bible is one of a kind. No other religious book can match its reliability or authenticity. G.B. Hardy makes this point with great eloquence in his delightful book, *Countdown*:

"When you consider the great writings of the Egyptians, the Babylonians, the Greeks and the Romans, how they are saturated with mythology, superstition, and fantasy … replete with scientific blunders, surely it is impossible the Bible could escape without error. Still it stands without a single proven error after thirty-four centuries of scholarship."[345]

If the Bible is God's Word, it must not contradict God's world.[346] If God spoke through the Bible one would expect it to speak accurately about the facts and events in history.

Josephus, the Jewish historian and contemporary of Christ, provided powerful evidence for the reliability of the New Testament. His work, *Antiquities*, offers abundant references, facts, figures and characters found in the New Testament. Dr F.F. Bruce, who was Rylands Professor of Biblical Criticism and Exegesis in the University of Manchester, summed up the historical evidence:

"Here, in the pages of Josephus, we meet many figures who are well known to us from the New Testament: the colourful family of the Herods; the Roman emperors Augustus, Tiberius, Claudius, and Nero; Quirinius, the governor of Syria; Pilate, Felix, and Festus, the procurators of Judea; the

342. He was also an ardent Darwinian and eugenicist, so he is cited as a hostile witness—see Jerry Bergman, H.G. Wells: Darwin's disciple and eugenicist extraordinaire, *J. Creation* **18**(3):116–120, 2004; creation.com/wells.
343. H.G. Wells, *The Outline of History*, Volume **I**, Doubleday, New York, p. 420, 1971.
344. Riss, R., *The Evidence for the Resurrection of Jesus Christ*, Bethany Fellowship, Minneapolis, MN, p. 103, 1977.
345. Hardy, G.B., *Countdown: A Time to Choose*, Moody, Chicago, p. 34, 1972.
346. For refutation of many skeptical claims, see "Bible 'contradictions' and 'errors'", creation.com/skeptics-bible-errors.

high-priestly families—Annas, Caiaphas, Ananias, and the rest; the Pharisees and Sadducees; and so on."[347]

III. THE MANUSCRIPTS SUPPORT IT

Authentic record

How do we know what the Bible said in the beginning? How can we know that the text we have is what was originally written, i.e. is *authentic*? Many skeptics doubt that we even have the original New Testament.

This issue can only be settled by using standard bibliographical tests for reliability, similar to what would be used to judge the *Iliad* or Caesar's writings.

In fact, the manuscript evidence is overwhelming, both in the time gap between them and the original, and the number. For example, the earliest known New Testament manuscript is the John Rylands papyrus fragment of John's Gospel known as $\mathfrak{P}^{52}$, containing John 18:31–33, 37–38, dated to c. AD 125. Compare this to other great works in this table:

THE ANCIENT MANUSCRIPTS				
Author	Original	Earliest Copy	Timespan	Copies
Plato	400 BC	AD 900	1,200 yrs	7
Caesar	100 BC	AD 900	1,000 yrs	10
Aristotle	300 BC	AD 1,100	1,400 yrs	5
Tacitus	AD 100	AD 1,100	1,000 yrs	20
Herodotus	400 BC	AD 900	1,300 yrs	8
Thucydides	AD 400	AD 900	1,300 yrs	8
Livy	AD 30	AD 900	900 yrs	20
New Testament	AD 100	AD 200	100 yrs	5,300

Thus Sir Frederic Kenyon (1863–1952), principal librarian and Director of the British Museum for 21 years, put this into perspective:

> *"This may sound a considerable interval, but it is nothing to that which parts most of the great classical authors from their earliest manuscripts. We believe that we have in all essentials an accurate text of the seven extant plays of Sophocles; yet the earliest substantial manuscript upon which it is based was written more than 1,400 years after the poet's death."[348]*

Almost 40 years later, Kenyon wrote:

347. Bruce, F.F., *The New Testament Documents: Are they Reliable?* Inter-Varsity, London, p. 104, 1968.
348. Kenyon, F.G., *Handbook to the Textual Criticism of the New Testament*, MacMillan and Co., London, p. 4, 1901.

"The interval then between the dates of original composition and the earliest extant evidence becomes so small as to be in fact negligible, and the last foundation for any doubt that the Scriptures have come down to us substantially as they were written has now been removed. Both the authenticity and the general integrity of the books of the New Testament may be regarded as finally established."[349]

Kenyon summed up the evidence:

"The Christian can take the whole Bible in his hand and say without fear or hesitation that he holds in it the true Word of God, handed down without essential loss from generation to generation throughout the centuries."[350]

So, by applying the tightest standards scholars can muster (without eliminating all the other classical works), we can conclude that the NT we have is a trustworthy copy of the original. NT scholar F.F. Bruce wrote:

"The evidence for our New Testament writings is ever so much greater than the evidence for many writings of classical authors, the authenticity of which no-one dreams of questioning. And if the New Testament were a collection of secular writings, their authenticity would generally be regarded as beyond all doubt. It is a curious fact that historians have often been much readier to trust the New Testament records than have many theologians. Somehow or other, there are people who regard a 'sacred book' as ipso facto *under suspicion, and demand much more corroborative evidence for such a work than they would for an ordinary secular or pagan writing. From the viewpoint of the historian, the same standards must be applied to both. But we do not quarrel with those who want more evidence for the New Testament than for other writings; firstly, because the universal claims which the New Testament makes upon mankind are so absolute, and the character and works of its chief Figure so unparalleled, that we want to be as sure of its truth as we possibly can."[351]*

In the light of the overwhelming evidence we fully concur with Francis Piper that "what the church lacks in our day is not a reliable text of the Bible, but the faith in the sufficiently reliable text."[352]

Accurate originals

The above shows that we have an *authentic* text, i.e. one that faithfully represents the original. But was the original *accurate*?

Skeptics have long argued that the Gospels were written long after the events they recorded. However, there are cogent arguments by J.A.T. Robinson, who was a liberal and Bishop of

349. Kenyon, F.G., *The Bible and Archaeology*, Harper & Row, NY, p. 288, 1940.
350. Kenyon, F.G., *Our Bible and the Ancient Manuscripts*, Harper, New York, p. 55, 1958.
351. Bruce, ref. 347, p. 15.
352. McGuiggan, J., *If God Came*, Montex Pub., Lubbock, TX, p. 204, 1980.

Woolwich, for redating the Gospels between AD 40 and 65,[353] except probably John that was closer to AD 85.[354]

John Wenham, scholar of New Testament Greek, points out that this was the teaching of the early Church, which was closer to the events than any modern skeptic:

> "The [Church] fathers are almost unanimous in asserting that Matthew the tax-collector was the author, writing first, for Hebrews in the Hebrew language: Papias (c. 60–130), Irenaeus (c. 130–200), Pantaenus (died c. 190), Origen (c. 185–254), Eusebius (c. 260–340), Epiphanius of Salamis (c. 315–403), Cyril of Jerusalem (c. 315–86) and others write in this vein. The Medieval Hebrew gospel of Matthew in Even Bohan could be a corrupted version of the original. Though unrivaled, the tradition has been discounted on various grounds, particularly on the alleged unreliability of Papias, from whom some would derive the whole tradition."[355]

This suggests that the Gospels were written in the lifetimes of people who knew Jesus personally (~6 BC – ~ AD 30 for His earthly lifetime).

Matthew and Luke record Jesus' prophecy of Jerusalem's demise (Matthew 24:2, Luke 21:20–24) but do not record its fulfilment in AD 70. Matthew, especially, would not have failed to record yet another fulfilled prophecy if he had written after the event. Acts, written after Luke, mentions neither the fall of Jerusalem, and the horrific Neronian persecutions (mid 60s) although other persecutions are mentioned, nor the martyrdoms of James (61), Paul (64) and Peter (65), so was probably written before then.

Here is an analogy: imagine you find a tourist guidebook of New York City. Then you see that it describes the Twin Towers as a notable landmark and worthy tourist attraction. What would you conclude about the date of this guidebook? Presumably, that it was written before the terrorists destroyed the towers on 11 September 2001. This is the same logic that would be applied to the Gospel dating.[356]

And not only were the Gospels written within the lifetimes of those who knew Christ, they were written in a culture that fostered an accurate memory. The Swedish scholar Birger Gerhardsson has shown that the canonical Gospels drew on a collective communal memory made strong by the oral teaching methods of the time. These techniques would have enabled "very accurate communication between Jesus and his followers" and would have ensured "excellent semantic recall".[357]

---

353. Robinson, J.A.T., *Redating the New Testament*, SCM, London, 1976.

354. For a summary of the evidence, see Grigg, R., Date of John's Gospel, creation.com/john-gospel-date, 2010.

355. Wenham, J.W., *Redating Matthew, Mark and Luke: A Fresh Assault on the Synoptic Problem*, IVP, 1992.

356. NB: This is *not* an 'argument from silence'. (That form of argument would be an example of the *fallacy of denying the antecedent*.) Instead, we are using arguments from *conspicuous absence*, which is a form of valid argument known as the *destructive hypothetical syllogism* or *denying the consequent*. See Clark, G.H., *Logic*, The Trinity Foundation, Jefferson, Maryland, 1985, 2nd edition 1988; Sarfati, J., Loving God with all your mind: logic and creation, *J. Creation* **12**(2):142–151 1998; creation.com/logic.

357. Gerhardsson, B., *Memory and Manuscript*, translated by Sharp, E., Villadsen og Christensen, Copenhagen, 1964.

This close time gap and excellent cultural memory make it incredible that the Gospels would be legendary. Julius Müller (1801–1878) challenged 19th-century skeptics to show anywhere in history where within 30 years, legends had accumulated around a historical person and become firmly fixed.[358] A.N. Sherwin-White (1911–1993), the eminent classical historian from Oxford University, conducted a careful study of Greek and Roman history to determine the rate at which legend accumulates. The evidence revealed that not even two full generations would be enough for legendary development to wipe out the historical core of a historical story, as he says:

> *"The agnostic type of form-criticism would be much more credible if the compilation of the Gospels were much later in time … Herodotus enables us to test the tempo of myth-making, [showing that] even two generations are too short a span to allow the mythical tendency to prevail over the hard historic core."[359]*

The brilliant New Testament Princeton scholar, J. Gresham Machen (1881–1937), concludes:

> *"We know that the gospel story is true partly because of the early date of the documents in which it appears, the evidence as to their authorship, the internal evidence of their truth, the impossibility of explaining them as being based upon deception or upon myth."[360]*

How about the Old Testament? The accidental discovery of the Dead Sea Scrolls at Khirbet Qumran in 1947 was a bombshell. These papyrus documents come from the Jewish sect of the Essenes, and date to 150–70 BC. Among other things, they included manuscripts of the Hebrew Old Testament.

Such an amazing find provided an opportunity to test the accuracy of copying over the centuries. That's because the DSS are about 1,000 years older than the earliest Masoretic manuscripts of the Old Testament (these were compiled by specialist copiers called Masoretes, and the basis for modern Hebrew Bibles). But upon comparison, they were found to be word-for-word identical for 95% of the text. This is amazing testimony to the accuracy of copying over a whole millennium.

Consider that wonderful chapter 53 of Isaiah, the prophecy of Jesus' atoning death and resurrection. Of the 166 words, only 17 letters are different. Ten are spelling variants, and four more are stylistic changes. The remaining three letters spell the word 'light' in Isaiah 53:11, and may make more sense that way, although it doesn't greatly affect the meaning of the passage. So overall, the DSS increase our already high respect for the Masoretic Text.[361]

358. Müller, J., *The Theory of Myths, in Its Application to the Gospel History Examined and Confuted*, John Chapman, London, p. 26, 1844.
359. Sherwin-White, A.N., *Roman Society and Roman Law in the New Testament*, Clarendon Press, Oxford, pp. 189–190, 1963.
360. Machen, J.G., *Christianity and Liberalism*, Eerdmans, Grand Rapids, p. 72.
361. Sarfati, J., Who wrote Isaiah? creation.com/isaiah-author-date, 8 November 2011.

IV. ARCHAEOLOGY SUPPORTS IT

The accuracy of the Bible is abundantly confirmed by the science of archaeology. Australian church historian Dr James H. Jauncey states that "Archaeology is the science which investigates the ruins of ancient civilizations with a view to reconstructing their history and finding out the truth with regard to their customs and ways of living."[362]

The significance of archaeology to the Bible is twofold: Firstly, it provides objective evidence for the accuracy of biblical accounts. Secondly, it offers greater insight and factual information to biblical narrative. The Bible makes innumerable references to historical events and characters. These references include dates, customs, people, behaviour, places and cities. Archaeological research done in Bible lands has amazingly confirmed the reliability and historicity of the Scriptures in so many areas. Every part of the Bible that could be checked by archaeology now provides the most positive proofs for the accuracy of the Bible. Archaeologist Dr Joseph Free, in his book *Archaeology and Bible History*, writes, "Archaeology has confirmed countless passages which have been rejected by critics as unhistorical or contradictory to known facts."[363] We concur with the judgement of Jack Cottrell, professor of theology at Cincinnati Christian University, who contends:

> *"Through the wealth of data uncovered by historical and archaeological research, we are able to measure the Bible's historical accuracy. In every case where its claims can be thus tested, the Bible proves to be accurate and reliable."[364]*

During the nineteenth century, when liberal theology was at its height, the Bible was commonly treated as a book of legends, myths and fiction. Many of its characters and events were rejected as unhistorical. Many liberal critics argued that the Hittite race never existed and Abraham was just a mythological figure. The critics strongly charged that Moses could not have written the first books of the Bible since writing was not invented then. The gospel of John was supposed to have been written by a second-century individual who had no contact with the event reported. The unbelieving critics insisted that the book of Acts was a legendary account with no historical basis and not written by Luke but by an unknown author living in the second century.

Today, archaeology has refuted the skepticism of the critics and confirmed the reliability of biblical history. No eminent scholar would share the liberal view of the nineteenth-century critics. The liberal, critical view has no historical basis and cannot be maintained intellectually on the basis of archaeology. It has

362. Jauncey, J.H., *Science Returns to God*, Zondervan, Grand Rapids, p. 77, 1971.
363. Free, J., *Archaeology and Bible History*, Scripture Press, Wheaton, IL, p. 1, 1969.
364. Cottrell, J., *The Authority of the Bible*, Baker, Grand Rapids, pp. 48–49, 1979.

been wisely said that every time the spade goes into the ground, a liberal theory is buried. The world-renowned archaeologist and palaeographer Dr William F. Albright, of Harvard University, rightly points out:

> *"The excessive skepticism shown toward the Bible by important historical schools of the eighteenth and nineteenth centuries, certain phases of which still appear periodically, has been progressively discredited."*[365]

Jauncey fully agrees with the above conviction when he declares, "In almost every area where the Bible was criticized on subjective or theorizing grounds, it has already been vindicated on this objective basis."[366] Using the Bible as a guide, the renowned Jewish archaeologist Nelson Glueck has discovered over a thousand ancient sites in Trans-Jordan and 500 more in the Negev. In writing a review on Werner Keller's best-selling book, *The Bible as History* (1955), in *The New York Times*, Professor Glueck states:

> *"The reviewer has spent many years in biblical archaeology, and, in company with his colleagues, has made discoveries confirming in outline or in detail historical statements in the Bible. He is prepared to go further and say that no archaeological discovery has ever been made that contradicts or controverts historical statements in Scripture."*[367]

Archaeology has confirmed the culture and customs of Abraham's day, and has brought to light the great Hittite empire previously unknown to historians. It has proven the accuracy of Luke's writings at every point where it is possible to verify. The classic works of A.T. Robertson, *Luke the Historian in the Light of Historical Research*, and of Sir William Mitchell Ramsay (1851–1939), *St. Paul the Traveller and the Roman Citizen*, record these findings. Ramsay, as a young professor, set out to uncover contradictions between the biblical records and actual archaeological findings. But after years of doing archaeological research in Asia Minor and Greece, Ramsay was forced to reverse his opinion. His research confirmed the reliability of the Bible and he became a firm believer in the authority of the Scriptures—so convincing was the evidence that he became a Christian. Ramsay describes his conviction:

> *"I take the view that Luke's history is unsurpassed in regard to his trustworthiness … You may press the words of Luke in a degree beyond any other historian's and they stand the keenest scrutiny and the hardest treatment."*[368]

Norman L. Geisler writes, "It has been largely due to the archaeological efforts of the late great Sir William Ramsay that the critical views of New Testament history have been overthrown and its historicity established."[369] Millar Burrows of Yale University, writing on archaeology, points out:

365. Albright, W.F., *The Archaeology of Palestine and the Bible*, Revell, New York, p. 127, 1935.
366. Jauncey, ref. 362, p. 79.
367. Glueck, N., "Book Review", *The New York Times*, 28 October 1956. Keller's book sold about ten million copies.
368. Ramsay, W.M., *Luke, The Physician*, Hodder & Stoughton, London, pp. 177–179, 1908.
369. Geisler, N.L., *Christian Apologetics*, Baker, Grand Rapids, p. 326, 1976.

"On the whole, however, archaeological work has unquestionably strengthened confidence in the reliability of the Scriptural record. More than one archaeologist has found his respect for the Bible increased by the experience of excavation in Palestine."[370]

Donald J. Wiseman, the director of the British Museum and a specialist in the field of archaeology, informs us that:

"The geography of Bible lands and visible remains of antiquity were gradually recorded until today more than 25,000 sites within this region and dating to Old Testament times, in their broadest sense, have been located."[371]

It is amazing how an ancient book can receive such overwhelming support from the science of archaeology. The logic of Dr Jauncey cannot be faulted, "If the Bible has been shown to be truthful in these obscure details, it is very unlikely that any part of it is the work of a forger."[372]

If all the lines of evidence demonstrate the reliability of the Bible, then the Bible's own claims to being God's inspired Word should be taken seriously.

V. PROPHECY PROVES IT

One of the most powerful evidences for the divine origin of the Bible is the remarkable number of fulfilled prophecies found in it. The Bible contains numerous predictions of events which were actually fulfilled. The successful fulfilments of these prophecies are valid proof of divine direction and supernatural assistance. God alone knows the future and He is the only being who has the ability to predict future events with 100% accuracy. Bernard Ramm adds:

"Prophecy is thus by its nature a manifestation of the supernatural light of God. The reason for this is derived from an inspection of the powers of the human mind. We can probe into the past by the means of the science of historiography. We can probe into space by virtue of the telescope and the ancillary sciences developed around astronomy ... but there is no knowledge of the future that compares in certainty and accuracy with our knowledge of past time and outer space."[373]

370. Burrows, M., *What Mean These Stones?* American Schools of Oriental Research, New Haven, CN, p. 1, 1941.
371. Wiseman, D.J., "Archaeological Confirmation of the Old Testament," in Henry, C.F.H. (Ed.), *Revelation and the Bible*, Baker, Grand Rapids, pp. 301–302, 1958.
372. Jauncey, ref. 362, p. 85.
373. Ramm, ref. 332, p. 82–83.

The Bible itself makes the fulfilment of prophecy a test for its own validity, and thus the reputation of the Bible stands on prophecy. It has been estimated that prophecy constitutes thirty-four percent of the entire content of the Bible. God Himself agrees to let His statements stand or fall by the test of prophecy and He invites others to do the same:

> *"'Present your case,' the Lord says. 'Bring forward your strong* arguments,' The King *of Jacob says. Let them bring forth and declare to us what is going to take place; as for the former* events, declare what they were, That we may consider them, and know their outcome; Or announce to us what is coming. Declare the things that are going to come afterward, That we may know that you are gods" (Isaiah 41:21–23 NASB).*

> *"I am God, and there is none like me. I make known the end from the beginning, from ancient times, what is still to come" (Isaiah 46:9–10).*

"But there is a God in heaven who reveals mysteries. He has shown … what will happen" (Daniel 2:28). The Bible contains prophetic statements which only God could reveal. For example, Old Testament scholar Gleason Archer points out that Isaiah 6:13 is "a clear prediction of the total devastation and depopulation of Judah meted out by Nebuchadnezzar in 587 BC, over 150 years later!"[374] Some skeptics have claimed parts of the book of Isaiah had more than one author, and the prophecies were written around the time of the events they foretold. But this prediction undermines this, because it comes from an undisputably early part of the book. So Archer says, "Isaiah 6:13 therefore destroys the basic premise of the entire Deutero-Isaiah theory, which assumes that it would be impossible for an eighth-century Hebrew prophet to foretell or even foreknow the events of 587 and 539–537 BC (the Fall of Babylon and the return of the first settlers to Jerusalem)."[374]

And most importantly, the Bible gives us specific details about the coming of the Messiah.

- In Genesis 3:15 the Messiah is called the seed of the woman; the Messiah will be born into a human family, and with no human father.[375]

- In Genesis 12:1–3 the Messiah will be of the lineage of Abraham.

- In Genesis 49:9,10 the Messiah will come out of the tribe of Judah.

- In 1 Chronicles 1:24 the Messiah will be born of the lineage of Shem.

- In Isaiah 11:1,2,10 the Messiah will come out of the lineage of Jesse.

- In Isaiah 7:14 the Messiah will be born of a virgin.[375]

- In Isaiah 9:6,7[376] and 16:5 the Messiah will be the Son of David.

- In Micah 5:2 the Messiah will be born in Bethlehem.

374. Archer, G.L., *Encyclopedia of Bible Difficulties*, Zondervan, Grand Rapids, Michigan, pp. 263–264, 1982.
375. Sarfati, J., The Virginal Conception of Christ, *Apologia* **3**(2):4–11, 1994; creation.com/virgin.
376. Sarfati, J., Isaiah 9:6–7: The coming Child who would be called 'Mighty God'; messiah.com.es, creation.com/isaiah96, 2010.

- In Psalm 22:14–18 the Messiah will be crucified.

- In Psalm 16:9–11 the Messiah will be resurrected.

- In Daniel 9, the "seventy sevens": the Messiah will be "cut off" after 96 seven-year periods after Cyrus' decree to rebuild Jerusalem.

These were clearly fulfilled by Jesus of Nazareth, and *only* by Him. No counterfeit claimant could arise today, because the timeline of Daniel 9 (point 11) has long run out. Also, when the Romans destroyed Jerusalem in AD 70, all genealogical records were destroyed, except for the Levites (for the Priesthood). So no claimant after that could prove his descent from Judah, Jesse, or David (points 3, 5, 7).

After His Resurrection, Christ spoke to His disciples: "This is what I told you while I was still with you: Everything must be fulfilled that is written about me in the Law of Moses, the Prophets and the Psalms" (Luke 24:44).[377] We agree with G.B. Hardy:

> *"Only the supernatural mind can have prior knowledge to the natural mind. If then the Bible has foreknowledge, historical and scientific, beyond the permutation of chance ... it truly then bears the fingerprint of God."[378]*

VI. CHRIST CONFIRMED IT

One good reason why anyone should believe the Bible to be God's Word is because of the testimony of Jesus Christ. Arthur Rendle Short (1880–1953), professor of surgery at Bristol University, UK, correctly argues that, "The most serious reason for regarding the Bible as the Word of God is because of the respect in which it was held by Jesus Christ."[379] Kenneth Kantzer represents the opinions of many scholars when he wrote, "Christians hold the Bible to be the Word of God (and inerrant) because they are convinced that Jesus, the Lord of the church, believed it and taught His disciples to believe it."[380] On the same note, the British writer John W. Wenham, in his very popular work *Christ and the Bible*, rightly points out, "To Christ the Bible is true, authoritative, inspired, to him the God of the Bible is the living God, and the teaching of the Bible is the teaching of the living God. To Him what Scripture says, God says."[381] Jesus Christ accepted the Bible as the infallible Word of God. Clark Pinnock is right, "The Bible is not infallible because it says so—but because He says so. There is no more reliable witness to the nature of Scripture than the one who died and rose to be our Saviour."[382] Jesus believed that God has spoken in His written revelation therefore Scripture

377. See Fruchtenbaum, A., *Messianic Christology*, Ariel Ministries, 1998; Ankerberg, J., Weldon, J. and Kaiser, W., *The Case for Jesus the Messiah: Incredible Prophecies that Prove God Exists*, Harvest House, Eugene, OR, 1989.
378. Hardy, ref. 345, p. 35.
379. Rendle Short, A., *Why Believe*, Inter-Varsity Fellowship, London, p. 63, 1964.
380. Archer, G.L., *Encyclopedia of Bible Difficulties*, Zondervan, Grand Rapids, p. 7, 1982.
381. Wenham, J.W., *Christ and the Bible*, Baker, Grand Rapids, p. 188, 1984.
382. Pinnock, ref. 340, p. 100.

is God's Word (Matthew 5:18; 19:4; John 10:35; Acts 4:25; 28:25; Hebrews 10:15).

Theologian John H. Gerstner correctly observes:

> *"The evidence that Christ did regard the Old Testament Scriptures as inspired is so persuasive that it is seldom contested today even by those who themselves do not accept this inspiration but think that Jesus was mistaken, a victim of the 'errors' of his day.*[383]

Along the same line, the brilliant Old Testament scholar Edward J. Young affirms, "Not only did Jesus Christ look upon the Old Testament as forming an organic whole but also he believed that both as a unit and in its several parts it was finally and absolutely authoritative."[384]

For Christ, the Bible is the Word of God. In fact, He used the phrase, "The Word of God," when He referred to certain Old Testament passages. When dealing with the Pharisees, Jesus charged them with replacing the commandment of God with their own tradition hence they were guilty of "invalidating the Word of God" (Mark 7:13). When He was debating with them about His claim to deity He appealed to the Scriptures as final and fully authoritative and therefore "the Scripture cannot be broken" (John 10:35). Christ's frequent and continued appeal to the Scriptures indicates His high view of Scripture.

In fact, Jesus affirmed the reality (historicity) of the following people and events, *often the targets of severe skeptical and liberal mockery:*[385]

- God created Adam and Eve as the first man and woman, "from the beginning of creation", and this was the basis for marriage (Matthew 19:3–6, Mark 10:5–9).

- Abel (Luke 11:51).

- Noah and the Flood. (Matthew 24:37–39, Luke 17:26–27).

- Abraham (John 8:56–58).

- Sodom and Gomorrah (Matthew 10:15; 11:23–24, Luke 10:12).

- Lot (and wife!) (Luke 17:28–32).

- Abraham, Isaac and Jacob (Matthew 8:11, Luke 13:28).

- Manna from heaven (John 6:31, 49, 58).

- Moses and the bronze serpent (John 3:14).

383. Gerstner, J.H., *Reasons For Faith*, Baker, Grand Rapids, p. 87, 1967.
384. Young, E.J., "The Authority of the Old Testament" in Wooley, P. (Ed.), *The Infallible Word*, Presbyterian & Reformed, Nutley, NJ, pp. 58–59.
385. Livingston, D., *Jesus Christ on the infallibility of Scripture*, from "A Critique of Dewey Beegle's book titled: Inspiration of Scripture", M.A. Thesis, 2003; creation.com/jesus_bible.

- Jonah and the great sea creature (Matthew 12:39–41).

- Queen of Sheba (Matthew 12:42).

- Moses as inspired author of the Pentateuch (Luke 16:31, John 5:46–47).

- Daniel the Prophet as author of the book of Daniel (Matthew 24:15, citing Daniel 9:27).

In the same line, Professor F.F. Bruce, in his excellent work *The Books and the Parchments*, notes:

> *"In many points He condemned the Jewish tradition, but not with respect to the canonicity of Scriptures. His complaint, indeed, was that by other traditions they had invalidated in practice the Word of God recorded in canonical Scripture."*[386]

It is a fact of history that Christ accepted the Scriptures as God's Word. "But," the critics, argue, "why should anyone accept the authority of Jesus?" "If we could accept the words of Jesus, why not accept the authority of Mohammed or Buddha or even Karl Marx? What makes Jesus so special?" Or, "this is just circular reasoning: using the Bible to prove the Bible." This is an important challenge for which we have an excellent reply that breaks the circle.

Here are the answers:

It is not circular to use Matthew to prove Genesis (Matthew 19:3–6, cf. Genesis 1:27, 2:4), Paul to prove Luke (1 Timothy 5:18, cf. Luke 10:7) or Peter to prove Paul (2 Peter 3:15–16).

It is also not circular to use Jesus' clear statements to prove the Bible. His statements such as, "Scripture cannot be broken" (John 10:35) and the repeated, "It is written …" show that for Jesus, what Scripture said is what God said.[387] Indeed, He defended many of the doctrines that skeptics love to scoff at, as shown above. Even without accepting Scripture as the authority, many liberal theologians believe that there is overwhelming historical evidence that Christ affirmed biblical inerrancy, although they disagree with Him.[388]

At the early part of our discussion, we documented that the Scriptures are reliable materials; a fact accepted by leading historians. Their reliability is further supported by the findings of archaeology. Hence, one could logically affirm that the Scriptures are historically reliable. We could argue that the Scriptures, which are reliable, provide information about Jesus Christ, who claimed to be God and proved His claims by rising from the dead (cf. Acts 17:31). This *independent historical evidence breaks the circle*. That's because only God has the power of resurrection; Jesus had the power of resurrection, therefore Jesus is God. Whatever

386. Bruce, F.F., *The Books and the Parchments*, Pickering & Inglis, London, p. 102, 1950.
387. Sarfati, J., The Authority of Scripture, *Apologia* **3**(2):12–16, 1994; creation.com/authority.
388. Harold Lindsell cites the liberal scholars H.J. Cadbury, Adolph Harnack, Rudolf Bultmann and F.C. Grant to prove this point, *The Battle for the Bible*, Zondervan, Grand Rapids, MI, pp. 43–45, 1976.

God says is true. Jesus, who is God, says the Bible is God's Word, therefore the Bible is God's Word.

VII. THE BIBLE LED TO MODERN SCIENCE[389]

This might be a surprising line of evidence for many, because many anti-Christians claim that Christianity and science have been enemies for centuries. But the truth is diametrically opposed. Informed historians of science, including non-Christians, have pointed out that modern science first flourished under a Christian worldview while it was *stillborn* in other cultures such as ancient Greece, China and Arabia.[390]

This should be no surprise when we ask why science works at all. There are certain essential prerequisites that make science possible, and they simply did not exist in non-Christian cultures.[391]

1. There is such a thing as objective truth.

Jesus said, "I am the way, and the truth, and the life. No one comes to the Father except through me" (John 14:6). But postmodernism, for example, denies objective truth. One example is, "What's true for you is not true for me." So maybe they should try jumping off a cliff to see if the Law of Gravity is true for them. Another postmodern claim is, "there is no truth"—so is *that* statement true?; or "we can't know truth"—so how do they *know* that? (For more, see ch. 7 on the Eastern Mind).

2. The universe is *real*, because God created the heavens and the earth (Genesis 1).

This sounds obvious, but many eastern philosophies believe that everything is an illusion (so is *that* belief an illusion as well?). There is no point in trying to investigate an illusion by experimenting on it.

3. The universe is *orderly*, because God is a God of order not of confusion—1 Corinthians 14:33.

But if there is no creator, or if Zeus and his gang were in charge, why should there

---

389. Largely based on Sarfati, J., (1) Why does science work at all? *Creation* **31**(3):12–14, 2009; creation.com/whyscience, and (2) The biblical roots of modern science, *Creation* **32**(4), 2010; creation.com/roots.

390. Stark, R., *For the Glory of God: How monotheism led to reformations, science, witch-hunts and the end of slavery,* Princeton University Press, 2003; see also review by Williams, A., The biblical origins of science, *J. Creation* **18**(2):49–52, 2004; creation.com/stark.

391. I acknowledge Sean Wieland's input into such a list.

be any order at all? If some Eastern religions were right that the universe is a great Thought, then it could change its mind at any moment.

It is impossible to prove from nature that it is orderly, because the proofs would have to presuppose this very order to try to prove it. Also, in this *fallen* world with natural disasters and thunderstorms and general chaos, it is not so obvious that it was made by an orderly Creator. This is a major message of the book of Ecclesiastes—if we try to live our lives only according to what is under the sun, the result is futility. Hence our chief end is to "Fear God and keep his commandments" (Ecclesiastes 12:13).

A fundamental facet of science is deriving laws that provide for predictable outcomes. This is only possible because the universe is orderly.

4. Since God is sovereign, He was free to create as He pleased.

So the only way to find out how His creation works is to *investigate* and *experiment*, not rely on man-made philosophies as did the ancient Greeks.

This is illustrated with Galileo Galilei (1564–1642). He showed by experiment that different weights fall at the same speed (apart from air resistance), which refuted the Greek philosophy that heavy objects fall faster. He also showed by *observation* that the sun had spots, refuting the Greek idea that the heavenly bodies are perfect.[392]

Another example is Johannes Kepler (1571–1630), who discovered that planets moved in ellipses around the sun. This refuted the Greek philosophies that insisted on circles because they are the most 'perfect' shapes, which then needed the addition of an increasingly cumbersome system of circles upon circles called *epicycles* to try to accommodate the observations.

But when it comes to *origins* as opposed to understanding how things *work*,[393] God has revealed that He created about 6,000 years ago over six normal-length days, and judged the earth with a globe-covering flood about 4,500 years ago. It's thus no accident that Johannes Kepler calculated a creation date of 3992 BC, and Isaac Newton (1643–1727), probably the greatest scientist of all time, also strongly defended biblical chronology.

5. Man *can and should investigate* the world, because God gave us *dominion* over His creation (Genesis 1:28); creation is not divine.

So we don't need to sacrifice to the forest god to cut down a tree, or appease the water spirits to measure the boiling point of water. On the contrary, many other founders of modern science saw their scientific research as bringing glory to God.

6. Man can *initiate* thoughts and actions; they are not fully determined by deterministic laws of brain chemistry.

This is a deduction from the biblical teaching that man has both a material and

---

392. A common skeptical charge against Christianity is the alleged 'church vs Galileo' affair. In reality, Galileo was first challenged by the Aristotelian science establishment before the Church. It was really science vs science and papal personality politics. See Sarfati, J., Galileo Quadricentennial: Myth vs fact, *Creation* **31**(3): 49–51, 2009; creation.com/galileo-quadricentennial.

393. See Sarfati, J., Naturalism, Origins and Operational Science, creation.com/naturalism, 2000.

immaterial aspect (e.g. Genesis 35:18, 1 Kings 17:21–22, Matthew 10:28). This immaterial aspect of man means that he is more than matter, so his thoughts are likewise not bound by the material makeup of his brain.

But if materialism were true, then 'thought' is just an epiphenomenon of the brain, and the results of the laws of chemistry. Thus, *given their own presuppositions*, materialists have not freely arrived at their conclusion that materialism is true, because their conclusion was *predetermined by brain chemistry*. But then, why should their brain chemistry be trusted over mine, since both obey the same infallible laws of chemistry? So in reality, if materialists were right, then they can't even help what they believe (including their belief in materialism!). Yet they often call themselves 'freethinkers', overlooking the glaring irony. Genuine initiation of thought is an insuperable problem for materialism, as is consciousness itself.[394]

7. Man can think rationally and logically, and logic itself is objective.

This is a deduction from the fact that he was created in God's image (Genesis 1:26–27), and from the fact that Jesus, the Second Person of the Trinity (see ch. 4 as well as ch. 8 p. 187), is the *logos* (John 1:1–3). This ability to think logically has been impaired *but not eliminated* by the Fall of man into sinful rebellion against his Creator. (The Fall means that sometimes the reasoning is flawed, and sometimes the reasoning is valid but from the wrong premises. So it is folly to elevate man's reasoning above what God has revealed in Scripture.[395]) But if evolution were true, then there would be selection only for survival advantage, not rationality.

8. Results should be reported *honestly*, because God has forbidden false witness (Exodus 20:16).

But if evolution were true, then why not lie? It is not that surprising that scientific fraud[396] is now "a serious, deeply rooted problem".[397] "[T]he dozen or so proven cases of falsification that have cropped up in the past five years have occurred in some of the world's most distinguished research institutions—Cornell, Harvard, Sloan-Kettering, Yale and so on."[398] This was said in 1981 and evolution has even more of a strangle-hold on thinking today.

Note, it's important to understand the point here—*not* that atheists can't be moral but that they have *no objective basis for this morality from within their own system* (see ch. 1, section III, p. 34). The Apostle of Antitheism, Richard Dawkins himself, admits that our "best impulses have no basis in nature,"[399] and his fellow anti-theistic evolutionary biologist William Provine said that evolution means, "There is no ultimate foundation for ethics, no ultimate meaning in life, and no free will for humans, either."[400]

394. Thompson, B. and Harrub, B., Consciousness: the king of evolutionary problems, *CRSQ* **41**(2):113–130, 2004; see review by Tate, D., Consciousness: a problem for naturalism, *J. Creation* **21**(1):29–32, 2007.
395. Sarfati, J., Loving God with all your mind: Logic and creation, *J. Creation* **12**(2):142–151, 1998; creation.com/logic.
396. Bergman, J., Why the epidemic of fraud exists in science today, *J. Creation* **18**(3):104–109, 2005.
397. Roman, M., When good scientists turn bad, *Discover* **9**(4):50–58, 1986; p. 58.
398. Editorial: Is science really a pack of lies? *Nature* **303**(5916):361–362, 1983; p. 361.
399. Evolution: The dissent of Darwin, *Psychology Today*, p. 62, January/February 1997.
400. Provine, W.B. (Professor of Biological Sciences, Cornell University, USA), *Origins Research* **16**(1/2):9, 1994.

Scientific jump after the Reformation

Europe in the Middle Ages had a Judeo-Christian worldview, what Oxford don C.S. Lewis[401] (1898–1963) called "Mere Christianity" in a famous book of that name. So it's not surprising that there were very significant advances in science at that time. But it took the Reformation to recover specific biblical authority. With this came the recovery of a plain or historical-grammatical understanding of the Bible,[402] recovering the understanding of the New Testament authors[403] and most of the early Church Fathers.[404] This turned out to have a huge positive impact on the development of modern science. This is so counter to common (mis)understanding, yet it is well documented by Peter Harrison, then a professor of history and philosophy at Bond University in Queensland, Australia (and now Andreas Idreos Professor of Science and Religion at the University of Oxford):

> "It is commonly supposed that when in the early modern period individuals began to look at the world in a different way, they could no longer believe what they read in the Bible. In this book I shall suggest that the reverse is the case: that when in the sixteenth century people began to read the Bible in a different way, they found themselves forced to jettison traditional conceptions of the world."[405]

As Prof. Harrison explained:

> "Strange as it may seem, the Bible played a positive role in the development of science. … Had it not been for the rise of the literal interpretation of the Bible and the subsequent appropriation of biblical narratives by early modern scientists, modern science may not have arisen at all. In sum, the Bible and its literal interpretation have played a vital role in the development of Western science."[406]

Stephen Snobelen, Assistant Professor of History of Science and Technology, University of King's College, Halifax, Canada, writes in a similar vein, and also explains the somewhat misleading term 'literal interpretation':[407]

> "Here is a final paradox. Recent work on early modern science has demonstrated a direct (and positive) relationship between the resurgence of the Hebraic, literal exegesis of the Bible in the Protestant Reformation, and the rise of the empirical method in modern science. I'm not referring to wooden literalism, but the sophisticated literal-historical hermeneutics that Martin Luther and others (including Newton) championed."[408]

401. See also Bergman, J., "C.S. Lewis: creationist and anti-evolutionist" *J. Creation* **23**(3):110–115, 2009.
402. Kulikovsky, A., The Bible and hermeneutics, *J. Creation* **19**(3):14–20, 2005; creation.com/hermeneutics.
403. Sarfati, J., Genesis: Bible authors believed it to be history, *Creation* **28**(2):21–23, 2006; creation.com/gen-hist.
404. Q&A: Genesis: Early Church Fathers; creation.com/fathers.
405. Harrison, P., *The Bible, Protestantism and the rise of natural science*, Cambridge University Press, 2001; see review by Weinberger, L., *J. Creation* **23**(3):21–24, 2009.
406. Harrison, P., The Bible and the rise of science, *Australasian Science* **23**(3):14–15, 2002.
407. Grigg, R., Should Genesis be taken literally? *Creation* **16**(1):38–41, 1993; creation.com/literal.
408. Snobelen, S., "Isaac Newton and Apocalypse Now: a response to Tom Harpur's 'Newton's strange bedfellows'; A longer version of the letter published in the 26 February 2004 *Toronto Star*"; isaacnewton.ca/media/Reply_to_Tom_Harpur-Feb_26.pdf.

Prof. Snobelen explains the reason why: scientists started to study nature in the same way they studied the Bible. Just as they studied what the Bible really said, rather than imposing outside philosophies and traditions upon it, they likewise studied how nature really did work, rather than accept philosophical ideas about how it should work (extending allegorizing readings of Scripture to the natural world[406]).

> *"It was, in part, when this method was transferred to science, when students of nature moved on from studying nature as symbols, allegories and metaphors to observing nature directly in an inductive and empirical way, that modern science was born. In this, Newton also played a pivotal role. As strange as it may sound, science will forever be in the debt of millenarians and biblical literalists."*[408]

It is thus no accident that science has flowered since the Reformation, where the Bible's authority (see ch. 5) was rediscovered. And it is no accident that the country with the strongest remnants of Bible-based Christian faith, the USA, the one Dawkins disparages because 40% of its population believe in creation, leads the world by a mile in the output of useful science.

RECOMMENDED READING

- Ankerberg, John, John Weldon and Walter Kaiser, *The Case for Jesus the Messiah: Incredible Prophecies that Prove God Exists*, Harvest House, Eugene, OR, 1989.

- Archer, Gleason L., *Encyclopedia of Bible Difficulties*, Zondervan, 1982.

- Bible Questions and Answers, creation.com/bible.

- Boice, James Montgomery. *Standing on the Rock: Biblical Authority in a Secular Age*, Baker Books, Grand Rapids, MI, 1994.

- Bruce, F.F., *The New Testament Documents: Are they Reliable?* Eerdmans, Grand Rapids, 1956.

- Clark, Gordon H., *God's Hammer: The Bible and its Critics*, The Trinity Foundation, Jefferson, MD, 1982.

- Fruchtenbaum, Arnold, *Messianic Christology*, Ariel Ministries, 1998.

- Harrison, P., *The Bible, Protestantism and the rise of natural science*, Cambridge University Press, 2001.

- Harrison, P., *The Fall of Man and the Foundations of Science*, Cambridge University Press, 2007.

- Radmacher, Earl D. (Ed.), *Can We Trust the Bible?* Tyndale, Wheaton, 1979.

- Robinson, John A.T., *Can We Trust the New Testament?* Eerdmans, Grand Rapids, 1977.

- Stark, Rodney, *For the Glory of God: How monotheism led to reformations, science*, witch-hunts and the end of slavery, Princeton University Press, 2003.

- Staudinger, Hugo, *The Trustworthiness of the Gospels*, The Handsel Press, Edinburgh, 1981.

- Warfield, B.B., *The Inspiration and Authority of the Bible*, Presbyterian and Reformed, Philadelphia, 1958.

- Wenham, John W., *Christ and the Bible*, Inter-Varsity, Downer's Grove, 1972.

- Wenham, John W., *Redating Matthew, Mark and Luke: A Fresh Assault on the Synoptic Problem*, IVP, 1992.

If all religions lead to God, how come most of them, having been given a thousand years at least, haven't yet arrived?
— GORDON BAILEY

I believe in Christianity as I believe that the sun has risen not only because I see it, but because by it I see everything else.
— C.S. LEWIS

ONE WAY

6

....

WHAT ABOUT
OTHER RELIGIONS?

We live in the age of pluralism. Non-Christian religions are emerging in every sector of our society. There is much truth to the old African saying, "He who never visits thinks mother is the only cook." If we visit other countries, watch television and read the newspaper we cannot avoid confronting other religions. The Western world is no longer monolithic but pluralistic. Gone are those days when Christianity was looked upon as the only religion for the West. R.D. Clements, in his popular book *God and the Gurus*, writes, "It is quite likely that the whole of Western culture may become increasingly influenced by Eastern ideas."[409] Today, Christians not only face the need of proclaiming the Good News of Jesus Christ, but they also confront the gigantic task of demonstrating the uniqueness of Christianity in the midst of a plurality of religions.

I. DO ALL RELIGIONS LEAD TO GOD?

One basic assumption of the modern mind is that all religions are both fundamentally the same and superficially different. Those who advocate this view affirm that it does not matter which religion we belong to as long as we believe some sort of something. Mahatma Gandhi declared, "My position is that all the great religions are fundamentally equal." Rama Krishna asserts, "Truth is one; sages call it by various names."[410] This present conviction was strongly held by the Roman senator Quintus Aurelius Symmachus in his classic 4th-century debate with St Ambrose when he said, "The heart of so great a mystery cannot be reached by following one road only." Ambrose on the other hand affirmed the absolute truth of Christianity, which logically entailed that other religions are false.

Following Symmachus, the modern religious relativist argues, "All religions lead to God;

---

409. Clements, R.D., *God and the Gurus*, InterVarsity, London, p. 7, 1974.
410. Quoted in Ridenour, F., *So What's the Difference?* Regal Books, Glendale, CA, p. 99, 1967.

they are basically the same and no religion can be wrong." Gordon Bailey is right, "If all religions lead to God, how come most of them, having been given a thousand years at least, haven't yet arrived?"[411]

On the surface it appears very loving and tolerant to affirm that all religions are fundamentally equal, but in reality this view leads to the death of religion. We must tolerate the views of others and respect their right to hold their views but we have no right, in the name of tolerance, to declare that mutually contradictory views are equally true. R.C. Sproul observes, "We must note the difference between equal toleration under the law and equal validity according to truth."[412] The kind of religious tolerance which refuses to pronounce any religion true and others false misses the very truth of religion. Truth is by definition very narrow, and by its very essence is intolerant of error. He who says all religions are the same knows very little about religion. If all religions are the same, what are the fundamentals or the elements that unify all religions as being the same?

In the light of conflicting religious claims, one could either ignore the obvious contradictions among religions, which is a nice way to kill all religions, or consider the major contradictions as non-essentials. Such an approach will bring peace and tolerance, but peace at what price? We may achieve peace but we will miss the truth. If truth is what matters ultimately, then we cannot ignore conflicting truth-claims. Distinguished Welsh theologian and academic

411. Quoted in Green, M., *Faith for the Non-Religious*, Tyndale House, Wheaton, p. 63, 1976.
412. Sproul, R.C., *Objections Answered*, G/L Publications, California, p. 40, 1978.

Huw Owen (1926–1996) points out:

> *"So far as the transcendental truth claims of religion are concerned the question of objective truth remains. Thus divine reality cannot be both personal and impersonal. Also it cannot be validly interpreted both in theistic and monistic terms. To look at it from the human side, our final bliss cannot consist both in the attainment of Nirvana and in eternal fellowship with a personal God of love."*[413]

Love, sincerity, honesty and faith cannot be the basis for all religions. Hitler sincerely believed in what he was doing—but he was sincerely wrong! A Hindu might sincerely believe that bathing in the highly polluted Ganges river will bring healing, but the belief will not alter the facts. One may have faith that the ten dollars in one's pocket is a thousand dollars, but no amount of faith will change the fact. Faith must be based on fact; sincerity and love must be grounded in truth. Just because we worship some god doesn't mean that we worship the true God. As Brian Maiden correctly notes, "It is not enough to worship God; we must worship the God who really is. Otherwise we are not really worshipping God at all."[414] We must be certain that what we believe is true and have good evidence that our belief is worthy of our ultimate commitment. Dr Vernon Grounds (1914–2010), a leader at Denver Seminary for over 60 years, was not off the mark when he wrote:

> *"Unless a religion squares with the facts of history and human experience; and unless it agrees with the truth of God which is the underlying reality of all things, that religion, however sincere its followers may be, is not good enough."*[415]

It is not arrogant and unkind to tell the truth lovingly. In reality, those who condone false religion as true are cruel to those who follow a mistaken path. The most loving thing to do to a person on a wrong train is not to admire his sincerity and say, "It doesn't matter what you believe, all trains lead to the same place, have a pleasant trip!" Such an action denies the very essence of love and compassion. When a person is on a wrong train the most loving thing

413. Owen, H.P., *Christian Theism: A Study in its Principles*, T. & T. Clark, Edinburgh, pp. 143–144, 1984.
414. Maiden, B., *One Way to God?* Inter-Varsity, London, pp. 6–7, 1974.
415. Grounds, V.C., *The Reason for Our Hope*, Moody, Chicago, pp. 93–94, 1945.

we can do is to share the truth kindly and show him where to find the right one. As Michael Green suggests:

"It is not that Christians are narrow-minded or uncharitable about other faiths. But if Jesus is indeed, as the resurrection asserts, God himself come to our rescue, then to reject him, or even to neglect him, is ultimate folly."[416]

All religions differ about who and what is God. Religions make contrary claims. All religions cannot be equally true when they all contradict one another. Opposing convictions cannot both be true. If all religions contradict one another there are only two logical choices: Either they are all false, or there is only one true religion. If there is one true God, then there must be one true way to reach him. If God has communicated to man in Scripture as to how we should please Him, then to choose other ways is to deny God's truth and ignore His revelation. Honesty should move us to reflect, in the light of our sin and rebellion, not why there is only one way to God, but why there should be a way at all!

416. Green, M., *Man Alive*, Inter-Varsity, London, p. 61, 1967.

Professor Robert Zaehner (1913–1975), a leading British scholar on Eastern Religions, incisively notes:

> *"To maintain that all religions are paths leading to the same goal, as is so frequently done today, is to maintain something that is not true. Not only on the dogmatic, but also on the mystical plane, too, there is no agreement. It is then only too true that the basic principles of Eastern and Western, which in practice means Indian and Semitic, thought are, I will not say irreconcilably opposed; they are simply not starting from the same premises. The only common ground is that the function of religion is to provide release; there is no agreement at all as to what it is that man must be released from. The great religions are talking at cross purposes."[417]*

II. IS HINDUISM A VIABLE BELIEF SYSTEM?

Hinduism is one of the oldest religions in the world. It dates back to 3000 BC and its historical origin is untraceable. It involves a variety of beliefs and practices, and it has been rightly said that Hinduism is more a culture than a creed. According to one Indian, it is a museum of beliefs, a medley of rites, or a mere map, a geographical expression. The word *Hindu* is Persian for 'Indian'. The Hindu scholar K.M. Sen asserts, "The religious beliefs of different schools of Hindu thought vary and their religious practices also differ; … indeed Hinduism is a great storehouse of all kinds of religious experiments."[418] No less an authority than Radhakrishnan, one of the world's most respected Hindus, in defending Hinduism declares:

> *"While it gives absolute liberty in the world of thought, it enjoins a strict code of practice. The theist, the sceptic and the agnostic may all be Hindus if they accept the Hindu system of culture and life … what counts is conduct, not belief."[419]*

In one sense Hinduism is the mother of all eastern thinking. Popular Hinduism has as many as 330 million gods. In the West the question is, "Does God exist?" but in the East the question is, "Which god to worship?"

What major convictions influence the lives of millions of Hindus? Christopher E. Storrs rightly points out:

417. Quoted in Lewis, H.D. and Slater, R.L., *The Study of Religions*, Penguin, Middlesex, p. 145, 1969.
418. Sen, K.M., *Hinduism*, Penguin Books, Middlesex, p. 37, 1961.
419. Radhakrishnan, S., *The Hindu View of Life*, London, p. 38, 1931.

"The One-without-a-Second, the sole Reality; the mirage of this world; the ceaseless wandering from birth to birth; the iron law of Karma which fixes present and future status; Release or Moksha—salvation from an endless cycle in Nirvana."[420]

Central to Hinduism is the concept 'Brahman'; the impersonal, the ultimate reality, the supreme soul of the universe which is beyond all human description. Brahman is one without a second. There is nothing but the one. All reality is one: God is all and all is God. The Hindu affirms, "Truly this whole world is Brahma. In calmness let man worship It as that from which he came forth, as that into which he will be dissolved, as that in which he breathes."[421] Rabindranath Tagore insists:

"According to some interpretations of the Vedanta doctrine Brahman is the absolute Truth, the impersonal It, in which there can be no distinction of this and that, the good and the evil, the beautiful and its opposite, having no other quality except its ineffable blissfulness in the eternal solitude of its consciousness utterly devoid of all things and all thoughts."[422]

The Hindu philosopher Shankara asserts, "Brahman alone is real, the phenomenal world is unreal, or mere illusion."[423] As Jack C. Winslow aptly observes:

"Brahma is conceived as beyond all attributes, including moral attributes. Brahma is neither holy nor unholy, loving nor unloving. Thus the moral challenge contained for the Jew and the Christian in the divine command, 'Be ye holy, for I am holy' is lacking in Hinduism … morality belongs to the world of maya, not to the world of ultimate reality."[424]

Sri Ramakrishna, admired by many as one of the greatest philosophers of nineteenth-century Hinduism, illustrates adequately the Hindu view of ultimate reality which resides within the seeker. In a popular parable he states:

"A man woke up at midnight and wanted to have a smoke. Needing a light, he went to his neighbour's house and knocked on the door. When the neighbour asked what his midnight visitor wanted, he replied, 'I wish to smoke. Can you give me a light?' To which the neighbour answered, 'Bah! What's the matter with you? Here you have taken all this trouble to come over here, to say nothing of wakening me, to get a light, when in your own hand you hold a lighted lantern!'

"'Likewise,' continues Sri Ramakrishna with the moral, 'what a man wants is already within him; but he still wanders here and there in search of it.'"[425]

The Hindu quest for reality is expressed in the following:

420. Storrs, C.E., *Many Creeds: One Cross*, SCM, London, p. 35, 1945.
421. Quoted in Winslow, J.C., *The Christian Approach to the Hindu*, Lutterworth, London, p. 13, 1974.
422. Tagore, R., *The Religion of Man*, Allen & Unwin, London, p. 127, 1931.
423. Quoted in Ferm, V. (Ed.), *An Encyclopedia of Religion*, The Philosophical Library, New York, p. 707, 1945.
424. Winslow, ref. 421, pp. 48–49.
425. Quoted in Potter, C.F., *The Faith Men Live By*, The World's Work, Kingswood, Surrey, p. 25, 1955.

"Why dost thou go to the forest in search of God? He lives in all, is yet ever distinct: he abides with thee too. As fragrance dwells in a flower, or reflection in a mirror, so does God dwell inside everything; seek him therefore in the heart."[426]

Mahatma Gandhi outlined the Hindu worldview remarkably well:

"To me God is Truth and Love, God is Ethics and morality, God is fearlessness. God is the source of light and life, and yet he is above and beyond all these. God is conscience. He is even the atheism of the atheist. He transcends speech and reason. He is a personal God to those who need his personal presence. He is embodied to those who need his touch … He is all things to all men."[18]

In Hinduism God is not separate from man, God is man. God is the one reality and man has no individual existence outside the reality of God. God is the reality both manifest and unmanifest, transcendent and immanent, infinite and finite, formed and formless, temporal and timeless, the one beyond all definition and distinction, above our classification of subjective and objective.

426. Quoted in Kenny, J.P., *Christ Outside Christianity*, Spectrum, Melbourne, p. 20, 1971.

The Hindu concept of God is foreign to Christianity. For the rational mind the concept of a pantheistic God raises a number of logical difficulties.[427] The pantheist may suggest that God is beyond reason and continues to affirm the view but such a leap of faith provides no comfort or hope to a seeking mind. However, if everything is God then in reality nothing is God. By calling the universe 'God', we do not change one single fact of reality, rather we commit the intellectual sin of word-magic, where something supposedly receives new life by giving it a new name. But a rose by a different name is still a rose.

If everything is God, then God is both good and evil. If God is both good and evil, there is no difference between loving or killing someone. Where all is divine, all is good. The Hindu idea of God provides no basis for religious experience. If only God exists then there are no creatures to experience God, and love is totally impossible in this context, for an impersonal God cannot love man. American scholar Ian Barbour (1923–) states the fundamental difference between Hinduism and Christianity on the subject of selfhood when he points out that for Hindus, "It is the self as such which is the problem, and man should escape the self by detachment from all desires and emotions, or by absorption in the divine." But for the Christians, he states, "Self-centeredness rather than selfhood itself is the problem, and love toward God and man is the true fulfilment of individuality."[428] Ultimately, the Hindu belief system is very inadequate; to tell a man earnestly seeking God that he is God, is like telling a beggar that he is food! Christopher E. Storrs says:

427. For a good discussion see Geisler, N., *Christian Apologetics*, Baker Book House, Grand Rapids, pp. 173–192, 1976.
428. Barbour, I., *Issues in Science and Religion*, Prentice-Hall, Englewood Cliffs, NJ, p. 234, 1966.

"Hinduism stands poles apart from the faith of the Hebrew prophets with their clear-cut certainty of truth and falsehood, and with their inspired intolerance of false belief or make-believe."[429]

In essence Hinduism is man's attempt to reach the Transcendent with the brilliance of his wisdom and virtue. It is a remarkable (but vain) compliment to human achievement. The reality is, man may ask the question but only God is big enough to give us the answer.

Hinduism offers no cleansing power from guilt and sins. As the common saying goes: "I came to Allahabad; I washed, but my sins came away with me."[430]

HINDUISM		VS		CHRISTIANITY
Pantheism	■——	METAPHYSICS	——■	Theism
Impersonal	■——	GOD	——■	Personal
Subjective	■——	TRUTH	——■	Objective
Divine	■——	MAN	——■	Sinner
Relative	■——	ETHICS	——■	Absolute
Self-effort	■——	SALVATION	——■	Grace
Ignorance	■——	SIN	——■	Rebellion

III. DOES BUDDHISM ANSWER THE PROBLEM OF LIFE?

There are some 600 million Buddhists around the world. Buddhism was founded in India by Siddhartha Gautama a little more than 500 years before Christ. During the course of many years, it spread to various parts of Asia. In one sense Buddhism is a Hindu heresy (just as Islam could be considered a Judeo-Christian heresy). Buddhism is largely divided into two main groups: the Buddhism that was introduced to China, Japan, and Korea is generally called *Mahayana Buddhism* meaning the 'Great Vehicle', but the Buddhism of Sri Lanka, Burma, Cambodia, Laos and Thailand is called *Theravada Buddhism* meaning the 'Lesser Vehicle.' Various sects and schools have arisen from the two main groups. Buddha developed his teachings in the context of Hinduism, seeking to provide a better solution to the problem

---

429. Storrs, ref. 420, p. 25.
430. Winslow, ref. 421, p. 49.

of human suffering. The Buddhist scholar Shoyu Hanayama notes, "The universal and fundamental doctrines of Buddhism were naturally expounded by Sakyamuni, the founder of [Mahayana] Buddhism, but they were not invented by Sakyamuni."[431]

In his book *The Path of Buddha*, Kenneth W. Morgan suggests, "In Buddhism, there is no such thing as belief in a Supreme Being, a creator of the universe, the reality of an immortal soul, a personal Saviour."[432] According to Ninian Smart (1927–2001), a leading scholar in comparative religion, Buddhism is "Mysticism without God".[433] Equally renowned for his contribution to comparative religion, H.D. Lewis from London University asserts that Buddha dismissed "all speculation about other ultimate questions as a useless and even misleading diversion of energy."[434] Buddha taught the 'Four Noble Truths' and the 'Eight-fold Path' to achieve the ultimate. He never spoke about God or ways to approach Him. In the light of this, Buddhism is a philosophy of life rather than a philosophy of God.

BUDDHISM'S FOUR NOBLE TRUTHS

The Fact of Suffering

The Cause of Suffering

The Cessation of Suffering

The Path to Cessation of Suffering

BUDDHISM'S EIGHT-FOLD PATH

Right views (right understanding of the Buddha's teachings)

Right consideration (of the truth)

Right words (which are true)

Right conduct (in everyday life)

Right way of life (in society)

Right efforts (to attain the enlightenment)

Right mind (right use of the intellect)

Right meditation (to enter Buddhahood)

431. Hanayama, S., "Buddhism" in Chalmers, R.C. and Irving, J.A. (Eds.), *The Meaning of Life in Five Great Religions*, Westminster, Philadelphia, p. 41, 1965.
432. Morgan, K.W. (Ed.), *The Path of Buddha*, Ronald Press, New York, p. 71, 1956.
433. Smart, N., *The Religious Experience of Mankind*, Scribners, New York, p. 81, 1969.
434. Lewis and Slater, ref. 9, p. 159.

The desire of every Buddhist is to be free from the problems of life; to be free from pain and suffering. As their saying goes, "As the water of the sea tastes of salt, so all life tastes of suffering. To live is to suffer." Their goal is to develop a detachment from life. Hanayama declares, "The existence of the Self or Ego, which is believed in many religions to exist permanently and apart from one's body, is completely denied in Buddhism."[435] D.T. Suzuki reminds us, "To think that there is the self is the start of all errors and evils. Ignorance is at the root of all things that go wrong."[436]

Buddha taught that desire is the root of all evil. To exist is to suffer and the answer to suffering is Nirvana (annihilation) which is achievable by successive reincarnation. Hence Buddhism insists, "Those who love a hundred have a hundred woes. Those who love ten have ten woes. Those who love one have one woe. Those who love none have no woes." The goal of life is to reach the stage of desirelessness. When we cease to desire we have overcome the burden of life. How one is supposed to be desireless without *desiring* to be desireless is a problem few have any time to answer.

According to Buddhism God is beyond any description, hence it would be proper to include Buddhism in the category of agnosticism. Leading Buddhist scholar, Christmas Humphreys, explains:

> *"The Buddhist teaching on God, in the sense of an ultimate Reality, is neither agnostic, as is sometimes claimed, nor vague, but clear and logical. Whatever Reality may be, it is beyond the conception of the finite intellect; it follows that attempts at description are misleading, unprofitable, and a waste of time. For these good reasons the Buddha maintained about Reality 'a noble silence.' If there is a Causeless Cause of all Causes, an Ultimate Reality, a Boundless Light, an Eternal Noumenon behind phenomena, it must clearly be infinite, unlimited, unconditioned and without attributes. We, on the other hand, are clearly finite, and limited and conditioned by, and in a sense composed of, innumerable attributes. It follows that we can neither define, describe, nor usefully discuss the nature of THAT which is beyond the comprehension of our finite consciousness. It may be indicated by negatives and described indirectly by analogy and symbols, but otherwise it must ever remain in its truest sense unknown and unexpressed, as being to us in our present state unknowable."[437]*

Though Buddha was profoundly moved by human suffering he did not offer a solution to alleviate human suffering. His ethos was not to take the physical reality seriously. Reality according to Buddha is not the external 'What' but rather the internal 'How'. He did not regard himself as divine nor did he offer any help except his teaching. According to Buddha,

---

435. Hanayama, ref. 431, p. 46.
436. Suzuki, D.T., *Mysticism, Christian and Buddhist*, Harper & Row, New York, p. 153, 1957.
437. Quoted in Chapman, C., *Christianity on Trial*, Volume **II**, Lion, Herts, England, p. 26, 1974.

"Man is born alone, lives alone and dies alone, and it is he alone who can blaze the way which leads him to Nirvana." The Buddha Annual of Ceylon says, "Buddhism is that religion which without starting with a God, leads men to a stage where God's help is not necessary." There is no God or a Saviour to help man from the problem of life; man must save himself. A Buddhist monk in prayer was once asked by a Christian what he was doing. The Buddhist replied, "I am praying to nobody for nothing." English writer and apologist G.K. Chesterton (1874–1936) rightly notes, "We may call Buddhism a faith; though to us it seems more like a doubt."[438] The idea of the Cross is foreign to the Buddhist. G. Parrinder speaks of a Buddhist who said, "I cannot help thinking of the gap that lies deep between Christianity and Buddhism. The crucified Christ is a terrible sight and I cannot help associating it with the sadistic impulse of a psychically affected brain."[439]

Despite its popularity and simplicity Buddhism seriously fails to meet the basic problems of life. Alan Watts, the popular Buddhist writer, aptly describes the Buddhist answer, "The solution for us is not solution, but only solution via dissolution."[440] There is a profound difference between the serene and passionless Buddha of Buddhism and the tortured Christ on the Cross of Christianity. As philosopher Alfred North Whitehead (1861–1947) observed, "Buddha gave his doctrine; Christ gave His life." Man cannot solve his own problem for there is no human solution to the human problem. However good the Eightfold Path may be, no human self-improvement projects are good enough to make a person perfect before a holy God. Former Archbishop of Canterbury George Carey (1935–) is right, "There is a world of difference between the passive and serene figure of Buddha and the active, suffering figure of Christ."[441] According to G.K. Chesterton, "It was fitting that the Buddha be pictured with his eyes closed; there is nothing important to see."

BUDDHISM	VS	CHRISTIANITY
Monism	■————■	Dualism
Agnostic	■————■	Theistic
Mystical	■————■	Historical
Self-effort	■————■	Divine Assistance
Detachment	■————■	Involvement
Enlightenment	■————■	Regeneration
Reincarnation	■————■	Resurrection

438. Chesterton, G.K., *The Everlasting Man*, Hodder & Stoughton, London, p. 21, 1947.
439. Parrinder, G., *Avatar and Incarnation*, Faber & Faber, London, p. 214, 1970.
440. Quoted in Petersen, W.J., *Those Curious New Cults*, Keats Publishing, New Canaan, CT, p. 172, 1975.
441. Carey, G., *God Incarnate*, Inter-Varsity, Leicester, p. 52, 1977.

IV. DOES ISLAM OFFER A RELIABLE REVELATION?

Islam is the second-largest religion in the world. The Pew Research Center reports:

> *"A comprehensive demographic study of more than 200 countries finds that there are 1.57 billion Muslims of all ages living in the world today, representing 23% of an estimated 2009 world population of 6.8 billion."[442]*

Thus it deserves a whole chapter (8) on answering its claims. The section here is mainly about describing its teaching.

The word *Islam* in Arabic means 'surrender', hence a Muslim is one who has surrendered to the sovereign will of Allah (God). It was founded by Mohammed in the early part of the 7th-century, and the claimed revelations of Mohammed are compiled in their sacred book called the Koran. As H. Kraemer points out, in Islam, "The Word did not become flesh: the Word became Book."[443] Every devoted Muslim believes that the Koran is the Word of God. The word *Koran* means 'The Readings' and is comprised of 114 surahs, or chapters. It must not be subjected to any form of question or criticism. Beside the Koran the Muslim believes the Hadith and Sunna. These are accepted with respect but they are not equal to the Koran. In his book *History of Religion*, the great scholar E.O. James writes:

> *"Islam, in fact, might be counted almost a Christian 'heresy' apart from this new direct revelation, supplementing and completing that vouchsafed through Christ and Hebrew prophets, since the Founder got most of his material from late forms of Judaism and Christianity, often curiously distorted and garbled."[444]*

The central teachings of Islam are the 'Five Pillars':

1. Confession that "There is no god but Allah, and Mohammed is his prophet."

2. Praying five times daily facing Mecca.

3. Giving alms to the poor.

4. Fasting during the month of Ramadan.

5. One pilgrimage to Mecca during a lifetime if possible.

Islam rejects the crucifixion and the Resurrection of Christ. In his book *Crises of Belief*, Stephen Neill correctly observes, "It is, however, clear that the vast majority of Muslims believe, and have been taught, that Jesus was not crucified but that God rescued him and carried him away to a safe place in the heavens."[445] Christopher E. Storrs adds, "Muhammed

---

442. *Mapping the Global Muslim Population: A Report on the Size and Distribution of the World's Muslim Population*, The Pew Forum on Religion and Public Life, 7 October 2009.
443. Kraemer, H., *The Christian Message in a Non-Christian World*, Kregel, Grand Rapids, p. 218, 1956.
444. James, E.O., *History of Religions*, English University Press, London, p. 190, 1956.
445. Neill, S., *Crises of Belief*, Hodder & Stoughton, London, pp. 81–82, 1984.

MECCA?... IS THAT IN LITTLE 'OLE ENGLAND?

would not even grant that the crucifixion was historical; for if God had thus failed one faithful prophet, might He not fail His final prophet?"[446] Jesus Christ is accepted as a prophet of God but His full divinity is denied. It is considered that the Bible was corrupted by later Christians, and the doctrine of sin distorted and forgiveness ignored.

Although they believe in one God, yet they deny that He is triune— three Persons: Father, Son and Holy Spirit, the Holy Trinity (for the evidence for this foundational Christian doctrine, see ch. 8, p. 187) Islamic convert and scholar Professor Watkin asserts, "The first principle of Islam is that there is nothing human in God, nothing divine in man."[447] Al-Junayd, the ninth-century mystic, adequately expresses the Islamic approach to God, "No one knows God save God Himself Most High, and therefore even to the best of His creatures He has only revealed His names in which He hides Himself."[448] God is so far removed from man that he is practically unknowable. A popular song suggests, "Whatsoever your mind can conceive, That Allah is not, you may believe."

Philosopher David Hugh Freeman observes, "In twenty passages of the Koran Allah is said 'to lead men astray'."[449] There is no actual provision for sin, and there is nothing which Allah has done for the salvation of man that has cost him anything. There is no assurance of eternal life and their concept of heaven is far removed from the Christian understanding of heavenly existence. Heaven is a place of sensual pleasures. In Surah 56:15–24, the Koran says:

446. Storrs, ref. 420, p. 80.
447. Quoted in Storrs, Ref, 420, p. 68.
448. Quoted in Zwemer, S.M., A Moslem Seeker After God, Revell, p. 182, 1920.
449. Freeman, D.H., A Philosophical Study of Religion, Craig Press, Nutley, NJ, p. 124, 1964.

"They shall recline on jewelled couches face to face, and there shall wait on them immortal youths with bowls and ewers and a cup of purest wine (that will neither pain their heads nor take away their reason); with fruits of their own choice and flesh of fowls that they relish. And theirs shall be the dark-eyed houris, chaste as hidden pearls: a guerdon for their deeds."

Many scholars suggest that Mohammed was unsure when he first received his revelations and they were accompanied by several fits and foaming at the mouth.[450] He first commanded his followers to pray like Daniel towards Jerusalem, but when the Jews and Christians did not accept his message, he directed them to face Mecca. As Dr Robert Morey observes:

"Muhammad had at first tried to encourage the Jews to accept his prophethood by preaching monotheism, observing the Jewish sabbath, praying toward Jerusalem, appealing to Abraham and the patriarchs, adopting some of their dietary laws, and praising their Scriptures."[451]

He taught an apostolic succession of prophets who came with parts of God's revelation—Abraham, Moses, Christ—but he was the final prophet (Seal of Prophecy) to confirm and seal all previous revelation before the day of Judgement. He never claimed to be divine, "I am no more than all men; I am only human", nor performed any miracles to verify his claims. He admitted that he was a sinner and even expressed that he needed help by asking his followers to pray for him.[452]

Christopher E. Storrs writes, "Muhammad indeed confessed to be a human prophet, sinful, and on occasions fallible; but his revelations were infallible."[453]

Islam: warrior cult

While many people attack Christianity because of the Crusades, an increasing number of historians regard them as a belated and justifiable response to *centuries* of Islamic aggression. (See the books by Robert Spencer and Rodney Stark in the bibliography.)

The Muslims quickly conquered the Iberian Peninsula well before the Crusades. They would have almost certainly conquered Europe if the Frankish king Charles Martel's infantry had not defeated the Muslim cavalry at the Battle of Tours/Poitiers in a brilliant defensive strategy.

Also, just think about the historic centres of Christianity such as Jerusalem, Antioch, Alexandria and the rest of North Africa—they are now Muslim lands, converted at the point of the sword. And *after* the crusades, the Muslim Turks conquered the ancient land of Asia

---

450. See Anderson, N., *The World's Religions*, IVP, London, p. 94, 1950.
451. Morey, R., *The Islamic Invasion*, Harvest House, Eugene, OR, p. 82, 1992.
452. Morey, ref. 451, p. 94.
453. Storrs, ref. 420, p. 65.

Minor, the birthplace of the Apostle Paul, the site of many of his missionary journeys and home of the Seven Churches of the book of Revelation. Furthermore, when they conquered Constantinople (now Istanbul) in 1453, they turned Hagia Sophia ('Holy Wisdom'), the world's biggest church of its day and centre of Eastern Orthodox Christianity, into a mosque.

In this, they were following the example of Muhammad himself. Evangelist Lowell Lundstrom observes, "During Muhammad's ten years in Medina, he planned 65 military campaigns and raids, and he personally led 27 of them."[454] In Surah 66:9, the Koran exhorts, "O Prophet! Strive against the disbelievers and the hypocrites and be stern with them. Hell will be their home, a hapless journey's end." Historian Sir Steven Runciman notes, "Unlike Christianity, which preached a peace that it never achieved, Islam unashamedly came with the sword."[455] So while atrocities committed in the name of Christ, such as during the Crusades, were inconsistent with the teachings of Christ, the atrocities committed by Muslims are *consistent with* Muhammad's teachings and actions.[456]

The Koran is believed to be eternal and uncreated, which would imply that it has an existence apart from God. Allah allows the Bible to be corrupted, but the Koran is eternally preserved. Mohammed regarded Jesus Christ as the greatest of the prophets before his own appearance. He described Christ as "a Word of God", "Apostle of God" (Sura 4:169) and "a Spirit of God". He admitted that Christ was sinless (Sura 3:36,37 & 19:19), born of a virgin and performed miracles.

V. THE UNIQUENESS OF CHRISTIANITY

Christianity is unique. There is no faith like the Christian faith. Christianity differs from all other religions in its basic teaching regarding who God is, what man is, how God redeems man, and what sin is. All other religions teach salvation by good works, but Christianity offers salvation by grace alone through faith. In other religions man is constantly seeking God, but in Christianity God is in search of man. Billy Graham is right, "There are many religions in the world, but only one Christianity, for only Christianity has a God who gave Himself for mankind. World religions attempt to reach up to God; Christianity is God reaching down to man."[457]

In the world's religions we have man's answers to man's problem, but in Christianity we have God's answer to man's problems. What man has long hoped for religiously through the centuries has taken place in Christ. The infinite has become finite, the abstract concrete, the invisible visible; God became man. This position should not be regarded as narrow-minded

454. Lundstrom, L., *The Muslims are Coming*, Lowell Lundstrom Ministries, Sisseton, SD, p. 37, 1980. Lundstrom served for ten years as president and chancellor of Trinity Bible College, in Ellendale, North Dakota.
455. Quoted in Lundstrom, ref. 454, p. 37.
456. See Sarfati, J., Unfair to Islam? creation.com/islamunfair, 2008.
457. Quoted in Adair, J.R. and Miller, T. (Eds.), *Escape from Darkness*, Victor Books, Wheaton, p. 51, 1982.

exclusivism but an invitation to share the joy of Christ, as George Carey so aptly describes: "The supreme gift we bring to others, not arrogantly nor with pride, is that in Jesus our Lord we find the final and complete answer to man's needs."[458]

Christianity answers the questions of history, offers a solution to the problem of sin, removes the burden of guilt, releases from the fear of death, reverses despair into hope, and provides power to live a victorious life with God. Stephen Neill's conclusion is therefore completely logical, "For the human sickness there is one specific remedy, and this is it. There is no other."[459]

In one profound sense all other religions have views, but in Christianity we have news—the Good News that God has done something of eternal value for the salvation of man in Jesus Christ. J. Gresham Machen was right when he wrote:

> *"All the ideas of Christianity might be discovered in some other religion, yet there would be in that other religion no Christianity. For Christianity depends, not upon a complex of ideas, but upon the narration of an event."*[460]

Christianity is unique because Jesus Christ is different from all the leaders of the world. He is not just one bead on the necklace of God or "one note of the flute that Divinity blows".[461] In Jesus Christ we have something unique. The Apostle Paul gives us good reasons why Christ cannot be put alongside of Buddha, Mohammed, Confucius, Socrates and Plato. In his letter to the Philippians Paul writes, "He became obedient unto death, even death on a cross. Therefore God has highly exalted him and bestowed on him the name which is above every name, that at the name of Jesus every knee should bow, in heaven and on earth and under the earth." (2:8,9)

1. Reliable Revelation

The Christian revelation is unlike all other claims to revelation; the Christian revelation is totally reliable. There is more historical evidence for the reliability of the New Testament than any ten pieces of classical literature put together. To briefly summarise the evidence (explained in more detail in the section on manuscript evidence for the Bible, ch. 5, p. 118):

The New Testament is one of the most highly researched books of the ancient world. The earliest copy of the writings of Tacitus, the Roman historian, is about a thousand years from the time of the original. A thousand years separate the writing of Caesar's *Gaelic War* from the date of the oldest manuscripts, and we have only ten copies. Thirteen hundred years separate the earliest extant manuscripts of Plato from the time he wrote the originals. The

458. Carey, ref. 441, p. 58.
459. Neill, S., *Christian Faith and Other Faiths*, Oxford University Press, London, p. 17f, 1961.
460. Machen, J.G., *Christianity and Liberalism*, Eerdmans, Grand Rapids, p. 70, 1923.
461. Heiner, W., *Jesus is Different*, Paternoster, Exeter, p. 12, 1982.

earliest writings of Aristotle which we possess date back fourteen hundred years from the original, but when we come to the New Testament the gap between the original copies and the existing copies is 30, 100 and 200 years. F.F. Bruce, the Ryland's Professor of Biblical Criticism at the University of Manchester, writes:

> "The evidence for our New Testament writings is ever so much greater than the evidence for many writings of classical authors, the authenticity of which no-one dreams of questioning."[462]

If anyone rejects the reliability of the New Testament then on the same ground he or she must be prepared to reject all the documents for ancient and classical history. The agnostic historian H.G. Wells agrees that the Gospels existed in the first century. He says that, "Information about the personality of Jesus is derived from the four gospels, all of which were certainly in existence a few decades after his death."[463] Sir Frederic Kenyon, former director and principal librarian of the British Museum, concluded shortly before his death, "Both the authenticity and the general integrity of the books of the New Testament may be regarded as finally established."[464]

2. Resurrected Redeemer

The Christian faith is based on a historical event—the Resurrection. All other major world religions are based on a philosophical or theological system but Christianity is founded on a space-time event. There is one event in the life of Christ that separates Him from every person that ever lived in the history of the world—the Resurrection. There is absolutely nothing in any philosophy or religion that compares with what is found in Jesus Christ. G.B. Hardy states it eloquently:

There are but two essential requirements:

1. Has anyone cheated death and proved it?
2. Is it available to me? Here is the complete record:

- Confucius' tomb—occupied,

- Buddha's tomb—occupied,

- Mohammed's tomb—occupied,

- Jesus' tomb—EMPTY.

- Argue as you will … THERE IS NO POINT IN FOLLOWING A LOSER.[465]

462. Bruce, F.F., *The New Testament Documents: Are They Reliable?* Eerdmans, Grand Rapids, p. 15, 1977.
463. Wells, H.G., *Outline of History*, Volume **I**, p. 15, 1920.
464. Kenyon, F., *The Bible and Archaeology*, Harper & Row, New York, p. 289, 1940.
465. Hardy, G.B., *Countdown: A Time to Choose*, Moody, Chicago, p. 32, 1963.

The fact that all the founders of the world's religions could not conquer their own death is good evidence that they do not represent ultimate truth. Jesus Christ demonstrates that He is the truth by dying and rising from the grave. If Jesus Christ defeated death, which is man's greatest enemy, then He is the greatest authority on Truth and He can be trusted to speak with absolute reliability on all the greatest questions of life, God and death. Philosopher H.D. Lewis rightly summed it up, "He came in complete human form to meet a universal need in a way that is adequate for all times and places and is without parallel or substitute."[466]

There is more historical evidence for the Resurrection of Jesus Christ than there is for the fact that Napoleon was defeated at the battle of Waterloo or that Julius Caesar was a Roman Emperor. No theory has ever been produced which could logically refute the reality of the Resurrection while adequately considering all the available evidence. The Cambridge scholar Bishop Westcott writing on the resurrection states:

> "Indeed, taking all the evidence together, it is not too much to say that there is no single historic incident better or more variously supported than the resurrection of Christ."[467]

466. Lewis and Slater, ref. 417, p. 193.
467. Westcott, B.F., *The Gospel of the Resurrection*, London, pp. 4–6, 1879.

3. Resourceful Relationship

Christianity is not merely a religion but a relationship. The Christian faith provides a right relationship between man and God through Jesus Christ. In all the world's major religions man tries to work his way to God but in Christianity God reaches out to save man. In other religions man seeks to redeem himself by his own effort but in Christianity God redeems man from his sin and failures. God does for man what he cannot do for himself. Religion gives good advice but Christ offers power and strength to overcome sin and evil.

The story is told that Sadhu Sundar Singh, the great Indian saint, was once travelling in a train with a number of learned Brahmin. "Tell us," they said, "what belief do you have in Christianity that is not found in Hinduism?" Sadhu responded, "I have Christ." They repeated the question and again Sadhu replied, "I have Christ." They asked him for the third time, "What belief do you have in Christianity that is not found in Hinduism?" And again Sadhu replied, "I have Christ." Christianity is Jesus Christ! It would be fair to affirm that of all the great religious leaders of the world Jesus Christ alone makes the remarkable claim that He is God:

- I and the Father are one (John 10:30).

- The Son of Man has authority on earth to forgive sins (Mark 2:10).

- Before Abraham was born, I am (John 8:58 and Isaiah 46:4).

- He who does not honour the Son does not honour the Father who sent him (John 5:23).

- Behold, I am coming soon! My reward is with me, and I will give to everyone according to what he has done. I am the Alpha and the Omega, the First and the Last, the Beginning and the End (Revelation 22:12,13).

Hendrik Kraemer captured the truth when he declared that "Christ is the crisis of all religions."[468] Without Him Christianity would be dead wood. He makes all the difference. Christ is not just a fact to be believed or a topic just for discussion but a living reality to encounter. He is a vital person to know and to love. Only Christianity provides a resource and a solution to face the problem of sin. The Bible states, "But God demonstrates his own love for us in this: While we were still sinners, Christ died for us" (Romans 5:8). The founders of the world's religions say, "Do! Do! Do!" but Christ says, "Done! It is finished!" Sir Norman Anderson says:

> *"This is the unique element in the gospel, which tells us that what we could never do, God has done. We cannot climb up to heaven to discover God, but God has come to earth, in the person of His Son, to reveal Himself to us in the only way we could*

---

468. Kraemer, ref. 443, ch. IV.

really understand: in terms of a human life."[469]

This is what makes Christianity so special; in Jesus Christ:

- Our sins are forgiven.

- Our guilt is removed.

- Our fear of death is destroyed.

- Our faith is founded on a personal God.

- Our search for truth is satisfied.

- Our security and identity are complete.

- Our lives are now based on a new hope.

The basic difference between Christianity and the world's religions is this: As a Hindu I [S.K] was drowning in a large lake and I did not know how to swim. The religious leaders and gurus came by and gave me lectures on how to swim. Confucius taught, "You should have followed my teaching and then you would never have fallen." Mohammed advised,

469. Anderson, N., *Jesus Christ: The Witness of History*, InterVarsity, pp. 156–157, 1985.

"Allah wills whatsoever he wills." Buddha came by and said, "It's all an illusion in the mind, change your mind and you will change the problem." Krishna came along and said, "It's your karma that you have fallen into the lake. You deserve it." Then Jesus Christ came. He did not give a lecture or some good advice. He said, "I have come to seek and to save those who are lost," and He came right into the lake and lifted me out of it and changed my life and put a new song in my heart. The songwriter captures my sentiment when he wrote, "From sinking sand He lifted me, with tender hands He lifted me. From shades of night to plains of light. Oh, praise His name, He lifted me." I now understand the experience of the psalmist when he said:

> *"I waited patiently for the Lord; he turned to me and heard my cry. He lifted me out of the slimy pit, out of the mud and mire; he set my feet on a rock and gave me a firm place to stand. He put a new song in my mouth, a hymn of praise to our God. Many will see and fear and put their trust in the Lord"* (Psalm 40:1–3).

RECOMMENDED READING

- Anderson, Sir Norman (Ed.), *The World's Religions*, Eerdmans, Grand Rapids, 1976.

- Bavinck, J.H., *The Church Between Temple and Mosque*, Eerdmans, Grand Rapids, 1981.

- Fernando, Ajith, *The Christian's Attitude Toward World Religions*, Tyndale House, Wheaton, 1978.

- Hesselgrave, David J., *Communicating Christ Cross-Culturally*, Zondervan, Grand Rapids, 1978.

- Hume, Robert E., *The World's Living Religions*, Scribner's, New York, 1929.

- Neill, Stephen, *Crises of Belief*, Hodder and Stoughton, London, 1984.

- Newbigin, Lesslie, *The Finality of Christ*, John Knox, Richmond, 1969.

- Spencer, Robert, The *Politically Incorrect Guide to Islam (And the Crusades)*, Regnery Press, 2005.

- Spencer, Robert, *Religion of Peace?: Why Christianity Is and Islam Isn't,* Regnery Publishing, 2007.

- Stark, Rodney, *God's Battalions: The Case for the Crusades*, HarperOne, 2009.

- Zacharias, Ravi, Why Jesus?: *Rediscovering His Truth in an Age of Mass Marketed Spirituality,* FaithWords, 2012.

If, when I was asleep I was a man dreaming I was a butterfly,
how do I know when I am awake I am not a butterfly
dreaming I am a man?
— LAO-TSE

The gods love the obscure and hate the obvious.
— UPANISHADS

The answer to every problem is that there is no problem. Let
man perceive this truth and then he is without problems.
— MAHARISHI MAHESH YOGI

7

ANSWERING THE EASTERN MIND

"The East is East and West is West and never the Twain shall meet",[470] said Rudyard Kipling a century ago. But today one would be naive to hold such a view. The East and the West are no longer apart but are becoming one. Although the West is influencing the East through its science and technology, the East is making its impact on the West through its religious ideology. Canadian communication theorist Marshall McLuhan (1911–1980) observes that the East may be going West in terms of the goal-oriented outer trip, but the West is going East in terms of the inner trip. Theologian Nels F. Ferre (1908–1971) says, "The supernatural, personalistic, classical Christian faith is now being undermined by an ultimately non-dualistic, impersonal or trans-personal faith. The winds are blowing gale-strong out of the Orient."[471]

Gone are those days when the East was looked upon as dark and depraved. Many Westerners now admire the East and cherish it as a place to discover spiritual wisdom. Youth, disillusioned with the Western life-style and humanistic materialism, are turning East with a hope of finding meaning for their existence. Eastern ideas and philosophies are penetrating every sector of Western culture. Eastern sects such as the Transcendental Meditation Movement, Divine Light Mission, Hare Krishna Movement, Soka Gakkai, Theosophy, and Zen Buddhism are rapidly increasing and gaining recognition in many areas.

Eastern movements cannot be dismissed as passing fads nor can they be ignored as obscure cults. Their influence and ideology have serious implications for social, psychological, philosophical and spiritual life. In the light of these it is imperative that we examine the basic premises of the Eastern worldview.

---

470. Rudyard Kipling, "The Ballad of East and West" in *Rudyard Kipling's Verse* (Garden City: Doubleday, Doran & Co., 1945).
471. Ferre, N.F., "Foreword" in Singh, S., *Christology and Personality*, Westminster Press, p. 14, 1961.

I. THE ROOTS OF EASTERN IDEAS

The historical roots of eastern thinking are most intriguing. The climate of opinion in many circles is that the eastern ideas are unique to the East and its basic presuppositions are foreign to the West. These convictions are simply fictional and have no historical ground.

The roots of Hinduism go back to an Indo-European–speaking people (sometimes called 'Aryans'), who introduced Vedic teaching to the Dravidian people of India, who were animist. This new ideology was similar in essence to that of the Greeks, as Jack C. Winslow points out:

> *"There is, for instance, Varuna, the Greek Ouranos, i.e. Heaven, who in Greek mythology is the father of Zeus, the bright sky. The Vedic equivalent of Zeus is Dyaus, often called Dyauspitar, or Father Dyaus—in Greek, Zeus pater and in Latin, Jupiter."*[472]

The origins of Aryan beliefs are deeply grounded in the mythology and philosophy of the ancient Greeks. Greek philosophers such as Parmenides, Heraclitus, Plotinus and Pythagoras held to views which are basic to Hinduism and Buddhism. Concepts like pantheism, monism, emanation and reincarnation were common doctrines among the Greeks. The Eastern views of time, history and existence are identical to those of the Greeks. The British Christian sociologist Os Guinness observes, "Both the Greeks and the Hindus viewed time as cyclical and limitless." He points out, "The Greeks viewed the physical universe as a world of shadow, less true or less real than the transcendent ideal which was beyond knowledge; for the Hindus the physical universe is a world of 'maya', or illusion."[473]

II. THE BASIC EASTERN BELIEF SYSTEM

Every religion has a belief system and the East has one which is contrary to Christianity. The test of a belief system must be that it is logically consistent, factually verifiable and existentially liveable. Any worldview which fails the above principles should be rejected. An unwise person may accept the absurd, but a wise person will choose the logical.

Eastern religion functions on the basis of certain theological and philosophical presuppositions. A presupposition is a belief or a conceptual framework of thought accepted as a premise to support one's basic view of life and through which one sees all realities. American philosopher and presuppositional apologist Gordon H. Clark (1902–1985) rightly affirms, "Every philosophy must have its first principles."[474] These presuppositions provide a basis for one's ethical, social and religious life. Behind the practice of Hinduism

---

472. Winslow, J.C., *The Christian Approach to the Hindu*, Lutterworth Press, London, p. 12, 1958.
473. Guinness, O., *The Dust of Death*, InterVarsity, Downers Grove, p. 197, 1973.
474. Clark, G.H., *Three Types of Religious Philosophy*, Presbyterian & Reformed, Nutley, NJ, p. 104, 1973.

and Buddhism lie several presuppositions which control the belief systems:

1. Reality Is One

Although Eastern religion embraces a wide range of ideas from polytheism to theism, its basic belief system is pantheism or monism. Pantheism affirms that there is only one ultimate reality—God—and everything is part of this reality. We agree with Mark Albrecht that "It may be said with some certainty that no religion or religious philosophy is any better than its conception of God."[475] From Shankara, Vivekenanda, and Radhakrishnan to Maharishi the main religious system is pantheistic. The *Upanishad* defines ultimate reality as, "That from which these beings are born, that in which born they live, and that into which they enter at their death is Brahman."[476] In the *Bhagavad Gita* Brahman itself speaks:

> *"All this universe is strung upon me, as rows of gems upon a thread. I am the taste in water, I am the light in moon and sun, sound in the ether, manhood in men. The pure scent in earth am I, and the light in fire; the life in all born beings am I, and the mortification of them that mortify the flesh. I am the understanding of them that understand, the splendour of the splendid."[477]*

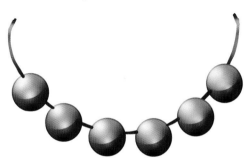

No words could describe Brahman for it is beyond framework. Brahman is God, being, awareness and bliss. Sarvapalli Radhakrishnan, known throughout the world as India's greatest philosopher of this century, when asked to define Brahman, remained silent and when pressed to respond, stated that, "The Absolute is silence."[478] It is "the divine darkness", and "that of which nothing can be said". Brahman is Atman, the One-without-a-Second. Radhakrishnan argues:

> *"He who knows Brahman becomes Brahman. Perfection is a state of mind, not contingent of time or place … he who knows himself to be all can have no desire. When the Supreme is seen, the knots of the heart are cut asunder … There can be no sorrow or pain or fear when there is no other."[479]*

In pantheistic thinking there is no room for any other. The *Upanishad* summed up Brahman as "Thou art That" *Tat tuam asi*:

> "Place this salt in water and come to me tomorrow morning."

475. Albrecht, M., *Reincarnation: A Christian Appraisal*, InterVarsity Press, Downers Grove, p. 106, 1982.
476. Radhakrishnan, S., *The Principal Upanishads*, Allen & Unwin, London, p. 55, 1958.
477. *Bhagavad Gita*, Volume **7**, pp. 7–10.
478. Quoted in Storrs, C.E., *Many Creeds: One Cross*, SCM Press, London, p. 33, 1945.
479. Radhakrishnan, ref. 476, p. 18.

Svetaketu did as he was commanded, and in the morning his father said to him: "Bring me the salt you put into the water last night."

Svetaketu looked into the water, but could not find it, for it had dissolved.

His father then said: "Taste the water from this side. How is it?"

"It is salt."

"Taste it from the middle. How is it?"

"It is salt."

"Taste it from that side. How is it?"

"It is salt."

"Look for the salt again and come again to me."

The son did so, saying: "I cannot see the salt. I only see the water."

His father then said: "In the same way, O my son, you cannot see the spirit. But in truth he is there. An invisible and subtle essence is the Spirit of the whole universe. That is Reality. That is Truth. Thou art That!"[480]

Brahman is the only reality, all else is illusionary as the Hindu philosopher Shankara asserts, "Brahman alone is real, the phenomenal world is unreal, or mere illusion."[481] Where all is divine everything is one. The logic is, if God is All, there cannot be anything but God. The goal of Eastern pantheism is the ontological merging of Atman (self) with Brahman (the Absolute), as consciousness of the self is radically transcended to the oblivion. The true experience of Atman leads to the knowledge of Brahman. The experience of Atman is not objective but subjective, intuitive and immediate. The pantheist argues that our physical senses often create the impression that we are separate, isolated and individual, but this is due to ignorance. Once we lose the false sense of individuality, we experience pure conscious cosmic unity with Brahman. Commenting on Atman and Brahman the *Upanishads* declare:

> *"This soul of mine within the heart is smaller than a grain of rice, or a barley-corn, or a mustard-seed, or a grain of millet, or the kernel of a grain of millet; this soul of mine within the heart is greater than the earth, greater than the atmosphere, greater than the sky, greater then the worlds … This soul of mine within the heart, this is Brahman."[482]*

As one author puts it "'The doer and the Causer to do are one.' 'God tells the thief to go and steal, and at the same time warns the householder against the thief.'"[483] The logic of Stephen

480. *Chandogya Upanishad* **VI**:11ff.
481. Ferm, V. (Ed.), *An Encyclopedia of Religion*, The Philosophical Library, New York, p. 707, 1945.
482. *Chandogya Upanishads* 3.14.2–3.
483. Storrs, ref. 478, p. 36.

Neill is inescapable, "If in fact Brahman and I are one, there is no one to be offended."[484] The quest of every Hindu is reflected in the prayer of the *Upanishads*, "Lead me from the unreal to the real. Lead me from darkness to the light. Lead me from death to immortality."[485]

The conception that reality is ultimately one is not only the metaphysical view of classical Hinduism but also historical Buddhism. D.T. Suzuki, the leading advocate of Zen Buddhism, asserts:

> *"Simple people conceive that we are to see God as if He stood on that side and we on this. It is not so; God and I are one in the act of my perceiving Him. In this absolute oneness of things, Zen establishes the foundation of its philosophy."[486]*

According to Mahayana Buddhism, reality is beyond any categories of existence:

> *"Suchness (reality) is neither that which is existence nor that which is non-existence; neither that which is at once existence and non-existence; nor that which is not at once existence; and non-existence; it is neither that which is unity nor that which is plurality; neither that which is at once unity and plurality, nor that which is not at once unity and plurality."[487]*

Is God the rock, the tree and energy that emits from them? Are we not insulting God by reducing Him to the level of plants and animals? Is there no difference between a painter

484. Neill, S., *Christian Faith and Other Faiths*, Oxford University Press, London, p. 97, 1961.
485. *Brihadaranyaka Upanishad* **I**:3,28.
486. Suzuki, D.T., in Barrett, W. (Ed.), *Zen Buddhism, Selected Writings*, ed. William Barrett, Doubleday, New York, p. 115, 1956.
487. Suzuki, D.T., *Outline of Mahayana Buddhism*, Schocken Books, New York, pp. 101–102, 1963.

and his painting, a creator and his creation? Is pantheism really an intellectual option for modern man? When one seriously reflects on the pantheistic idea that reality is one, it should not take too long to discover the impossibility and the difficulty of such a notion. If reality is ultimately one, then there are no finite individuals. But to assert, 'reality is one' in a strictly monistic context would be senseless. If only God exists, who is God talking to?

Pantheism is impossible. To affirm "God exists but I do not" is self-contradictory since one must exist in order to make the statement. The denial of dualism and the affirmation of pantheism is irrational since the pantheist must exist as a separate individual (which refutes pantheism) to make statements on the nature of existence. If pantheism is true, no pantheist should advocate pantheism since such an activity presupposes the existence of other beings that need to be convinced about pantheism.

The logic of Norman L. Geisler should challenge every pantheist:

> *"When we cross a busy street and see three lanes of traffic coming towards us, should we not even worry about it because it is merely an illusion? Indeed, should we even bother to look for cars when we cross the street, if we, the traffic and the street do not really exist? If pantheists actually lived out their pantheism consistently, would there be any pantheists left?"*[488]

The leading Indian-born Christian apologist Ravi Zacharias (1946–) also said, "Yes, even in India we look both ways before we cross the street because it is either me or the bus, not both of us!"[489]

Pantheists teach that man is deceived in thinking of his individual existence. If this were the case, how could the pantheist know that he is not mistaken when he thinks reality is one? If the real is unreal and the obvious is false, how do we know that the pantheists are really telling us the truth? On what basis is the pantheist so sure that he is not mistaken? Do the pantheists possess a special pipeline to reality? If reality were one, relationship and religious experience would be impossible and meaningless. If God alone exists, God and not

488. Geisler, N.L. and Watkins, W., *Perspectives: Understanding and Evaluating Today's World Views*, Here's Life Publishers, San Bernardino, CA, p. 92, 1984.
489. See Dr Zacharias' books in the bibliography. The article "Proven Western Logic vs Flawed Eastern Logic" at forums. canadiancontent.net is the source of this interesting dialogue.

the pantheist is having the experience. Professor John Warwick Montgomery's insightful analysis of pantheism is worth noting:

> *"Pantheism … is neither true nor false; it is something much worse, viz., entirely trivial. We had little doubt that the universe was here anyway; by giving it a new name ('God') we explain nothing. We actually commit the venerable intellectual sin of Word Magic, wherein the naming of something is supposed to give added power either to the thing named or to the semantic magician himself."[490]*

Writing on the same issue, C.E.M. Joad (1891–1953), former professor of philosophy at London University, in his book *Guide to Philosophy* insists that:

> *"If we assume that Substance in the original definition means simply 'all that there is,' then it is the conclusion. Such a conclusion is not worth proving. It is, indeed, merely a tautology—that is to say, an asserting of the same thing in two different ways."[491]*

Eastern thought vs good and evil

The fallacy of pantheism is not only a logical error but it has serious moral implications. If God is All and All is God, then evil is part of God. "Since the pantheist God", writes Mark Albrecht, "is of one essence with creation and consciousness, God is thus the origin of the imperfection and evil in our world; the foulest deeds and thoughts of humanity literally become attributes of God."[492]

Francis Schaeffer illustrates the serious implication of pantheism:

490. Montgomery, J.W., *The Suicide of Christian Theology*, Bethany, Minneapolis, p. 252, 1975.
491. Quoted in Montgomery, ref. 490, p. 252.
492. Albrecht, ref. 475, p. 106.

"One day I was talking to a group of people in the digs of a young South African in Cambridge. Among others, there was present a young Indian who was of Sikh background but a Hindu by religion. He started to speak strongly against Christianity, but did not really understand the problems of his own beliefs. So I said, 'Am I not correct in saying that on the basis of your system, cruelty and non-cruelty are ultimately equal, that there is no intrinsic difference between them?' He agreed … the student, in whose room we met, who had clearly understood the implications of what the Sikh had admitted, picked up his kettle of boiling water with which he was about to make tea, and stood with it steaming over the Indian's head. The man looked up and asked him what he was doing and he said, with a cold yet gentle finality, 'There is no difference between cruelty and non-cruelty.' Thereupon the Hindu walked out into the night."[493]

Samuel M. Thompson's brilliant philosophical critique of pantheism deserves our attention. The philosopher writes:

"Any attempt to identify God and the world is bound to fail just so far as it recognizes the slightest distinction between the world as such and God as such; for any distinction whatever is enough to destroy the identity. On the other hand if there is no distinction then we do not have two things to identify with each other, and so again the basic pantheistic doctrine fails."[494]

There is much wisdom in the words of Anglican/Reformed theologian J.I. Packer, "If God's being is an aspect of my own, 'the depth in me,' all attempts to worship Him become self-worship."[495] At this point one can hardly avoid the temptation of citing Professor C.E.M. Joad's eloquent remarks:

"If there is only God, how can there be illusions? Can God's mind create and nourish them? No. Can mine? I think that it can. But, if it can, my mind must be other than God's, and all is not God."[496]

Dr E. Stanley Jones' insightful truism must not escape our notice:

"I have searched India from the Himalaya to Cape Cormorin for over a half century to

493. Schaeffer, F., *The God Who is There*, InterVarsity Press, Downers Grove, p. 101, 1968.
494. Thompson, S.M., *A Modern Philosophy of Religion*, Henry Regnery, Chicago, p. 237, 1955.
495. Packer, J.I., *Keep Yourself from Idols*, Church Book Room, London, p. 13, 1964.
496. Joad, C.E.M., *Return to Philosophy*, Faber and Faber, London, p. 35, 1958.

find a person who has arrived at the realization of the self and become the Self, become God. I have never found one. It is illusion … A creature can never become the Creator."[497]

2. Reality is Illogical

Basic to all Eastern thinking is that reality is illogical and reason cannot lead to God. It is often asserted that "God is greater than logic." Buddha's advice to his disciples was, "Do not go by reasoning, nor by inferring, nor by argument."[498] It is said that "The Buddha preached for forty nine years and in all that time found it not necessary to speak one word."[499] Writing on Zen Buddhism, D.T. Suzuki points out, "Zen is one thing and logic another. When we fail to make this distinction and expect Zen to give us something logically consistent and intellectually illuminating, we altogether misinterpret the signification of Zen."[500] Suzuki goes far in asserting that "All our theorization fails to touch reality."[501] The 1960s rock band Sopwith Camel rightly expressed the Eastern approach in a song that said, "Stamp out reality before reality stamps out you."[502] Social and political activist Abbie Hoffman (1936–1989) argued along the same line when he wrote in his 1968 book *Revolution for the Hell of It*, "Listen to touches, Listen to silence … Don't listen to words, Don't listen to words. Don't listen to words."[503] For the East, the mind is a drunken monkey. Hare Krishna speaks about the garbage-pail mind.[504]

Reason has no essence in Eastern thinking. It insists, "Don't think, when you are thinking that you are thinking." We are told that "Shiva gave birth to Shakti and Shakti gave birth to Shiva. But only the sages can comprehend this secret." Guru Maharaji Ji contends, "Mind always projects what is false. Mind is a black light."[505]

The Hindu argues that God is both personal and impersonal; Shankara, the impersonal, and Ramanuja, the personal. W. Cantwell Smith reminds us, "No Hindu has said anything that some other Hindu has not contradicted."[506] The Hindu is not embarrassed that his concept violates the law of the excluded middle in logic. He considers God totally other, far removed, contrary to all our thinking. God is everything our mind cannot conceive. The *Upanishads* suggest:

"Him (Brahman) the eye does not see, nor the tongue express, nor the mind grasp.

497. Jones, E.S., *The Victory Through Surrender*, Abingdon Press, Nashville, p. 27, 1966.
498. Woodward, F.L., *Some Sayings of Buddha*, Oxford, p. 283.
499. Reps, P., *Zen Flesh, Zen Bones: A Collection of Zen and Pre-Zen Writings*, Anchor Books, New York, p. 45.
500. Suzuki, ref. 486, p. 19.
501. Suzuki, D.T., *An Introduction to Zen Buddhism*, Grove Press, New York, p. 41, 1964.
502. Petersen, W.J., *Those Curious New Cults*, Keats Publishing, New Canaan, CT, p. 173, 1975.
503. Unfortunately (though consistent with this outlook), he committed suicide by swallowing 150 barbiturate pills with strong alcohol.
504. Quoted in Cohen, D., *The New Believers: Young Religion in America*, M. Evans & Co., New York, p. 112, 1975.
505. Quoted in Clements, R.D., *God and the Gurus*, Inter-Varsity, London, p. 27, 1974.
506. Smith, W.C., *Question of Religious Truth*, Scribners, New York, p. 74, 1967.

Him we neither know nor are able to teach. Different is he from the known, and … from the unknown …

"He truly knows Brahman who knows him as beyond knowledge; he who thinks that he knows, knows not. The ignorant think that Brahman is known, but the wise know him to be beyond knowledge."[507]

This irrational approach to reality is so typical of the Zen movement. An ancient Zen master would lift one of his fingers whenever he was asked the meaning of Zen—this was his answer. Others would slap the inquirer or kick a ball. A Zen student says, "I owe everything to my teacher because he taught me nothing." According to them, "When you don't understand, then you will know." This is in keeping with Lao-tse's famous aphorism "He who knows doesn't speak; he who speaks doesn't know." One Zen master goes so far as saying, "When the mouth opens, all are wrong."[508] Shankara, the famous Hindu philosopher, illustrates Eastern agnosticism. "Sir," said a pupil to his master, "teach me the nature of Brahman." The master did not reply. When a second and a third time he was importuned, he answered, "I teach you indeed, but you do not follow. His name is silence."[509]

The problem with the notion that 'reality is illogical' is not immediately apparent when one accepts the notion without reflection. Conditioned to think in this way, people seldom question the validity of the premise. If reality is illogical, how could one know reality? If reality is totally irrational, how does one differentiate between reality and fantasy? The Chinese mystic Lao-tse, founder of Taoism, points this out, "If, when I was asleep I was a man dreaming I was a butterfly, how do I know when I am awake I am not a butterfly dreaming I am a man." How could one judge falsity from truth if one cannot comprehend rationally? If God is beyond my conception then the very concept that 'God is one' would be meaningless.

What does one possibly understand by the following statement that was attributed to Buddha?

"I have not elucidated that the world is eternal, and I have not elucidated that the world is not eternal. I have not elucidated that the saint exists after death, I have not elucidated that the saint does not exist after death. I have not elucidated that the

507. *The Upanishads*, translated by Prabhavananda, S. and Manchester, F., Mentor Books, NY, pp. 30–31, 1957.
508. Reps, P., compiled by, *Zen Flesh and Zen Bones*, Penguin Books, Harmondsworth, p. 118, 1972.
509. Quoted in Prabhavananda, S., *The Spiritual Heritage of India*, Vedanta Press, Hollywood, p. 45, 1963.

saint both exists and does not exist after death."[510]

These esoteric statements sound very profound and impressive but no-one understands what they mean, not even the guru who made them. R.C. Sproul puts this delightfully:

> *"Absurdities often sound profound because they are incapable of being understood. When we hear things we do not understand, sometimes we think they are simply too deep or weighty for us to grasp when in fact they are merely unintelligible statements like 'one-hand clapping'."*[511]

Pantheists can't live consistently with their premise. If reality is illogical, why speak and write on reality? To speak and write one must use logic, without which no communication is possible. If the pantheist is not saying anything logical about ultimate reality, why should anyone follow the pantheist? Why is he advocating pantheism, and not theism or atheism? If logic does not matter why not accept any other belief system?

It is at this point that pantheism reveals its serious inconsistency. The position of the pantheist is either self-refuting or meaningless—there is no third possibility. If there is such a third possibility, is that rational? If it is not then it's irrational. It makes no sense to speak of a third category which transcends reason when the pantheist offers no evidence of ever crossing it. The Oxford scholar C.S. Lewis declares, "Unless human reasoning is valid no science can be true."[512] (See also ch. 5 section VII, The Bible led to modern science, p. 129).

If reality is not rational, then this statement, which says reality is not rational, is either saying something rational about reality, or it is not saying anything rational about reality. If it is not saying anything rational about reality then the pantheist in reality has said nothing about reality. If the statement is saying something true about reality then reality is not beyond reason. For if it is beyond reason how could the pantheist make reasonable statements of that which is beyond reason?

The following exchange is most instructive. After one of Dr Ravi Zacharias's university presentations on the uniqueness of Christ a professor challenged him with:

> *"Dr Zacharias, your presentation about Christ claiming and proving to be the only way to salvation is wrong for people in India because you're using 'either-or' logic. In the East we don't use 'either-or' logic—that's Western. In the East we use 'both-and' logic. So salvation is not either through Christ or nothing else, but both Christ and other ways."*[489]

The irony was not lost on people: an American-born professor in the West lecturing a man who was born and raised in India on how Indians think!

510. Quoted in Head, J. and Cranston, S.L. (Eds.), *Reincarnation: The Phoenix Fire Mystery*, Warner Books, New York, p. 61, 1977.
511. Sproul, R.C., *Knowing Scripture*, InterVarsity, Downers Grove, p. 17, 1978.
512. Lewis, C.S., *Miracles*, Fontana Books, London, p. 18, 1960.

The professor insisted that there were two types of logic. Ravi said, "Professor, I think we can resolve this debate very quickly with just one question." This was: "Are you saying that when I'm in India, I must use **either** the 'both-and logic' **or** nothing else?" The professor was speechless, so Ravi asked him again: "Are you saying that when I'm in India, I must use *either*," Ravi paused for effect, "the 'both-and logic' or," another pause, "nothing else?" The professor had to concede, "The either-or does seem to emerge, doesn't it."[489]

If reality is unreasonable then one has no basis for making reasonable statements about reality. A professor once started his class by saying, "Today our topic is 'The Inadequacy of Language'," and he proceeded with his lecture. After some time a student raised his hand and said, "Professor, if language is inadequate, then would it be pointless for us to sit here and listen to your words?" Another student understood the problem and stood up and proposed, "Yes! We are wasting our time if language is an inadequate tool for communication. We'd better leave this place and play squash." One by one the students left the class leaving the professor lecturing to himself. If words and reasons are inadequate why use them at all? R.C. Sproul is right, "When the laws of logic are violated, intelligible communication ceases."[513]

If God is beyond all thought, He is beyond the thought that He is beyond all thought. And He is beyond this thought as well and also the thought that this is so. If it is true that God is beyond thought, then the thought which says "God is beyond thought" is not true, hence it is false to say God is beyond thought. We cannot give a rational account of that which is absolutely irrational for then the irrational would be rational and it would not be absolutely irrational. If reality is totally irrational then how did I get to know so much about reality in order to make rational statements about ultimate reality? When logic is murdered, one is forced to attend the funeral of truth. The death of truth is inevitable when logic and common sense is abandoned.

513. Sproul, R.C., Gerstner, J. and Lindsley, A., *Classical Apologetics*, Zondervan, Grand Rapids, p. 76, 1984.

Very often, in order to justify their position, pantheistic mystics assert that their views could only be expressed in symbols. But under close analysis, this approach is no better. Professor C.E.M. Joad, after examining this position, concludes:

> *"I have never been able to make anything of symbolism. A symbol I understand to be a sign for something else. Either the symbolist knows what the something else is, in which case I cannot see why he should not tell us what it is straight out, instead of obscurely hinting at it in symbols, or he does not, in which case not knowing what the symbols stand for he cannot expect his readers to find out for him. Usually, I suspect, he does not, and his symbolism is merely a device to conceal his muddled thinking."*[514]

If a belief system is logically incoherent then it fails to pass the test for truth. It provides no sensible ground for belief. Philosopher H.J. Paton's wisdom is much needed at this point, "To declare war upon reason is to alienate all who care for truth and to hold open the door for the imposter and the zealot."[515]

3. Reality is Experience

Since pantheists say reality is irrational and the mind is incapable of conceiving reality, the door to reality is experience. The major emphasis of Eastern religion is meditation: looking into one's own nature, learning to control consciousness, becoming part of the cosmic oneness, losing one's identity and being one with the one. Mahatma Gandhi once told his followers to "turn the spotlight inward." A guru once told Os Guinness (1941–):

> *"To the Christian, talk of God is rather like the great bulk of an iceberg, whereas his experience of God is only the tiny tip of the iceberg; but for the Easterner the experience of God is the bulk of the iceberg, whereas his talk about God is only the tip."*[516]

Alan Watts (1915–1973), who was a leading advocate of Zen Buddhism, asserts, "It is one's own spiritual realization that makes the difference and the mind is its own place, and of itself can make a heaven of hell, a hell of heaven."[517] Sohaku Ogata in his *Zen*

514. Joad, C.E.M., *The Book of Joad*, Faber & Faber, London, pp. 72–73, 1944.
515. Paton, H.J., *The Modern Predicament*, Macmillan Press, London, p. 58, 1955. Paton (1887–1969) was Professor of Logic and Rhetoric at the University of Glasgow.
516. Guinness, ref. 473, p. 210.
517. Watts, A., *The Spirit of Zen*, Grove Press, New York, p. 80, 1958.

for the West writes:

> "The eye by which I see God is the same eye by which God sees me. My eye and God's are one and the same—one in seeing, one in knowing and one in loving … When I have shut the doors of my five senses, earnestly desiring God, I find him in my soul as clearly and as joyful as he is in eternity … Meditation, high thinking, and union with God, have drawn me to heaven."[518]

The *Upanishads* express that the non-rational final experience 'Turiya' (the state of highest blessedness):

> "Is not that which is conscious of the inner world … nor the outer world … nor both. It is not simple consciousness nor is it unconsciousness. It is unperceived, unrelated, incomprehensible, uninferable, unthinkable, and undescribable … it is the cessation of all phenomena; It is all peace, all bliss, non-dual."[519]

The underlying presupposition behind the view that reality can only be experienced is the notion that experience proves reality. But does subjective experience prove what we believe? When we reflect on experience it is worth remembering the remarks of philosopher Bertrand Russell who said, "We can make no distinction between the man who eats little and sees heaven and the man who drinks much and sees snakes." People who seek to prove their metaphysical beliefs on the basis of experience think metaphysics and experience are synonymous. What they fail to see is that experience is something one has and metaphysics is the interpretation of that experience. One should also remember that experiences are capable of many interpretations. No experience is, in the final analysis, self-interpreting. People with Eastern religious experience often say. "I had an experience but I cannot describe it to you." Persons with this mentality fail to see that experiences are meaningless unless describable. In other words, how can you know what you don't know? Experience is too weak a base on which to build one's eternal destiny. Followers of religions from Zen Buddhism to Mormonism have all used subjective experience to back up their beliefs. The fact that their beliefs conflict with one another disproves the claim that experience could validate one's belief system. An experience could be any number of things. It could be psychological, physiological, biblical or even demonic. Theologian Clark Pinnock substantiates this mode of thinking when he writes:

> "Religious sensation by itself can only prove itself. The assertion 'God exists' simply does not follow from the assertion 'I had an experience of God.' A psychological datum cannot automatically lead to a metaphysical discovery. However unique an experience may be, it is capable of a number of radically differing interpretations. It may be only an encounter with one's own subconscious."[520]

518. Ogata, S., *Zen for the West*, Dial Press, New York, pp. 17–19, 1959.
519. *Mandukya Upanishads* 7.
520. Pinnock, C.H., *Set Forth Your Case*, Craig Press, Nutley, NJ, p. 46, 1967.

Our psychological experience must be supported by objective, external criteria in order to validate our belief system. Professor Joad's insight is particularly valuable when he contrasts knowledge (truth) and feeling (experience). He wisely points out:

> *"Now the reason why knowledge is communicable and feeling is not is to be found in the fact that knowledge is of something other than and external to itself, whereas feeling reports nothing but the fact of the feeling. Knowledge, in short, involves a reference to something else, namely, that which is known; feeling does not."[521]*

At this point Paul T. Arveson's eloquent response to Eastern metaphysics should be noted, "Only when the axis of truth-value is accepted is it possible to communicate, live, and share in a society."[522] By starting from experience one simply has no means of checking his or her experience, for the simple reason that a subjective experience is too soft a ground to build the foundation of one's eternal hope. Subjectivism cannot be the basis for truth.

"What we learn from experience", argues C.S. Lewis, "depends on the kind of philosophy we bring to experience. It is therefore useless to appeal to experience before we have settled, as well as we can, the philosophical question."[523] Psychiatrist and minister Dr Walter Pahnke (1931–1971) rightly suggests, "It is misleading even to use the words 'I experienced' since during the peak of experience … there was no duality between myself and what I experienced."[524]

Carl Jung's striking remarks should be heeded, "We can never decide definitely whether a person is really enlightened, or whether he merely imagines it, we have no criterion of

521. Joad, C.E.M., *The Recovery of Belief*, Faber & Faber, London, p. 98, 1952.
522. Arveson, P.T., Dialogic—A Systems Approach to Understanding, *Journal of American Scientific Affiliation*, p. 51, June 1978.
523. Lewis, C.S., *Miracles*, Macmillan, New York, p. 11, 1948.
524. Pahnke, W., in DeBold, R. and Russell Leaf, R. (Eds.), *LSD, Man and Society*, Faber & Faber, London, p. 70, 1969.

this."[525] How can one be sure that it is God he is experiencing and not the devil, the Holy Spirit and not an evil spirit?

Beside the above reason, one should also carefully consider the element of psychological and spiritual dangers. When one totally depends on the sensuous, one could end up being senseless. Mystical experience is extremely dangerous, as William J. Petersen indicates, "The founder of the Krishna sect, Chaitanya, 'danced in such ecstasy, repeating the name of Hare, that he danced on into the sea at Puri and was drowned.'"[526] Masters and Houston wisely remark:

> "The history of transcendental experience bears testimony to the thin line that often separates the sublime from the demonic, and to the frequency with which the one may cross over into the other."[527]

The danger of mystical experience should not be overlooked. Consider the experience of Julio Ruibal, a former yoga master and guru who finally came to understand the powers of darkness in mystical experience. His comment is worth noting:

> "I advanced in the occult sphere so fast that I soon became the youngest guru in the Western Hemisphere, and one of the most advanced and powerful. Twice a week I taught yoga on television. Hatha-Yoga sounds like a nice simple set of exercises; everyone thinks it is just gymnastics. I want to warn that it is just the beginning of a devilish trap. After I became an instructor in Hatha-Yoga, my guru showed me that

525. Suzuki, D.T., *Introduction to Zen Buddhism*, Foreword, p. 15.
526. Petersen, ref. 502, p. 172.
527. Masters, R.E.L. and Houston, H., *Varieties of Psychedelic Experience*, Turnstone, London, p. 252, 1966.

the only thing these exercises do is open your appetite for the occult. They are like marijuana; they usually lead you on to a drug that is worse and stronger, binding you so completely that only Christ can deliver you. Many people think that occult power is just the power of the mind. This is not true. There is a point beyond which the power of the mind ends and the demonic power takes over."[528]

The wisdom of Princeton theologian B.B. Warfield (1851–1921) is remarkably relevant to those who are seeking for God in the wrong direction, "He who begins by seeking God within himself may end by confusing himself with God."[529] Divinity is not in humanity.

To look for God in man is like looking at yourself in the mirror and saying, "Here is God." Man beginning with himself has no basis of knowing the validity of his experience. Unless God has revealed Himself objectively and given us the content of his revelation, humans are lost and live in darkness.

III. THE CHRISTIAN ANSWER

The credibility of a religion depends on the justifiability of its truth claims. There are three basic criteria we commonly employ to determine the validity and truthfulness of a worldview. These criteria affirm that in order for a religion to be true it must be:

1. Logically Consistent,

2. Factually Verifiable,

3. Existentially Liveable.

It is meaningless to say that reality is beyond logic or that religion is a matter of faith and devoid of reason, for this very statement presupposes logic. Every meaningful statement is either logical or illogical. If it is logical then reality is logical but if the statement is not logical then it is meaningless, for a meaningless statement affirms nothing. David Freeman notes, "If beliefs are to make sense they must be consistent and not contradictory."[530]

528. Quoted in Weightman, C. and McCarthy, R.W., *A Mirage from the East*, Lutheran Publishing House, Adelaide, Australia, p. 8, 1977.

529. Warfield, B.B., *Biblical and Theological Studies*, Presbyterian and Reformed, Philadelphia, p. 455, 1952.

530. Freeman, D.H., *Know Your Self*, Craig Press, Nutley, NJ, p. 79, 1976.

The Christian faith is logically consistent, for it affirms the logically possible. Absurdities which are expressed in Hinduism and Buddhism (e.g. only God exists, the world is an illusion, no individuality, evil is an illusion, etc.) are not found in Christianity. The logical basis of Christianity is carefully argued in the writings of Thomas Aquinas, Augustine, James Oliver Buswell, Gordon H. Clark, E.J. Carnell, C. Stephen Evans, David Freeman, Stuart Hackett, William Hasker, C.F.H. Henry, Peter Kreeft, C.S. Lewis, Ronald Nash, Alvin Plantinga, Richard Purtill, David L. Wolfe, William Young, Ravi Zacharias, and others.

Secondly, the Christian faith is grounded and rooted in history. Unlike Eastern religion, which bases its teachings on abstract concepts, Christianity presents the reality of a living Christ who died and rose again for the salvation and liberation of man from sin. The facts of Christ and His Resurrection are historically verifiable like all other historical events that are verifiable. The works of John Warwick Montgomery, F.F. Bruce, Clark Pinnock, Craig Blomberg, William Lane Craig, Gary Habermas, J.P. Moreland, Bernard Ramm, William Ramsay, N.T. Wright, Mike Licona, James Patrick Holding, and others indicate beyond reasonable doubt that the Christian faith is based on good historical evidence.

Finally, the Christian worldview is existentially liveable. Christianity affirms the reality of a universe which has meaning, purpose and order. Everyone lives on the basis of the Christian concept of reality although few believe it. The point is that we must be able to live what we believe and believe what we live. Fine minds like G.K. Chesterton, Francis Schaeffer, Os Guinness, H. Blamires, Dinesh D'Souza, and others have provided excellent insights on how Christianity fits the facts of human life and experience.

Christianity provides a resource for the dignity, morality and the worthwhileness of humanity. Human beings are not just a cosmic accident, a speck of dust or a drop of water in an impersonal ocean. We are created in the image of God and are designed to have a meaningful relationship with our Creator. Professor Paul Krishna, a former Hindu, testifies to the reality of the resource found in Christ:

> *"As a Hindu I endured self-discipline and much study for one purpose—to better myself, to achieve heaven by my own deeds. Christianity starts with man's weakness. It asks us to accept our selfishness and inabilities, then promises a new nature. Christ came to heal the sick, not the well or self-sufficient."*[531]

Human beings need not despair and go on an eternal search for the Eternal, for the Eternal has come to the temporal: Jesus said, "I have come that they may have life, and have it to the full" (John 10:10).

---

531. Quoted in ref. 502, p. 172.

RECOMMENDED READING

- Chang, Lit-Sen, *Zen-Existentialism*, Presbyterian and Reformed, Philadelphia, 1969.

- Clark, David K., *The Pantheism of Alan Watts*, Inter-Varsity Press, Downers Grove, 1978.

- Hackett, Stuart, *Oriental Philosophy: A Westerner's Guide to Eastern Thought*, University of Wisconsin Press, Madison, 1979.

- Hunt, John, *Pantheism and Christianity*, Kennikat Press, New York, 1970.

- Means, Pat, *The Mystical Maze*, Campus Crusade for Christ, 1976.

- Zaehner, R.C., *Mysticism, Sacred and Profane*, Clarendon Press, Oxford Paperbacks, Oxford, 1961.

- Zacharias, Ravi, *New Birth or Rebirth? Jesus Talks with Krishna* (Great Conversations), Multnomah Books, 2008.

- Zacharias, Ravi, *The Lotus and the Cross: Jesus Talks with Buddha* (Great Conversations), Multnomah Books, 2010.

Muslims do not read the Quran and conclude that it is divine; rather they believe that it is divine, and then they read it.
— **WILFRED CANTWELL SMITH**

The Word did not become Flesh: the Word became a Book.
— **HENDRIK KRAEMER**

Islam confronts what is immutable in God with what is permanent in man.
— **FRITHJOF SCHUON**

8

THE CHALLENGE OF ISLAM

Over 30 years ago already, in a significant article on Islam, *Time* magazine declared, "Muslims are rediscovering their spiritual roots and reasserting the political power of the Islamic way of life." *Time* goes on to say, "The West can no longer afford to ignore or dismiss the living power of the prophet's message."[532]

As documented in ch. 6, almost a quarter of the world's population is Islamic. The continuing crisis in the Middle East illustrates the reality of its existence. "God may be dead in the West," asserts one observer, "but He is very much alive in the Middle East." And it's not just the middle East—Islam is making a great impact, both religiously and politically, around the globe.

From Malaysia to Morocco converts are being won to the Islamic faith. New centres for the propagation of Islam are emerging around the world. In some parts of Africa, Muslims are winning ten times as many converts as Christians.

Where Muslims gain power, it usually results in persecution of Christians. For example, "The last public Christian church in Afghanistan was razed in March 2010, according to the State Department's latest International Religious Freedom Report."[533]

The *Wall Street Journal* reports, "At least 54 Iraqi churches have been bombed and at least 905 Christians killed in various acts of violence since the U.S. invasion toppled Hussein in 2003 … Hundreds of thousands of Iraqi Christians have fled."[534]

Since Egypt's President Hosni Mubarak's regime started toppling in 2010, Islamic mobs have destroyed Coptic Christian churches and vandalized Copts' homes. For example,

532. *Time*, pp. 40,49, 16 April 1979.
533. Mora, E., Not a single Christian church left in Afghanistan, says State Department, cnsnews.com, 10 October 2011.
534. Dagher, S., An 'Arab Winter' chills Christians, online.wsj.com, 5 December 2011.

a car bomb exploded near one church, killing 21 and injuring 79 more.[535] Then the army slaughtered several dozen Copts when they protested against the destruction, and tens of thousands have fled.[536]

The Western world is not immune either. It was shocked on that fateful morning of '9-11' in 2001, which proved *Time* right: Muslim terrorists murdered 3,000 people in America. But all this was a long time coming, and much of the West was asleep. The American theologian Bruce Demarest warned 30 years ago:

> *"Through such movements as the World Community of Islam, the religion of Mohammed is vigorously contending today for the souls of America. It boldly claims to possess the answers to evils such as alcoholism, promiscuity, the breakdown of the family, and racism that plague American life."[537]*

In the UK, London was hit with Muslim suicide bombers in July 2005. After this, the Egyptian-born Jewish political commentator in Britain, 'Bat Ye'or' (1933–), even wrote a book called *Eurabia* in 2005.[538] Another British Jewish writer, Melanie Phillips (1951–), wrote *Londonistan* in 2006.[539]

Europe also needs to face Islam, because many European cities have a large and growing Muslim population. Witness the riots around the world when Danish cartoons about Muhammad were published. Dutch film-maker Theo van Gogh was murdered in the street for criticizing Islam. Think of the riots throughout France. Ambulance and other service vehicles entering 'Muslim' suburbs in European cities now require security (police) escorts.

Legal scholar Dr Augusto Zimmerman, a Vice-President of the Australian Society of Legal Philosophy, writes:

> *"Every year, Freedom House, a secular organization, conducts a survey to analyze the situation of democracy and human rights across the globe. Year after year, it concludes that the most rights-based and democratic nations are the majority-Protestant ones. On the other hand, Islam and Marxism, the latter a secular religion, seem to offer the most serious obstacles for the realization of democracy and human rights. In fact, the denial of the broadest range of basic human rights comes precisely from Marxist and majority-Muslim countries. The worst violators of human rights are Libya, Saudi Arabia, Sudan, Syria, Turkmenistan, and the one-party Marxist regimes of Cuba and North Korea."[540]*

535. Ayoub, J., Were Coptic Christians better off under Hosni Mubarak? christianpost.com, 23 November 2011.
536. Jacoby, J., For Arab Christians, a Wintry 'Spring', *patriotpost.us*, 7 December 2011.
537. Demarest, B., *General Revelation,* Zondervan, Grand Rapids, p. 17, 1982.
538. Bat Ye'Or, *Eurabia: The Euro-Arab Axis,* Fairleigh Dickinson University Press, 2005. The author's pen name is Hebrew (בת יאור) for 'Daughter of the Nile'; her real name is Gisèle Littman, née Orebi.
539. Phillips, M., *Londonistan,* Encounter Books, 2006.
540. Zimmermann, A., The Christian foundations of the rule of law in the West: a legacy of liberty and resistance against tyranny, *J. Creation* **19**(2):67–73, 2005; creation.com/law.

Europe has proved vulnerable to Islamism precisely because the prevailing atheistic culture is too morally weak to cope with it (see ch. 3).[541,542] The great poet and playwright T.S. Eliot (1888–1965) had warned about this over 60 years ago:

> "It is in Christianity that our arts have developed; it is in Christianity that the laws of Europe have—until recently—been rooted. It is against a background of Christianity that all our thought has significance. An individual European may not believe that the Christian Faith is true, and yet what he says, and makes, and does, will all spring out of his heritage of Christian culture and depend upon that culture for its meaning. Only a Christian culture could have produced a Voltaire or a Nietzsche. I do not believe that the culture of Europe could survive the complete disappearance of the Christian faith. And I am convinced of that, not merely because I am a Christian myself, but as a student of social biology.
>
> "If Christianity goes, the whole of our culture goes. Then you must start painfully again, and you cannot put on a new culture ready made. You must wait for the grass to grow to feed the sheep to give the wool out of which your new coat will be made. You must pass through many centuries of barbarism. We should not live to see the new culture, nor would our great-great-great-grandchildren: and if we did, not one of us would be happy in it."[543]

In our own time, Peter Hitchens (1951–), a fairly recent convert to Christianity thus an opponent of his 'New Atheist' brother Christopher (1949–2011), writes:

> "Only one reliable force stands in the way of the power of the strong over the weak … Only one reliable force restrains the hand of the man of power. And in an age of power-worship, the Christian religion has become the principal obstacle to the desire of earthy utopians for absolute power."[544]

None other than Richard Dawkins tacitly admits this:

541. See Sarfati, J. and Catchpoole, D., When will Europe wake up? Council of Europe 'condemns creationism' (but it ought to reconsider where the 'threat to human and civic rights' is really coming from); creation.com/europe, 1 February 2008.
542. Phillips, M., *World Upside Down*, Encounter Books, NY, 2010. See review by British engineer and apologist Dominic Statham, A revealing insight into European and world politics, *J. Creation* **25**(1):30–32, 2011; creation.com/phillips.
543. Eliot, T.S., *Notes Towards the Definition of Culture*, 1948.
544. Hitchens, P., *The Rage Against God: How Atheism Led Me to Faith*, Zondervan, 2010.

"There are no Christians, as far as I know, blowing up buildings. I am not aware of any Christian suicide bombers. I am not aware of any major Christian denomination that believes the penalty for apostasy is death. I have mixed feelings about the decline of Christianity, in so far as Christianity might be a bulwark against something worse."[545]

So it's vital to defend the 'bulwark'. Nothing else will withstand such a strongly held belief system. Charles Colson, one of President Nixon's 'Watergate Seven' who converted to Christianity after conviction, has affirmed that Christianity, "has always provided not only a vigorous defence of human rights but also the sturdiest bulwark against tyranny."[546]

Sadly, even within the Church, there are those who have largely abandoned the power of the Gospel, preferring the empty 'social gospel' of liberal theology. Thus the Archbishop of Canterbury, Rowan Williams, stated a few years ago that adoption of sharia law in the UK seems unavoidable.[547]

I.   THE RELIABILITY OF THE NEW TESTAMENT

Islam, like Judaism and Christianity, claims to be the climax of divine revelation. The source of this revelation is the Koran. In his popular work *Understanding Islam* Frithjof Schuon epitomizes the Islamic approach:

"If the Quran contains elements of polemic concerning Christianity and, for stronger reasons, concerning Judaism, it is because Islam came after these religions, and this means that it was obliged … to put itself forward as an improvement on what came before it."[548]

The Muslim believes that the Koran is the Word of God given to their prophet Mohammed who is regarded as the greatest and the last (or seal) of the prophets. The Koran presents Adam, Noah, Abraham, Moses, Jesus and the other biblical characters as genuine prophets of God. Jesus Christ is given great titles, but His divinity is rejected. In many cases Jesus is presented in unusual terms and set forth as being superior to all other prophets; however Mohammed is accepted as the final prophet.

"The teachings of Islam are summarized in the Five Doctrines and the Five Pillars. Professor Norman Anderson points out that, 'It is these Five Pillars, and particularly the profession of the creed and the performance of prayer and fasting, which chiefly make up the practice of Islam to the average Muslim.'"[549]

545. Cited by Gledhill, R., Scandal and schism leave Christians praying for a 'new Reformation', *The Times* (UK), 2 April 2010.
546. Colson, C. and Pearcey, N., *How Now Shall We Live?* Tyndale, Wheaton, IL, p. 131, 1999.
547. Phillips, M., The Archbishop's speech, *Spectator.co.uk*, 7 February 2008. See also "Church of England apologises to Darwin"; creation.com/anglican, 20 September 2008.
548. Schuon, F., *Understanding Islam*, translated by Matheson, D.M., Penguin Books, Baltimore, MD, p. 56, 1972.
549. Anderson, N. (Ed.), *The World's Religions*, Inter-Varsity Press, London, p. 120, 1975.

Muslims believe that the Bible was corrupted by the early Christians. They argue that false ideas and teaching were introduced into the Scriptures thus distorting the original teachings of Jesus Christ. They teach that "the ungodly ones among them changed that word into another than that which had been told them" (Surah 7:162). It says "Woe to those who write the Book with their own hands, And then say: 'This is from God,' to traffic with it for a miserable price!" (2:79). The verse that disturbs most Muslim is Surah 10:94. This verse states "If you were in doubt as to what We have revealed unto you, then ask those who have been reading the Book from before you: the Truth has indeed come to you from your Lord: so be in no wise of those in doubt." To suggest that the Bible has been corrupted is to go against this verse.

Maurice Bucaille, an Islamic apologist, writes, "As for the Gospels nobody can claim that they invariably contain faithful accounts of Jesus' words or a description of His actions strictly in keeping with reality."[550] In his book *Muhammad and Christ*, Maulvi Muhammad Ali asserts, "The basis of Christian religion is based on the most unreliable record."[551] Bucaille goes so far as to say that "We do not in fact have an eye witness account from the life of Jesus, contrary to what many Christians imagine."[552]

However, contrary to popular opinion, the New Testament is supported by a wealth of manuscripts unlike most classical documents. F.F. Bruce, the New Testament scholar, writes:

> *"The evidence for our New Testament writing is ever so much greater than the evidence for many writings of classical authors, the authenticity of which no-one dreams of questioning."[553]*

The New Testament is unusual in its accuracy, history and archaeology. Leading textual scholars who have studied the materials conclude that they are reliable. This conviction is shared, not only by those who maintain a conservative position, but even by those who come from the radical left. One such scholar is John A.T. Robinson, whose radical theology is well expressed in his popular volume *Honest to God*. In 1976 Robinson authored a new book, *Redating the New Testament*, which shocked the scholarly world. His research provided many evidences for the reliability of the New Testament.

Professor Joachim Jeremias makes a valuable comment concerning the authenticity of the New Testament:

> *"The linguistic and stylistic evidence shows so much faithfulness and such respect towards the tradition of the sayings of Jesus that we are justified in drawing up the*

550. Bucaille, M., *The Bible, The Quran and Science*, North American Trust Publication, Paris, p. 127, 1978.
551. Maulvi Muhammad Ali, *Muhammad and Christ* (Lahore: Ahmadiah Anjuman-i-Ishaet-l-Islam, Lahore, p. 15, 1921.
552. Bucaille, ref. 550, p. 108.
553. Bruce, F.F., *The New Testament Documents: Are They Reliable?* Eerdmans, Grand Rapids, MI, p. 15, 1977.

following principle of method: in the synoptic tradition it is the inauthenticity, and not the authenticity, of the sayings of Jesus that must be demonstrated."[554]

These facts provide good reason for one to accept the authenticity of the New Testament. As Clark Pinnock remarks, "Pessimism concerning the trustworthiness of the New Testament is utterly unwarranted, and generally reflects ignorance of the facts."[555]

The Christian is in a far better position to argue for the New Testament than the Muslim is for his Koran. In his work *The Sacred Writings of the World's Great Religions*, Dr S.E. Frost writes:

> *"Consequently, some twelve years later Othman, third Caliph, commanded that all copies of the original work be destroyed and a new authentic version be prepared. This accepted volume contains scraps of beliefs from many religious sources, chief of which are Arabic traditions and folk lore, Zoroastrianism, the Jewish and Christian theology."[556]*

554. Jeremias, J., *New Testament Theology, The Proclamation of Jesus*, Scribner's, New York, p. 37, 1971.
555. Pinnock, C., *Set Forth Your Case*, Craig Press, Nutley, N J, p. 52, 1967.
556. Frost, S.E., *The Sacred Writings of the World's Great Religions*, The New Home Library Series, The Blakiston Co., Philadelphia, p. 67, 1948.

Josh McDowell and John Gilchrist assert that:

> *"There is concrete evidence in the best works of Islamic tradition (e.g. the* Sahih of Muslim, *the* Sahih of Bukhari, *the* Mishkat-ul-Masabih*), that from the start the Qur'an had numerous variant and conflicting readings."*[557]

II.   THE RATIONALITY OF THE TRINITY

Although there may be many similarities between Islam and Christianity, there is nothing which divides the two religions more radically than their views of God. As we said in ch. 6, p. 104, Christians believe the doctrine of the Trinity: that in the unity of the Godhead there are three eternal and co-equal Persons: Father, Son and Holy Spirit, the same in essence but distinct in role—three Persons (or three centres of consciousness) and one Being. This is a corollary of the Deity of Christ (see ch. 4).

A well educated Muslim once told a Christian, "Whenever you Christians speak of Jesus as the 'Son of God' it makes our blood boil."[558] The Muslim view of God is expressed in seven words: *La ilaha illa Allah, Mohammed rasul Allah*—"There is no god but Allah (and) Mohammed is the prophet of Allah." This is their fundamental conviction of God. Just to repeat this creed *ipso facto* one becomes a true believer.

According to philosopher David Freeman, "The fundamental conception of Allah or God is impersonal and negative. He is a vast monad[559] that has no resemblance to anything known or to any creature." He further adds, "God is so different from his creatures that very little can be postulated of him."[560] The Koran in Surah 112 claims, "There is not to him a single equal." This idea is well expressed in a popular song, "Whatsoever your mind can conceive, That Allah is not, you may believe." God is totally other and there is nothing by which he could be compared. If this be the case then in the Islamic context God is totally unknowable. William McElwee Miller (1892–1993), American missionary to Persia, is right:

> *"Such a God is therefore unknowable, for all that can be said of Him is that He is not this or that. While God's name is often on the lips of Moslems, He is to most of them an unknown Being."*[561]

Miller agrees with Raymond Lull (or Ramon Llull, 1232–1315), the first great missionary to Muslims, that, "The greatest deficiency in the Moslem religion is in its conception of God."[561]

One of the most serious deficiencies is that there is no way that the Muslim God can be said

557. McDowell, J. and Gilchrist, J., *The Islam Debate*, Here's Life Publishers, San Bernardino, CA, p. 50, 1983.

558. Cited in Jones, L.B., *The People of the Mosque*, YMCA Publishing House, Calcutta, p. 277, 1939.

559. 'Monad' is a term in Greek philosophy meaning a solitary, indivisible single divine being (from μονάς *monas*, 'unit' from μόνος *monos*, 'alone').

560. Freeman, D., *A Philosophical Study of Religion*, The Craig Press, Nutley, NJ, pp. 122–123, 1964.

561. Miller, W.M., "Islam", in Vos, H.F. (Ed.), *Religions in a Changing World*, Moody Press, Chicago, p. 70, 1959.

to be a 'God of Love'. But according to the Bible, "God is love" (1 John 4:8,16). A Unitarian God, such as Islam's Allah, could not be a God of Love *in his nature*, since by definition love requires *another person* to be the recipient. Allah might conceivably be able to love *after* he created, but that would make love *contingent on creation*, not an intrinsic property of Allah.

But with the true God of the Bible, the love between God the Father and God the Son has always existed, even before creation. Furthermore, the Bible reveals a third person who is God, the Holy Spirit. This enables an even more perfect love that includes not only individual love, but *collective* love. This is the sort that should occur in a family, where the husband and wife love not only each other, but combine their love towards their child.

Christians share with the Muslims their denial of polytheism—the pantheon of numerous gods. Mohammed is right, that if Christians believe in three gods they are no better. But this is where the founder of Islam sadly misunderstood Christianity. Thomas Hughes provides the reasons for this misunderstanding:

> *"The controversies regarding the nature and person of our Divine Lord had begotten a sect of Tri-theists led by a Syrian philosopher named John Philoponus of Alexandria, and are sufficient to account for Muhammed's conception of the Blessed Trinity. The worship of the Virgin Mary had also given rise to a religious controversy between the Antiduo-Marianites and the Collyruduabs … Under the circumstances, it is not surprising to find that the mind of the Arabian reformer turned away from Christianity and endeavoured to construct a religion on the lines of Judaism."[562]*

Mohammed's misconception of the doctrine of the Trinity is equally transparent in the Koran. His notions about the Trinity are far removed from biblical evidence. The Koran clearly contradicts the central teaching of Holy Scriptures on the divinity of Christ. Surah 5:78 states, "Jesus Christ the son of Mary was no more than an Apostle." According to Dr Phil Parshall, a missionary in Bangladesh for 21 years and author of nine books on Islam:

> *"Muslims generally believe the dynamic of the Trinity consists of God the Father's having sexual intercourse with Mary the mother of Jesus, who was the second member of the Trinity. This union resulted in the birth of Jesus as the third person of the Godhead."[563]*

In Surah 4:171 Mohammed eloquently states Muslims' dominant attitude toward the Christian God:

> *"O people of the Scripture! Do not exaggerate in your religion nor utter aught concerning Allah save the truth. The Messiah, Jesus son of Mary, was only a messenger of Allah, and His Word which He cast into Mary, and a spirit from Him.*

562. Hughes, T., *Dictionary of Islam*, Reference Book Publishers, Clifton, NJ, p. 53, 1965.
563. Parshall, P., *New Paths in Muslim Evangelism: Evangelical Approaches to Contextualization*, Baker Book House, Grand Rapids, MI, p. 142, 1980.

So believe in Allah and His messengers, and say not three—cease! (it is) better for you! Allah is only one God. Far is it removed from His transcendent majesty that He should have a son."

The Muslims conceive God in terms of mathematical unity, hence reasoning from this point of view, God is by definition indivisible. The logic by which the Muslim reasons is as follows: If Father is God, The Son is God and, The Holy Spirit is God, mathematically the answer is three Gods $(1 + 1 + 1 = 3)$.

$$GOD = 1 \times 1 \times 1 = 1$$

Thus the Muslims argue that the Christian God is irrational (they never consider the possibility that the correct mathematics is $1 \times 1 \times 1 = 1$!). But before answering, we must note a double standard. Do not the Muslims argue that Allah is unlike his creatures and there is nothing to equal him? If this is the case, why do the Muslims limit God to human dimension and limit God to the confines of their own understanding? God is not a man that He should fit into our categories.

But the Trinity is *not* irrational. The one-ness and three-nesses are used in difference senses, so there is no contradiction. God is one in *essence*, but three in *person*. To put it in another way, in God there is one What and three Whos. What is God? God is one in essence. Who is God? He is the Father, the Son and the Holy Spirit.

Anglican (Episcopal) Priest Robert Brow makes an important point, "The Christian vision of the unity of God is not mathematical but rather organic. The electron, proton and neutron in the simplest atom are not added to make three, but held together by atomic force to form one unit." Hence, argues Brow, "If God is a living God, we should not therefore be surprised to find a complexity within his unity."[564] Writing on the same subject, Phil Parshall states:

> *"Aristotle pointed out that the word* one *is used in more than one sense. It can be used to indicate oneness of quantity or oneness of essence. For instance, a molecule of water may be 'one' numerically without being one or single in its essence, as its formula H_2O indicates."[565]*

564. Brow, R., *Religion, Origins and Ideas*, Tyndale Press, London, pp. 89–90, 1966.
565. Parshall, ref. 563, p. 143.

NB: like all analogies, it can't be carried too far. Hydrogen and oxygen atoms are parts of the water molecule, but the three persons are NOT 'parts' of God, Indeed, each Person has the fullness of the Godhead (see Colossians 2:9). A better analogy is that space contains three dimensions, yet the dimensions are not 'parts'—the concept of 'space' is meaningless without all three dimensions.

One ancient analogy compares Father and Son to the sun and its light (and the Holy Spirit could be the heat): the light's source is the sun, but the sun's very nature is to emit light (as per Genesis 1:14 ff. God made the sun precisely as a lightgiver to earth). Similarly, God the Son is eternally begotten of the Father, while the Father's nature is to beget the Son eternally. This is reflected in the classic Nicene Creed of AD 325:

> *"We believe in one Lord, Jesus Christ, the only Son of God, eternally begotten of the Father, God from God, Light from Light, true God from true God, begotten, not made, of one Being with the Father. Through him all things were made."*

Thus the Trinity does not involve any contradiction as some believe. It does not violate the laws of logic. It may go beyond logic but never against it. The Trinity is neither a metaphysical absurdity nor a mathematical nonsense. Very often the doctrine of the Trinity is rejected not because it is illogical but, as Dale Rhoton correctly observes, "One of the main reasons people object to the doctrine of the Trinity is that they automatically think of God as a Being with one centre of consciousness."[566] If we approach God with this disposition our minds will always remain in the dark as to His truth and reality. We concur with the judgment of J.S. Wright:

> *"If we start with the fixed idea that the unity of the Godhead means a bare mathematical unity, and that the divine Son-ship inevitably means that the Father existed before the Son, Scripture then cannot be clear to us, since we have tried to fix it into an arbitrary pattern of thinking."*[567]

Dr John Warwick Montgomery's insightful remarks on the subject are worthy of note:

> *"The doctrine of the Trinity is not 'irrational'; what is irrational is to suppress the biblical evidence for Trinity in favour of Unity, or the evidence for Unity in favour of Trinity. Our data must take precedence over our models—or, stating it better, our models must sensitively reflect the full range of data."*[568]

The data of Scripture clearly points to a triune God. The greatest reason why Christians accept the doctrine of the Trinity is that we cannot make sense of many important biblical passages unless the Trinity is true. The New Testament is meaningless without the concept of the Trinity. This can be shown in logical steps (from creation.com/trinity):

566. Rhoton, D., *The Logic of Faith*, STL Books, Bromley, Kent, p. 74, 1972.
567. Wright, J.S., The perspicuity of Scripture, *Theological Student's Fellowship Bulletin* **24**:6–9, Summer 1959; p. 7.
568. Montgomery, J.W., *How Do We Know There is a God?* Bethany Fellowship, Minneapolis, MN, p. 14, 1973.

- There is only *one* God (Deuteronomy 6:4, Isaiah 44:8). Note that the Hebrew word for 'one' is *echad*, which means composite unity—it is used in Genesis 2:24 where the husband and wife become "one flesh". The word for absolute unity is *yachid*, which is never used of God in the Scripture.

- The *Father* is called God (John 6:27, Ephesians 4:6).

- The *Son* is called God (Hebrews 1:8. He is also called "I am" in John 8:58 cf. Exodus. 3:14). He has always existed (John 1:1–3, 8:56–58), but took on full human nature in addition to His divine nature at the Incarnation (John 1:14, Philippians 2:5–11).

- The *Holy Spirit* is called God (Acts 5:3–4), and is personal (Acts 13:2), not some impersonal force as the Jehovah's Witnesses believe.

- They are *distinct*, e.g. at the baptism of Jesus in Matthew 3:16–17 all three were present and distinct. The Son is baptized, the Father speaks from Heaven, and the Holy Spirit, in the form of a dove, flies down and lands on the Son. See the baptismal formula in Matthew 28:19 "baptizing them in the name of the Father and of the Son and of the Holy Ghost". Note that the word "name" is singular, showing that all three Persons are one Being.

All these propositions, when combined, form the Trinity doctrine. Thus the Bible teaches the Trinity by logical deduction.

The fact is that God has revealed Himself in the Bible as Father, Son and Holy Spirit. The evidence for this is clearly revealed in the following verses: Matthew 28:19; 2 Corinthians 1:21–22; 13:14; 1 Corinthians 6:11; 12:4,5; Galatians 3:11–14; 1 Thessalonians 5:18–19; 1 Peter 1:2; John 1:1–3; 10:30,33; 14:9; 20:17; Colossians 2:9.

What puzzles the rational mind is not the doctrine of the Trinity, but the teaching of the Koran. Jesus Christ is presented as far superior to Mohammed in birth, title, deeds, power and position yet we are asked to follow Mohammed. The Jesus of the Koran is something of a mystery. Why is Jesus unique if Mohammed is the greatest prophet? Why is Jesus called the Messiah? Why was His birth miraculous if He was not the greatest of God's messengers?

III. THE REALITY OF THE RESURRECTION

The Christian faith is not based on an abstract metaphysical concept nor an illusory esoteric principle. Christianity is grounded and rooted in an important historical spacetime event— the death and the Resurrection of Jesus Christ. It is not views but news. We explained the evidence for this in ch. 1, p. 41. The good news, that God in Jesus Christ has visited our planet and has solved our problem of sin and death.

The Apostle Paul in a significant chapter in the book of First Corinthians states, "If Christ has not been raised, your faith is futile; you are still in your sins … If only for this life we have hope in Christ, we are to be pitied more than all men" (15:17,19). Unlike Islam, Christianity appeals to historical facts and evidence to authenticate its claims and credibility. But Islam denies these claims and rejects the evidences. The Koran says, "But they killed him not, nor crucified him, but so it was made to appear to them" (4:157). Agreeing with this verse Yusuf Ali points out, "The Quranic teaching is that Christ was not crucified, nor killed by the Jews, notwithstanding certain apparent circumstances which produced that illusion in the minds of some of his enemies."[569] It is the basic conviction of most Muslims that Jesus never died on the Cross. They are uncertain as to what actually took place but they emphatically deny his death on the Cross.

Maulvi Muhammad Ali rightly sees the logic of the Christian position but wrongly denies its evidences. He writes:

> *"Christ never died on the cross and he never rose from the dead: the preaching of the Christian missionary is therefore vain and vain is also his faith. The Christian religion laid its foundation on the death of Christ on the cross and his subsequent rising; both these statements have been proved to be utterly wrong."[570]*

It stands to reason that if Christ did not die and rise from the dead, then the Christian faith is utterly false, but if Christ did rise from the dead, then logic dictates that Christianity is the truth.

The Muslim's rejection of the crucifixion is illogical and has no basis in history. This position actually poses more problems and creates numerous absurdities. One could only maintain this position at the expense of facts and evidences. This view implies that the Roman centurions who were responsible for the death of Jesus were careless and irresponsible. Dr John W. Montgomery rightly points out:

> *"Jesus surely died on the cross, for Roman crucifixion teams knew their business (they had enough practice). He could not possibly have rolled the heavy boulder from the door of the tomb after the crucifixion experience."[571]*

Furthermore, Christianity would have been dead at

569. Abdullah Yusuf Ali, *The Holy Quran: Text, Translation and Commentary* (Qatar National Printing Press, 1946), p. 230.
570. Maulvi Muhammed Ali, ref. 551, pp. 158–159.
571. Montgomery, J.W., *History and Christianity*, InterVarsity Press, Downers Grove, IL, p. 77, 1964.

birth if its enemies could have produced the body, with the distinctive crucifixion damage. Yet they were unable to. Paul told the cosmopolitan Corinthian church that Jesus had appeared to 500 people at once, and most were still alive so could be questioned.

The evidence for the Resurrection of Christ is unbeatable.

Those who examined the evidence with an open mind have been persuaded to believe it.[572] Lord Caldecote, Lord Chief Justice of England, wrote after examining the evidence, "The claims of Jesus Christ, namely His Resurrection, has led me as often as I have tried to examine the evidence to believe it as a fact beyond dispute."[573] Lord Lyndhurst was one of the greatest legal minds in the history of England. He was three times High Chancellor of England and was elected High Steward of Cambridge University. His verdict on the Resurrection is, "I know pretty well what evidence is; and, I tell you, such evidence as that for the Resurrection has never broken down yet."[574]

The British lawyer, Frank Morison, set out to write a book that would finally refute the Resurrection. Thinking that the Resurrection was nothing but a fairy-tale, he started his research, but after months of carefully sifting through the evidence he was forced to the opposite conclusion. He fell on his knees and accepted Christ as his own personal, living saviour. He then wrote a book with the title *Who Moved the Stone*, with the first chapter entitled "The Book that Refused to be Written." He could not logically refute the evidence but was forced by the facts to embrace the truth of the Resurrection.[575]

More recently, the lawyer Clarrie Briese, formerly Chief Magistrate of New South Wales, Australia, and famous corruption fighter, trained his legal mind on the Gospels.[576] He pointed out that the Gospel authors were men of great honesty:

> *"Now it is true that many people in history have died because they believed in and fought for a lie, but in every case these people did not believe it to be a lie. They thought it to be the truth, worth dying for."*

Briese also points out:

> *"Classical historians have shown that even two full generations would not be sufficient for myths to overcome a historical core. Thus the time gap between the Gospel writings and the events they record are not long enough to affect matters of substance in their accounts."*

---

572. See also Clifford, R., *Leading Lawyers Look at the Resurrection*, Australia/New Zealand: Albatross; UK: Lion; Canada: Canadian Institute for Law, Theology & Public, 1991.
573. Quoted in Linton, I.H., *A Lawyer Examines the Bible*, Baker Book House, Grand Rapids, MI, p. 11, 1943.
574. Quoted in Smith, W.M., *Therefore Stand*, Keats Publishing, New Caanan, CN, p. 425, 1981.
575. Morison, F., *Who Moved the Stone*, Faber and Faber, London, 1958.
576. Briese, C., Can we believe the Gospels? A former chief magistrate examines the witnesses to the resurrection; creation.com/gospeltrue, 28 March 2007.

Briese also shows that the Resurrection account is further supported by many witnesses and accuracy of detail. He concludes:

> *"To summarise, one is left to say that the only rational conclusion is that the witnesses to the resurrection of Jesus Christ are witnesses of the highest credibility. If we are unable to accept their histories, why would we accept the histories of any other incidents in the human race?"*

The existence of Islam indicates man's search for answers, but no matter how hard he tries he will never in Islam find the Answer. Unless God personally reveals His truth, man will forever remain in the dark regarding the purpose of his life and the meaning of his ultimate existence. The answer to Islam is the same answer which Christians have found in Jesus Christ. He is a living Saviour, while Muhammad stayed in his tomb. Former Muslim Daud Rahbar, professor in the Islamic Department of Punjab University in Pakistan, answers the question of every Muslim:

> *"If the Biblical narrative about Jesus is a myth and if the Creator is other than that Divine Martyr Jesus, then He is a Creator who ought to vacate His heavenly throne for the Superior Being Jesus. But the truth is that the Eternal Creator and the Divine Martyr Jesus are one and the same Being."*[577]

Indeed so. And that truth ultimately demands a response from each one of us. As this Eternal Creator made flesh, the great Logos of God, the Lord Jesus Christ, stated in John 3:16–18:

> *"For God so loved the world, that he gave his only Son, that whoever believes in him should not perish but have eternal life. For God did not send his Son into the world to condemn the world, but in order that the world might be saved through him. Whoever believes in him is not condemned, but whoever does not believe is condemned already, because he has not believed in the name of the only Son of God."*

577. Quoted in Rhoton, ref. 566, p. 90.

RECOMMENDED READING

- *Answering Islam: A Christian-Muslim Dialog and Apologetic*, answering-islam.org.

- Cragg, Kenneth, *The Call of the Minaret*, Oxford University Press, New York, 1956.

- Caner, Ergun Mehmet and Caner, Emir Fethi, *Unveiling Islam*, Kregel, Grand Rapids, MI, 2004.

- Geisler, Norman and Saleddb, Abdul, *Answering Islam*, Baker, Grand Rapids, 1993).

- Marrison, G.E., *The Christian Approach to the Muslim*, Edinburgh House Press, London, 1959.

- McDowell, Josh and Gilchrist, John, *The Islam Debate*, Here's Life Publishers, San Bernardino, CA, 1983.

- Miller, William McElwee, *A Christian's Response to Islam*, Presbyterian and Reformed, Philadelphia, 1976.

- Pfander, C.G. and Tisdall, William St. Clair, *The Mizan-Ul-Haqq*, The Religious Tract Society, London, 1910.

- Spencer, Robert, *The Politically Incorrect Guide to Islam (And the Crusades)*, Regnery, 2005.

- Spencer, Robert, *Religion of Peace? Why Christianity Is and Islam Isn't*, Regnery, 2007.

- Strobel, Lee, *The Case for the Real Jesus: A Journalist Investigates Current Attacks on the Identity of Christ*, Zondervan, Grand Rapids, MI, 2009.

- Strobel, Lee, *The Case for the Resurrection: A First-Century Investigative Reporter Probes History's Pivotal Event*, Zondervan, Grand Rapids, MI, 2010.

- Tisdall, W. St. Clair, *Christian Reply to Muslim Objections*, Light of Life, Villach, Austria, 1980.

BIBLIOGRAPHY

"give attention to reading"—the Apostle Paul
(1 Timothy 4:13, KJV)

- Adair, James R. and Miller, Ted (Eds.), *Escape from Darkness*, Victor Books, Wheaton, 1982.
- Albrecht, Mark, *Reincarnation: A Christian Appraisal*, InterVarsity, Downers Grove, 1982.
- Albright, W.F., *The Archaeology of Palestine and the Bible*, Revell, New York, 1935.
- Allen, Woody, My philosophy, *The New Yorker*, p. 25, 27 December 1969.
- Anderson, J.N.D., *Christianity and Comparative Religion*, Inter-Varsity Press, Downers Grove, 1970.
- Anderson, J.N.D., *Christianity: The Witness of History*, Tyndale, London, 1969.
- Anderson, Sir Norman, *Jesus Christ: The Witness of History*, InterVarsity, 1985.
- Anderson, Sir Norman (Ed.), *The World's Religions*, Eerdmans, Grand Rapids, 1976.
- John Ankerberg, John Weldon and Walter Kaiser, *The Case for Jesus the Messiah: Incredible Prophecies that Prove God Exists*, Harvest House, Eugene, OR, 1989.
- Archer, Gleason L., *Encyclopedia of Bible Difficulties*, Zondervan, Grand Rapids, 1982.
- Aristotle, *Metaphysics*, translated by Hope, R., University of Michigan Press, 1960.
- Arnold, Thomas, *Sermons on the Christian Life: Its Hopes, Its Fears, and Its Close*, London, 1859.
- Ayer, A.J., *Language, Truth and Logic*, Dover, New York, 1952.
- Bach, Marcus, *Major Religions of the World*, Abingdon Press, New York, 1959.
- Badham, Leslie, *Verdict on Jesus*, Hodder & Stoughton, London, 1950.
- Bahnsen, Greg vs Stein, Gordon, *The Great Debate: Does God Exist?* Debate held at the University of California, 1985, transcript available at bellevuechristian.org, last accessed 25 May 2011.
- Baisnée, Jules A. (Ed.), *Readings in Natural Theology*, Newman Press, Westminister, MD, 1962.
- Ballard, Frank, *Christianity Reality in Modern Light*, Kelley, London, 1916.
- Ballard, Frank, *The Miracles of Unbelief*, T. & T. Clark, Edinburgh, 1904.
- Barth, Karl, *Church Dogmatics*, The Doctrine of Word of God, Volume **1**, Clark, Edinburgh, 1936.
- Barth, Karl, *Church Dogmatics*. Volume **III**, Bromiley, G. and Torrance, T.F. (Eds.), Clark, Edinburgh, 1960.
- Bavinck, J.H., *The Church Between Temple and Mosque*, Eerdmans, Grand Rapids, 1981.
- Berger, Peter, *A Rumor of Angels: Modern Society and the Rediscovery of the Supernatural*, Doubleday, Garden City, NY, 1970.
- Betz, Otto, *What Do We Know About Jesus?* SCM, London, 1968.
- Blamires, Harry, *The Christian Mind*, SPCK, London, 1963.
- Blanshard, Brand, *Reason and Belief*, London, 1962.
- Bouillard, Henri, *The Logic of the Faith*, Sheed and Ward, New York, 1967.
- Bloesch, Donald, *The Ground of Certainty*, Eerdmans, Grand Rapids, 1976.
- Blomberg, Craig, *The Historical Reliability of the Gospels*, InterVarsity, Downers Grove, 1987.
- Boettner, Loraine, *Studies in Theology*, Presbyterian and Reformed, Philadelphia, 1970.
- Boice, James Montgomery, *Standing on the Rock: Biblical Authority in a Secular Age*, Baker Books,

Grand Rapids, MI, 1994.

- Borne, Etienne, *Atheism*, Hawthorn Books, New York, 1961.
- Brow, Robert, *Religion, Origins and Ideas*, Tyndale Press, London, 1966.
- Brown, Colin, *Miracles and the Critical Mind*, Eerdmans, Grand Rapids, 1984.
- Brown, Colin, *Philosophy and the Christian Faith*, Tyndale Press, London, 1971.
- Bruce, F.F., *The Apostolic Defense of the Gospel.* London: Inter-Varsity Press, 1959.
- Bruce, F.F., *The Books and the Parchments*, Pickering & Inglis, London, 1950.
- Bruce, F.F., *The New Testament Documents*, Inter-Varsity, London, 1968.
- Bucaille, Maurice, *The Bible, The Quran and Science*, North American Trust Publications, Paris, 1978.
- Buell, Jon A. and Hyder, Quentin O., *Jesus: God, Ghost or Guru?* Zondervan, Grand Rapids, 1978.
- Burleigh, J.H.S. (Ed.), *Augustine: Earlier Writings*, Westminster, Philadelphia, 1953.
- Burrill, Donald R., *The Cosmological Arguments*, Anchor Books, Garden City, NY, 1967.
- Burrows, Millar, *What Mean These Stones?* American Schools of Oriental Research, New Haven, 1941.
- Bush, L. Russ., *A Handbook for Christian Philosophy*, Zondervan, Grand Rapids, 1991.
- Buswell, J. Oliver, Jr, "Review of Clark's *Christian View of Men and Things*", *Journal of the American Scientific Affiliation* **5**(4):8–9, December 1953.
- Buswell, J. Oliver, Jr, *A Christian View of Being and Knowing*, Zondervan, Grand Rapids, 1960.
- Buswell, J. Oliver, Jr, *A Systematic Theology of the Christian Religion*, Volume **I**, Zondervan, Grand Rapids, 1962.
- Butterfield, Herbert, *Christianity and History*, George Bell & Sons, London, 1950.
- Cairns, David, *The Reasonableness of the Christian Faith*, Hodder & Stoughton, London, New York.
- Camus, Albert, *The Plague,* translated by Gilbert, Stuart, Modern Library, New York, 1948.
- Cannaerts, Emile, "Why does Christ ask us to do the impossible?" in Wand, J.W.C. (Ed.), *Difficulties*, Mowbray, London, 1958.
- Carey, George, *God Incarnate*, Inter-Varsity Press, Leicester, 1977.
- Carnell, Edward J., *An Introduction to Christian Apologetics*, Eerdmans, Grand Rapids, 1978.
- Carnell, Edward J., *The Case For Biblical Christianity*, Ronald Nash (Ed.), Eerdmans, Grand Rapids, 1969.
- Carnell, Edward J., *Christian Commitment: An Apologetic*, Macmillan, New York, 1957.
- Cassels, Louis, *The Reality of God*, Herald Press, Scottdale, PA, 1972.
- Chang, Lit-Sen, *Zen-Existentialism*, Presbyterian and Reformed, Philadelphia, 1969.
- Chapman, Colin, *Christianity on Trial*, Volume **II**, Lion, Herts, England, 1974.
- Chesterton, G.K., *The Everlasting Man*, Hodder & Stoughton, London, 1947.
- Chesterton, G.K., *Orthodoxy*, Doubleday, Garden City, NJ, 1959.
- Clark, David K., *The Pantheism of Alan Watts*, Inter-Varsity Press, Downers Grove, 1978.
- Clark, Gordon H., *A Christian View of Men and Things*, Eerdmans, Grand Rapids, 1952.
- Clark, Gordon H., *God's Hammer: The Bible and its Critics*, Trinity Foundation, Jefferson, MD, 1982.
- Clark, Gordon H., *Karl Barth's Theological Method*, Presbyterian and Reformed, Philadelphia, 1963.
- Clark, Gordon H., *Religion, Reason and Revelation*, Presbyterian and Reformed, Philadelphia, 1961.
- Clark, Gordon H., *Thales to Dewey*, Houghton Mifflin, Boston, 1957.
- Clark, Gordon H., *Three Types of Religious Philosophy*, Presbyterian & Reformed, Nutley, 1977.
- Clements, R.D., *God and the Gurus*, Westminster, Philadelphia, 1961.
- Clifford, Ross, *Leading Lawyers Look at the Resurrection*, Australia/New Zealand: Albatross; UK: Lion; Canada: Canadian Institute for Law, Theology & Public, 1991.
- Coe, Richard, *Samuel Beckett*, Grove, New York, 1964.
- Cohen, Daniel, *The New Believers: Young Religion in America*, Evans & Co., NY, 1975.
- Collins, James, *God in Modern Philosophy*, Henry Regnery Co., Chicago, 1959.
- Cook, David, *Blind Alley Beliefs*, Pickering & Inglis, London, 1979.
- Copan, Paul and Craig, William Lane, *Contending with Christianity's Critics: Answering New Atheists and Other Objectors*, B&H Academic, 2009.
- Copleston, Fredrick, *The Existence of God*, Hick, John (Ed.), Macmillan, NY, 1968.
- Cottrell, Jack, *The Authority of the Bible*, Baker Book House, Grand Rapids, 1979.
- Coulson, C.A., *Science and Christian Belief*, Collins, London, 1958.
- Cragg, Kenneth, *The Call of the Minaret*, Oxford

University Press, New York, 1956.

- Craig, William Lane, *Apologetics: An Introduction*, Moody Press, Chicago, 1984.
- Craig, William Lane, *The Existence of God and the Beginning of the Universe*, Here's Life Publishers, San Bernardino, 1979.
- Craig, William Lane, *The Kalām Cosmological Argument*, Macmillan, New York, 1979.
- Craig, William Lane, *Knowing the Truth About the Resurrection*, Servant, Ann Arbor, MI, 1988.
- Craig, William Lane, *Reasonable Faith: Christian Truth and Apologetics*, 3rd edition, Crossway Books, Wheaton, 2008.
- Davis, John Jefferson, *Theology Primer*, Baker Book House, Grand Rapids, 1981.
- Davis, Stephen T., *Logic and the Nature of God*, Eerdmans, Grand Rapids, 1983.
- Dean, Robert J., *How Can We Believe?* Broadman, Nashville, 1978.
- Dehoff, George W., *Why We Believe the Bible*, Dehoff Publications, Murfreesboro, 1974.
- Deshmukh, I.O., *The Gospel and Islam*, Gospel Literature Service, Bombay, 1982.
- Demarest, Bruce, *General Revelation*, Zondervan, Grand Rapids, 1982.
- Demant, V.A., *Difficulties*, Mowbray, London, 1958.
- Diamond, Malcolm, *Contemporary Philosophy and Religious Thought*, McGraw-Hill, New York, 1974.
- D'Souza, Dinesh, *What's So Great About Christianity?* Regnery, Washington DC, 2007.
- Dyrness, William, *Christian Apologetics in a World Community*, Inter-Varsity Press, Downers Grove, 1983.
- Durant, Will, "Caesar and Christ," Volume **III**, *The Story of Civilization*, Simon and Schuster, New York, 1944.
- Edwards, Paul (Ed.), *The Encyclopedia of Philosophy*, Macmillan, London, 1972.
- Evans, C. Stephen, *The Quest for Faith: Pointers to God*, Inter-Varsity, Leicester, 1986.
- Fabro, Cornelio, *God in Exile*, Newman Press, New York, 1968.
- Farrer, Austin, *Finite and the Infinite*, The Seabury Press, New York, 1979.
- Ferm, Vergilius (Ed.), *An Encyclopedia of Religion*, Philosophical Library, New York, 1945.
- Fernando, Ajith, *The Christian's Attitude Toward World Religions*, Tyndale House, Wheaton, 1978.
- Ferre, Nels F., *Christology and Personality*, Westminster Press, 1961.

- Feuerbach, Ludwig, *The Essence of Christianity*, Harper Torchbooks, New York, 1957.
- Fisher, G.M., *Manual of Christian Evidences*, Scribner, New York, 1888.
- Fitchett, W.H., *The Beliefs of Unbelief*, Cassell, London, 1908.
- Flew, Antony, *God and Philosophy*, Hutchinson, London, 1966.
- Flew, Antony, *The Presumption of Atheism and Other Philosophical Essays on God, Freedom and Immortality*, Barnes & Noble, NY, 1976.
- Flew, Antony and MacIntyre, Alasdair, *New Essays in Philosophical Theory*, Macmillan, NY.
- Flew, Antony with Varghese, Roy, *There is No a God: How the world's most notorious atheist changed his mind*, Harper Collins, New York, 2007.
- Flew, Antony and Warren, Thomas B., *The Warren–Flew Debate*, National Christian Press, Jonesboro, AK, 1977.
- France, R.T., *The Evidence for Jesus*, Inter-Varsity, Downers Grove, 1976.
- Frazer, James, *The Golden Bough*, Volume **IX**, Studley Press, London, 1951.
- Free, Joseph, *Archaeology and Bible History*, Scripture Press, Wheaton, IL, 1969.
- Freeman, David H., *A Philosophical Study of Religion*, Craig Press, Nutley, NJ, 1964.
- Frost, S.E., *The Sacred Writings of the World's Great Religions*, Blakiston Co., Philadelphia, 1948.
- Fruchtenbaum, Arnold, *Messianic Christology*, Ariel Ministries, 1998.
- Fuller, D.P., *Easter Faith and History*, Eerdmans, Grand Rapids, 1965.
- Gange, Robert, *Origins and Destiny*, Word Books, Waco, TX, 1986.
- Garvie, A.E., *A Handbook of Christian Apologetics*, Charles Scribner's Sons, New York.
- Geehan, E.R. (Ed.), *Jerusalem and Athens*, Presbyterian and Reformed, Nutley, 1971.
- Geisler, Norman L., *Christian Apologetics*, Baker, Grand Rapids, 1976.
- Geisler, Norman L., *False Gods of Our Time*, Harvest House, Eugene, OR, 1985.
- Geisler, Norman L., *Miracles and Modern Thought*, Zondervan, Grand Rapids, 1982.
- Geisler, Norman L., *Options in Contemporary Christian Ethics*, Baker Books, Grand Rapids, 1981.
- Geisler, Norman L., *Philosophy of Religion*, Zondervan, Grand Rapids, 1974.
- Geisler, Norman L., *Roots of Evil*, Zondervan, Grand Rapids, 1978.
- Geisler, Norman L. and Corduan, Winfried,

Philosophy of Religion, Baker, Grand Rapids, 1989.

▪ Geisler, Norman L. and Turek, Frank, *I Don't Have Enough Faith to Be an Atheist*, Crossway Books, 2004.

▪ Geisler, Norman L. and Watkins, William, *Perspectives: Understanding and Evaluating Today's World Views*, Here's Life Publishers, San Bernardino, 1984.

▪ Gerhardsson, Birger, *Memory and Manuscript*, translated by Sharp, Eric, Villadsen og Christensen, Copenhagen, 1964.

▪ Gerstner, John H., *Reasons For Faith*, Baker, Grand Rapids, 1967.

▪ Gill, Jerry, *The Possibility of Religious Knowledge*, Eerdmans, Grand Rapids, 1971.

▪ Glueck, Nelson, "Book Review of *The Bible as History* by Werner Keller" *New York Times*, 28 October 1956.

▪ Green, Michael, *Faith for the Non-Religious*, Tyndale, Wheaton, 1970.

▪ Green, Michael, *Man Alive*, Inter-Varsity Fellowship, London, 1967.

▪ Green, Michael, *Runaway World*, Inter-Varsity Press, London, 1968.

▪ Grisez, Germain, *Beyond the New Theism*, University of Notre Dame Press, Notre Dame, IN, 1975.

▪ Grounds, Vernon C., *The Reason For Our Hope*, Moody, Chicago, 1945.

▪ Guinness, Os, *The Dust of Death*, InterVarsity Press, Downers Grove, 1973.

▪ Guinness, Os, *In Two Minds*, Inter-Varsity Press, London, 1977.

▪ Gundry, Stanley N. and Johnson, Alan F., *Tension in Contemporary Theology*, Moody, Chicago, 1976.

▪ Hackett, Stuart C., *Oriental Philosophy: A Westerner's Guide to Eastern Thought*, University of Wisconsin Press, Madison, 1984.

▪ Hackett, Stuart C., *The Resurrection of Theism*, Moody Press, Chicago, 1957.

▪ Halsey, Jim S., *For A Time Such As This*, Presbyterian and Reformed, Nutley, 1976.

▪ Hanayama, Shoyu, *The Meaning of Life in Five Great Religions*, Chalmers, R.C. and Irving, John A. (Eds.), Westminister, Philadelphia, 1965.

▪ Hardy, G.B., *Countdown*, Moody Press, Chicago, 1972.

▪ Harrison, P., *The Bible, Protestantism and the rise of natural scienc.*, Cambridge University Press, 2001.

▪ Harrison, P., *The Fall of Man and the Foundations of Science*, Cambridge University Press, 2007.

▪ Heiner, Wolfgang, *Jesus is Different*, Paternoster, Exeter, 1982.

▪ Henry, Carl F.H., *Giving Reasons for our Hope*, W.A. Wilde, Boston, 1949.

▪ Henry, Carl F.H., *God, Revelation and Authority*, Volume **I**, Word, Waco, 1976.

▪ Henry, Carl F.H., *Quest For Reality: Christianity and the Counter Culture*, Inter-Varsity Press, Downers Grove, 1973.

▪ Henry, Carl F.H., *Remaking the Modern Mind*, Eerdmans, Grand Rapids, 1948.

▪ Henry, Carl F.H. (Ed.), *Revelation and the Bible*, Baker, Grand Rapids, 1958.

▪ Hepburn, Ronald W., *Christianity and Paradox*, Watts, London, 1958.

▪ Hesselgrave, David J., *Communicating Christ Cross-Culturally*, Zondervan, Grand Rapids, 1978.

▪ Heydt, Henry J.A., *Comparison of World Religions*, Christian Literature Crusade, Philadelphia, 1976.

▪ Hick, John (Ed.), *Arguments for the Existence of God*, Herder, NY, 1971.

▪ Hick, John, *Christianity at the Centre*. London: SCM Press, 1968.

▪ Hick, John, *Evil and the God of Love*, Macmillan, New York, 1966.

▪ Hitchens, Peter, *The Rage Against God: How Atheism Led Me to Faith*, Zondervan, 2010.

▪ Hodgson, Leonard, *The Place of Reason in Christian Apologetics*, B. Backwell, New York, Oxford, 1925.

▪ Holding, James Patrick, *The Impossible Faith*, Florida, 2007; www.tektonics.org/lp/nowayjose.html

▪ Holmes, Arthur F., *All Truth Is God's Truth*, Eerdmans, Grand Rapids, 1977.

▪ Holmes, Arthur F., *Christian Philosophy in the 20th Century: An Essay in Philosophical Methodology*, Craig Press, Nutley, 1969.

▪ Holmes, Arthur F., *Faith Seeks Understanding*, Eerdmans, Grand Rapids, 1971.

▪ Holmes, Arthur F., *Philosophy: A Christian Perspective*, Inter-Varsity, Downers Grove, 1978.

▪ Hooper, Walter (Ed.), *Christian Reflection*, Eerdmans, Grand Rapids, 1967.

▪ Hoover, Arlie J., *Fallacies of Unbelief*, Biblical Research Press, Abilene, TX, 1975.

▪ Hopkins, Mark, *Evidences of Christianity*, T.R. Marvin & Son, 1909.

▪ Howe, Frederic R., *Challenge and Response*, Zondervan, Grand Rapids, 1982.

▪ Hume, David, *Dialogues Concerning Natural Religion*, Aiken, Henry D. (Ed.), Hafner, NY, 1948.

▪ Hume, Robert E., *The World's Living Religions*,

Scribner, New York, 1929.

- Hunt, John, *Pantheism and Christianity*, Kennikat Press, New York, 1970.
- *The Infallible Word*, Symposium by the members of the faculty of Westminster Theological Seminary, Presbyterian Guardian Publishing, Philadelphia, 1946.
- Jaki, Stanley L., *Cosmos and Creator*, Scottish Academy, Edinburgh, 1980.
- Jaki, Stanley L., *The Origin of Science and the Science of Its Origin*, Regnery/Gateway, South Bend, IN, 1978.
- Jaki, Stanley L., *The Roads of Science and the Ways to God*, University of Chicago Press, Chicago, 1978.
- James, E.O., *History of Religions*, English University Press, London, 1956.
- Jauncey, James H., *Science Returns to God*, Zondervan, Grand Rapids, 1971.
- Jeremias, Joachim, *New Testament Theology, The Proclamation of Jesus*, Scribner's, NY, 1971.
- Joad, C.E.M., *The Recovery of Belief*, Faber & Faber, London, 1952.
- Joad, C.E.M., *Return to Philosophy*, Faber & Faber, London, 1958.
- Jones, L. Bevan, *The People of the Mosque*, YMCA Publishing House, Calcutta, 1939.
- Jones, E. Stanley, *The Victory Through Surrender*, Abingdon Press, Nashville, 1966.
- Josephus, Flavius, *Antiquities of the Jews*, AD 93.
- Jung, Carl, *Modern Man In Search of a Soul*, translated by Dell and Bayress, Harcourt Brace, New York, 1933.
- Kaufmann, Walter, *Critique of Religion and Philosophy*, Doubleday, New York, 1961.
- Keller, Werner, *The Bible as History*, translated by Neil, William, William Morrow, New York, 1956.
- Kenny, J.P., *Christ Outside Christianity*, Spectrum, Melbourne, 1971.
- Kenyon, Frederic, *The Bible and Archaeology*, Harper, New York, 1940.
- Kenyon, Frederic, *The Bible and Modern Scholarship*, J. Murray, London, 1948.
- Kenyon, Frederic, *Our Bible and the Ancient Manuscripts*, Harper, NY, 1958.
- Keyser, L.S., *A System of Christian Evidence*, Lutheran Literary Board, Birlington, 1926.
- Kierkegaard, Søren, *Concluding Unscientific Postscripts*, translated by Swenson, David F. and Lowrie, Walter, Princeton University Press, 1941.
- Kierkegaard, Søren, *Philosophical Fragments*, Princeton University Press, 1936.
- Killen, R. Allan, "Apologetics" in *Wycliffe Bible Encyclopaedia*, Volume **I**, Moody Press, Chicago, 1975.
- Kraemer, H., *The Christian Message in a Non-Christian World*, Kregel, Grand Rapids, 1956.
- Kumar, Steve, *Answering the Counterfeit*.
- Kumar, Steve, *Christian Apologetics: Think Why You Believe*, New Zealand Apologetics Society, 1990.
- Kurtz, Paul, *Forbidden Fruit*, Prometheus Books, Buffalo, NY, 1988.
- Lecky, W.E.H., *History of European Morals From Augustus to Charlemagne*, Volume **II**, Longmans, Green, London, 1869.
- Lee, Francis Nigel, *A Christian Introduction to the History of Philosophy*, Craig Press, Nutley, 1969.
- Lepp, Ignace, *Atheism in Our Time*, Macmillan, New York, 1964.
- Lewis, C.S., "Miracles" in *The Best of C.S. Lewis*, Iversen, NY, 1969.
- Lewis, C.S., *God in the Dock: Essays on Theology and Ethics*, Hooper, Walter (Ed.), Eerdmans, Grand Rapids, 1970.
- Lewis, C.S., *Mere Christianity*, Macmillian, New York, 1952.
- Lewis, C.S., *Miracles*, Macmillian, New York, 1947.
- Lewis, C.S., *The Problem of Pain*, Macmillan, New York, 1948.
- Lewis, Gordon R., *Testing Christianity's Truth Claims*, Moody Press, Chicago, 1976.
- Lewis, H.D. and Slater, R.L., *The Study of Religions*, Penguin, Middlesex, 1969.
- Lewis, H.D. and Slater, R.L., *World Religions*, Watts, London, 1966.
- Licona, Mike, *The Resurrection of Jesus: A New Historiographical Approach*, IVP Academic, 2010.
- Linton, Irwin H., *A Lawyer Examines the Bible*, Baker, Grand Rapids, 1943.
- Little, Paul E., *Know Why You Believe*, Scripture Union, London, 1968.
- Lundstrom, Lowell, *The Muslims are Coming*, Lowell Lundstrom Ministries, Sisseton, SD, 1980.
- McDowell, Josh and Gilchrist, John, *The Islam Debate*, Here's Life Publishers, San Bernardino, CA, 1983.
- McGrath, Alister, *Bridge-Building*, Inter-Varsity, Leicester, England, 1992.
- McGuiggan, Jim, *If God Came*, Montex Publishing, Lubbock, 1980.
- Machen, J. Gresham, *Christianity and Liberalism*, Eerdmans, Grand Rapids.
- Mackie, J.L., *The Miracle of Theism*, Clarendon, Oxford, 1982.

- Maiden, Brian, *One Way to God?* Inter-Varsity, London, 1974.
- Malik, Charles H., *The Wonder of Being*, Word Books, Waco, TX, 1974.
- Marrison, G.E., *The Christian Approach to the Muslim*, Edinburgh House Press, London, 1959.
- Marshall, I. Howard, *I Believe in the Historical Jesus*, Eerdmans, Grand Rapids, 1977.
- Mascall E.J., *He Who is: A Study in Traditional Theism*, Darton, Longman & Todd, London, 1966.
- Masterson, Patrick, *Atheism and Alienation*, Penguin, Middlesex, 1971.
- Matson, W., *The Existence of God*, Cornell University, 1965.
- Matton, F.W. (Ed.), "The Existence of God," *Bales–Teller Debate*, Old Path Book Club.
- Mavrodes, George (Ed.), *The Rationality of Belief in God*, Prentice-Hall, Englewood Cliffs, 1970.
- Means, Pat, *The Mystical Maze*, Campus Crusade for Christ, 1976.
- Miethe, Terry L. (Ed.), *Did Jesus Rise From the Dead? The Resurrection Debate*, Harper & Row, San Francisco, 1987.
- Miller, E.L., *God and Reason: A Historical Approach to Philosophical Theology*, Macmillan, NY, 1972.
- Miller, William McElwee, *A Christian's Response to Islam*, Presbyterian and Reformed, Philadelphia, 1976.
- Miller, William McElwee, *Religions in a Changing World*, Vos, Howard F. (Ed.), Moody, Chicago, 1959.
- Mitchell, Basil, *Morality: Religious and Secular*, Clarendon, Oxford, 1980.
- Mitton, C. Leslie, *Jesus: The Fact Behind the Faith*, Eerdmans, Grand Rapids, 1977.
- Montgomery, John Warwick, *Faith Founded on Fact*, Thomas Nelson, Nashville, 1978.
- Montgomery, John Warwick (Ed.), *God's Inerrant Word*, Bethany, Minneapolis, 1974.
- Montgomery, John Warwick, *History and Christianity*, Inter-Varsity, Downers Grove, 1964.
- Montgomery, John Warwick, *How Do We Know There is a God?* Bethany, Minneapolis, 1973.
- Montgomery, John Warwick, *The Altizer–Montgomery Dialogue*, Inter-Varsity, Chicago, 1967.
- Montgomery, John Warwick, *The Shape of the Past*, Edwards, Ann Arbor, 1962.
- Montgomery, John Warwick, *The Suicide of Christian Theology*, Bethany Fellowship, Minneapolis, 1975.
- Montgomery, John Warwick, *Where Is History Going?* Zondervan, Grand Rapids, 1969.
- Moreland, J.P., *Scaling the Secular City*, Baker Grand Rapids, 1987.
- Moreland, J.P. and Nielsen, Kai, *Does God Exist?* Nelson, Nashville, 1990.
- Morey, Robert, *The Islamic Invasion*, Harvest House, Eugene, OR, 1992.
- Morey, Robert, *The New Atheism and the Erosion of Freedom*, Bethany, Minneapolis, 1986.
- Morgan, Kenneth W., *The Path of Buddha*, Ronald, New York, 1956.
- Morison, Frank, *Who Moved the Stone?* Faber & Faber, London, 1958.
- Morris, Henry M., *Many Infallible Proofs*, Creation-Life, San Diego, 1974.
- Morris, Thomas V. (Ed.), *The Concept of God*, Oxford University Press, 1987.
- Moule, C.F.D., *The Birth of the New Testament*, Harper & Row, San Francisco, 1981.
- Nash, Ronald H., *Christianity and the Hellenistic World*, Zondervan, Grand Rapids, 1984.
- Nash, Ronald H., *The Concept of God*, Zondervan, Grand Rapids, 1983.
- Nash, Ronald H., *Faith and Reason*, Zondervan, Grand Rapids, 1988.
- Nash, Ronald H., *The New Evangelicalism*, Zondervan, Grand Rapids, 1963.
- Neill, Stephen, *Christian Faith and Other Faiths*, Oxford University Press, London, 1961.
- Neill, Stephen, *Crises of Belief*, Hodder and Stoughton, London, 1984.
- Newbigin, Lesslie, *The Finality of Christ*, John Knox, Richmond, 1969.
- Nietzsche, Friedrich, *The Portable Nietzsche*, Kaufmann, Walter (Ed.), Princeton University Press, 1968.
- Nietzsche, Friedrich, *Thus Spoke Zarathustra*, Random House, New York.
- Ogata, Sohaku, *Zen for the West*, Dial Press, New York, 1959.
- *Oliphant–Smith Debate*, Gospel Advocate, Nashville, 1929.
- Orr, J. Edwin, *The Faith That Persuades*, Harper & Row, New York, 1977.
- Orr, J. Edwin, *The Resurrection of Jesus*, College Press, Joplin, 1972.
- Owen, H.P., *Christian Theism: A Study in its Principles*, T. & T. Clark, Edinburgh, 1984.
- Owen, H.P., *The Moral Argument for Christian Theism*, Allen & Unwin, London, 1965.
- Packer, J.I., *Keep Yourself from Idols*, Church Book Room, London, 1964.
- Pahnke, Walter, *LSD, Man and Society*, De Bold,

Richard and Leaf, Russell (Eds.), Faber & Faber, London, 1969.

▪ Parrinder, G., *Avatar and Incarnation*, Faber & Faber, London, 1970.

▪ Parshall, Phil, *New Paths in Muslim Evangelism*, Baker Book House, Grand Rapids, 1980.

▪ Petersen, William J., *Those Curious New Cults*, Keats Publishing, New Canaan, CT, 1975.

▪ Pfander, C.G., *The Mizan-Ul-Haqq (Balance of Truth)*, revised by Tisdall, W. St. Clair, Religious Tract Society, London, 1910.

▪ Pike, Nelson (Ed.), *God and Evil*, Prentice-Hall, Englewood Cliffs, NJ, 1964.

▪ Pinnock, Clark H., *Reason Enough: A Case for the Christian Faith*, Inter-Varsity Press, Downers Grove, 1980.

▪ Pinnock, Clark H., *Set Forth Your Case*, Moody Press, Chicago, 1971.

▪ Plantinga, Alvin, *God and Other Minds: A Study of the Rational Justification of Belief in God*, Cornell University Press, Ithaca, 1967.

▪ Plantinga, Alvin, *God, Freedom and Evil*, Eerdmans, Grand Rapids, 1974.

▪ Plantinga, Alvin and Wolterstorff, Nicholas, *Faith and Rationality: Reason and Belief in God*, University of Notre Dame Press, London, 1986.

▪ Potter, Charles Francis, *The Faith Men Live By*, The World's Work, Surrey, 1955.

▪ Purtill, Richard L., *Reason to Believe*, Eerdmans, Grand Rapids, 1974.

▪ Purtill, Richard L., *Thinking About Religion*, Prentice-Hall, Englewood Cliffs, 1978.

▪ Radhakrishnan, Sarvepail, *The Hindu View of Life*, Allen & Unwin, London, 1927.

▪ Radmacher, Earl D. (Ed.), *Can We Trust the Bible?* Tyndale, Wheaton, 1979.

▪ Ramm, Bernard L., *Protestant Christian Evidences*, Moody, Chicago, 1953.

▪ Ramm, Bernard L., *The God Who Makes a Difference*, Word Books, Waco, 1975.

▪ Ramsay, William M., *Luke, The Physician*, Hodder & Stoughton, London, 1908.

▪ Rashdall, Hasting, *The Theory of Good and Evil*, Clarendon, Oxford, 1907.

▪ Reichenbach, Bruce, *The Cosmological Argument: A Reassessment*, C. Thomas, Springfield, 1972.

▪ Reid, J.K.S., *Christian Apologetics*, Eerdmans, Grand Rapids, 1970.

▪ Rendle Short, A., *Why Believe*, Inter-Varsity Press, London, 1964.

▪ Reymond, Robert L., *The Justification of Knowledge*, Presbyterian and Reformed, Nutley, 1976.

▪ Rhoton, Dale, *The Logic of Faith*, STL Books, Bromley, Kent, 1972.

▪ Richardson, Alan, *Christian Apologetics*, Harper & Bro., New York, 1948.

▪ Richardson, Alan (Ed.), *A Dictionary of Christian Theology*, Westminister, Philadelphia, 1969.

▪ Ridenour, Fritz, *So What's the Difference*, Regal Books, Glendale, 1967.

▪ Riss, Richard, *The Evidence for the Resurrection of Jesus Christ*, Bethany Fellowship, Minneapolis, 1977.

▪ Robinson, John A.T., *Can We Trust the New Testament?* Eerdmans, Grand Rapids, 1977.

▪ Russell, Richard, Escape from reason, *International Reformed Bulletin* 43, Fall, 1970.

▪ Sarfati, Jonathan, *Refuting Evolution*, Creation Book Publishers, 1999/2012.

▪ Sarfati, Jonathan, *By Design: Evidence for nature's Intelligent Designer—the God of the Bible*, Creation Book Publishers, 2008

▪ Sarfati, Jonathan, *The Greatest Hoax On Earth? Refuting Dawkins on Evolution*, Creation Book Publishers, 2010.

▪ Sartre, Jean-Paul, *Existentialism and Humanism*, Methuen, London, 1948.

▪ Sartre, Jean-Paul, *Words*, George Brazillor, New York, 1964.

▪ Sartre, Jean-Paul, "Existentialism," translated by Frechtman, Bernard, in *Existentialism and Human Emotions*, Philosophical Library, New York, 1957.

▪ Schaeffer, Francis A., *Escape From Reason*, Inter-Varsity, London, 1975.

▪ Schaeffer, Francis A., *Genesis In Space and Time*, Inter-Varsity, Downers Grove, 1972.

▪ Schaeffer, Francis A., *He Is There and He Is Not Silent*, Hodder and Stoughton, London, 1972.

▪ Schaeffer, Francis A., *The God Who Is There*, Inter-Varsity, Downers Grove, 1968.

▪ Schaff, Philip, *The Person of Christ*, American Tract Society, New York, 1913.

▪ Schilling, S. Paul, *God in an Age of Atheism*, Abingdon, Nashville, 1969.

▪ Schuon, Frithjof, *Understanding Islam*, translated by Matheson, D.M., Penguin Books, Baltimore, MD, 1972.

▪ Scriven, Michael, *Primary Philosophy*, McGraw-Hill, New York, 1966.

▪ Sen, K.M., *Hinduism*, Penguin Books, Middlesex, 1961.

▪ Sillem, Edward, *Ways of Thinking About God*, Darton, Longman & Todd, London, 1961.

203

- Silvester, Hugh, *Arguing with God*, InterVarsity, Downers Grove, 1971.
- Smart, Ninian, *The Religious Experience of Mankind*, Scribners, NY, 1969.
- Smith, W. Cantwell, *Question of Religious Truth*, Scribners, NY, 1967.
- Smith, Wilbur M., *Therefore Stand*, Baker Book, Grand Rapids, 1969.
- Spiceland, James D., God Is Transcendent—But is Language? *Christianity Today* **22**:24–26, 5 May 1978.
- Spencer, Robert, *The Politically Incorrect Guide to Islam (And the Crusades)*, Regnery Press, 2005.
- Spencer, Robert, *Religion of Peace?: Why Christianity Is and Islam Isn't*, Regnery Publishing, 2007.
- Sproul, R.C., *Knowing Scripture*, Inter-Varsity, Downers Grove, 1978.
- Sproul, R.C., *Objections Answered*, Regal Books, Glendale, CA, 1978.
- Sproul, R.C., *The Psychology of Atheism*, Bethany, Minneapolis, 1974.
- Sproul, R.C., Gerstner, John and Lindsley, Arthur, *Classical Apologetics*, Zondervan, Grand Rapids, 1984.
- Stark, Rodney, *For The Glory of God: How Monotheism Led to Reformations, Science, Witch-hunts and the End of Slavery*, Princeton University Press, 2003.
- Stark, Rodney, *The Victory of Reason: How Christianity Led to Freedom, Capitalism, and Western Success*, Random House, New York, 2005.
- Stark, Rodney, *God's Battalions: The Case for the Crusades*, HarperOne, 2009.
- Stark, Rodney, *The Triumph of Christianity: How the Jesus Movement Became the World's Largest Religion*, HarperOne, 2011.
- Staudinger, Hugo, *The Trustworthiness of the Gospels*, Handsel Press, Edinburgh, 1981.
- Stauffer, Ethelbert, *Jesus and His Story*, Alfred P. Knopf, New York, 1959.
- Stewart, Don, *You Be The Judge*, Here's Life Publishers, San Bernardino, 1983.
- Storrs, Christopher E., *Many Creeds: One Cross*, SCM, London, 1945.
- Stott, John R.W., *Basic Christianity*, Inter-Varsity Press, Chicago, 1964.
- Stott, John R.W., *Your Mind Matters*, Inter-Varsity Press, Downers Grove, 1972.
- Strobel, Lee, *The Case for Christ: A Journalist's Personal Investigation of the Evidence for Jesus*, Zondervan, Grand Rapids, MI, 1998.
- Strobel, Lee, *The Case for Faith: A Journalist Investigates the Toughest Objections to Christianity*, Zondervan, Grand Rapids, MI, 2000.
- Strobel, Lee, *The Case for a Creator: A Journalist Investigates Scientific Evidence That Points Toward God*, Zondervan, Grand Rapids, MI, 2005.
- Strobel, Lee, *The Case for the Real Jesus: A Journalist Investigates Current Attacks on the Identity of Christ*, Zondervan, Grand Rapids, MI, 2009.
- Strobel, Lee, *The Case for the Resurrection: A First-Century Investigative Reporter Probes History's Pivotal Event*, Zondervan, Grand Rapids, MI, 2010.
- Strunk, Orlo,Jr, *The Choice Called Atheism*, Abingdon, Nashville, 1969.
- Suzuki, D.T., *An Introduction to Zen Buddhism*, Grove, New York, 1964.
- Suzuki, D.T., *Mysticism: Christian and Buddhist*, Harper & Row, NY, 1957.
- Suzuki, D.T., *Outline of Mahayana Buddhism*, Schocken, New York, 1963.
- Suzuki, D.T., *Zen Buddhism, Selected Writings*, Barrett, William (Ed.), Doubleday, New York, 1956.
- Swinburne, Richard, *The Coherence of Theism*. Oxford: Clarendon, 1977.
- Swinburne, Richard, *The Concept of Miracle*, St. Martin's Press, New York, 1970.
- Swinburne, Richard, *The Existence of God*, Clarendon Press, Oxford, 1979.
- Sylvester, Hugh, *Arguing with God*, InterVarsity, Downers Grove, 1971.
- Tagore, Rabindranath, *The Religion of Man*, Allen & Unwin, London, 1931.
- Taylor, Richard, *Ethics, Faith, and Reason*, Prentice-Hall, Englewood Cliffs, NJ, 1985.
- Tennant, F.R., *Philosophical Theology*, Cambridge University Press, 1956.
- Tenney, M.C., *The Reality of the Resurrection*, Moody Press, 1972.
- Tertullian, "On Prescription Against Heretics" in *The Anti-Nicene Fathers*, Volume **III**, Roberts, Alexander and Donaldson, J. (Eds.), Scribner's, NY, 1926.
- Thaxton, Charles B., Bradley, Walter L. and Olsen, Roger L., *The Mystery of Life's Origin*, Philosophical Library, NY, 1984.
- Thompson, Samuel M., *A Modern Philosophy of Religion*, Henry Regnery, Chicago, 1955.
- Thornhill, R. and Palmer, C.T., *A Natural History of Rape: Biological Bases of Sexual Coercion*, The MIT Press, Massachusetts, 2000.
- Tillich, Paul, *Systematic Theology*, Volume **I**, University of Chicago, 1957.

- Tisdall, W. St. Clair., *Christian Reply to Muslim Objections*, Light of Life, Villach, Austria, 1980.
- Toynbee, Arnold, *Civilization on Trial*, Oxford, New York, 1948.
- Trueblood, David Elton, *General Philosophy*, Baker, Grand Rapids, 1963.
- Trueblood, David Elton, *Philosophy of Religion*, Harper & Brothers, New York, 1957.
- Van Til, Cornelius, *An Introduction to Systematic Theology*, Presbyterian and Reformed, Philadelphia, 1971.
- Van Til, Cornelius, *Christian and Theistic Evidences*, Presbyterian and Reformed, Nutley, 1961.
- Van Til, Cornelius, *Common Grace*, Presbyterian and Reformed, Philadelphia, 1947.
- Van Til, Cornelius, *The Defense of Faith*, Presbyterian and Reformed, Philadelphia, 1955.
- Varghese, Roy Abraham (Ed.), *The Intellectuals Speak Out About God*, Regnery, Chicago, 1984.
- Verghese, Habel G., *Search for Inner Peace*, Bible Voice, Van Nuys, 1977.
- Wand, J.W.C., *Difficulties*, Mowbray, London, 1958.
- Warfield, B.B., *Biblical and Theological Studies*, Presbyterian and Reformed, Philadelphia, 1952.
- Warfield, B.B., *The Inspiration and Authority of the Bible*, Presbyterian & Reformed, Philadelphia, 1958.
- Warfield, B.B., *The Person and Work of Christ*, Puritan Reform, Philadelphia, 1950.
- Watts, Alan, *The Spirit of Zen*, Grove Press, New York, 1958.
- Weightman, Colin and McCarthy, Robert W., *A Mirage from the East*, Lutheran Publishing House, Adelaide, Australia, 1977.
- Wells, H.G., *The Outline of History*, Volume **I**, Doubleday, New York, 1971.
- Wenham, John W., *Christ and the Bible*, Baker, Grand Rapids, 1984.
- Wenham, John W., *The Goodness of God*, InterVarsity, Downers Grove, IL, 1974.
- Wenham, John W., *Redating Matthew, Mark and Luke: A Fresh Assault on the Synoptic Problem*, IVP, 1992.
- Westcott, Brooke Foss, *The Gospel of the Resurrection*, Macmillan, London, 1874.
- White, John Wesley, *Re-Entry*, Zondervan, Grand Rapids, 1970.
- Whitehead, A.N., *Religion in the Making*, Cambridge University Press, 1936.
- Wieland, Carl, *Beyond the Shadows: making sense of personal tragedy*, Creation Book Publishers, 2011.
- Wilder-Smith, A.E., *Why Does God Allow It?* Master, San Diego, 1980.
- Wilkins, Michael J. and Moreland, J.P., *Jesus Under Fire*, Zondervan, Grand Rapids, 1995.
- Winslow, Jack C., *The Christian Approach to the Hindu*, Lutterworth, London, 1958.
- Wiseman, Donald J., "Archaeological Confirmation of the Old Testament" in *Revelation and the Bible*, Baker, Grand Rapids, 1958.
- Wittgenstein, Ludwig, *Tractatus Logico-Philosophicus*, translated by Pears, D.F. and McGuinness, B.F., Routledge & Kegan Paul, London, 1969.
- Wright, N.T. (Tom), *Jesus and the Victory of God*, SPCK, 1993.
- Wright, N.T. (Tom), *Who Was Jesus?* Eerdmans, Grand Rapids, 1992.
- Wright, N.T. (Tom), *The Resurrection of the Son of God*, Fortress Press, 2003.
- Yandell, Keith E., *Christianity and Philosophy*, Eerdmans, Grand Rapids, 1984.
- Young, Edward J., "The Authority of the Old Testament" in *The Infallible Word*, Stonehouse, N.B. and Wooley, Paul (Eds.), Eerdmans, Grand Rapids, 1953.
- Young, John, *The Case Against Christ*, Church Pastoral Aid Society, London, 1978.
- Young, Warren C., *A Christian Approach to Philosophy*, Baker, Grand Rapids, 1954.
- Zacharias, Ravi, *Can Man Live without God?* Thomas Nelson, 1994.
- Zacharias, Ravi, *New Birth or Rebirth? Jesus Talks with Krishna* (Great Conversations), Multnomah Books, 2008.
- Zacharias, Ravi, *The Lotus and the Cross: Jesus Talks with Buddha* (Great Conversations), Multnomah Books, 2010.
- Zacharias, Ravi, *Why Jesus?: Rediscovering His Truth in an Age of Mass Marketed Spirituality*, FaithWords, 2012.
- Zacharias, Ravi and Strobel, Lee, *The End of Reason: A Response to the New Atheists*, Zondervan, 2008.
- Zacharias, Ravi and Geisler, Norman, *Is Your Church Ready?: Motivating Leaders to Live an Apologetic Life*, Zondervan, 2003.
- Zaehner, R.C., *Mysticism, Sacred and Profane*, Clarendon, Oxford, 1961.
- Zwemer, S.M., *A Moslem Seeker After God*, Revell, 1920.

ABOUT THE AUTHORS

Dr Steve Kumar

Living in a post-modern age, how should Christians stand firm and logically defend the faith? How can we speak with confidence to atheists, agnostics and skeptics? What are the facts and evidences that support our faith in the reality of God and Jesus Christ?

Dr Steve Kumar is an author, teacher, speaker, and apologist committed to answering the tough questions of the skeptics and equipping believers with the tools to think more clearly about their faith.

For almost thirty years Dr Kumar has been actively involved in speaking and writing about apologetics, philosophy and faith. As a prominent New Zealand Christian apologist, he is a sought-after speaker in academic and church settings around the world and has lectured at more than 75 theological colleges, universities and high schools in the USA, Canada, England, Australia, New Zealand and Asia. He is a frequent guest on television, radio, and news media programs and is an influential voice on issues that relate to the credibility of the Christian truth claims.

Dr Kumar was trained at faith Theological Seminary, Winbrenner Theological Seminary, Wittenburg University, and Covenant Theological Seminary, and gained his Ph.D. at California Graduate School of Theology. He has debated several notable skeptics and atheists, including Dr Alister Gunn (Head of Philosophy at the University of Waikato), Professor Keith Campbell (Head of Philosophy at Sydney University), and Dr Bill Cook, president of the NZ Rationalist society.

He co-founded and was President of the New Zealand Evangelical Apologetics Society and since then has been involved in working alongside Christian thinkers, activists, church-planters, and pastors. With a passion for communicating ideas in a way that is accessible and lively, Dr Kumar has spoken at many denominational settings, including camps, conferences, and church gatherings.

He has authored a number of books including *Christian Apologetics: Think Why You Believe* and *Answering the Counterfeit*. The original edition of this current book has previously won an 'Angel Award' for excellence in media, which is a major reason for producing this updated and expanded version.

Dr Jonathan Sarfati

Jonathan received his Ph.D. (Physical Chemistry) from Victoria University of Wellington, New Zealand. He has co-authored papers in mainstream scientific journals including one on high-temperature superconductors published in *Nature* when he was 22 years old.

He has long been interested in apologetics, and was a co-founder of the Wellington Christian Apologetics Society (New Zealand). It was through this that he first learned of Dr Kumar's work.

His first book *Refuting Evolution* (1999, 2008) was written to counter a teachers guidebook by the National Academy of Sciences (USA), *Teaching about Evolution and the Nature of Science*. It now has over half a million copies in print. He later wrote *Refuting Evolution 2* (2002, 2010) and the highly acclaimed *Refuting Compromise* (2004, 2010), both as responses to attacks on the biblical view of history.

In 2008, he finished *By Design: Evidence for nature's Intelligent Designer—the God of the Bible*. And in 2010, Dr Sarfati wrote *The Greatest Hoax on Earth? Refuting Dawkins on evolution*, a response to leading anti-theist Richard Dawkins' 2009 book *The Greatest Show on Earth: The Evidence for Evolution*.

He works full-time for *Creation Ministries International* in Atlanta GA, having relocated there in April 2010 from the Brisbane, Australia office. Jonathan is a co-editor of *Creation* magazine and also writes and reviews articles for the in-depth, peer-reviewed *Journal of Creation* (formerly *TJ*), as well as being active in speaking ministry.

Jonathan is also a former New Zealand Chess Champion, representing New Zealand in three Chess Olympiads (and drew with Boris Spassky, world champion 1969–1972). In 1988, the International Chess Federation awarded him the title of F.I.D.E. Master (FM). He regularly accepts challenges from multiple players while he is blindfolded. He then plays from memory with up to 12 players simultaneously.